EXCALIBUR

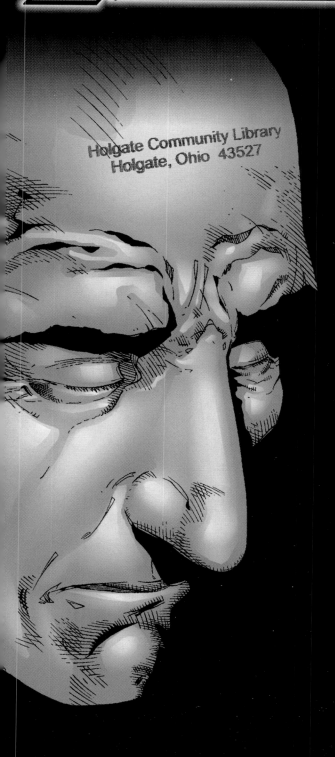

Holgate Community Library
Holgate, Ohio 43527

Writer
Chris Claremont

Penciler
Aaron Lopresti

Inkers
**Greg Adams
& Andrew Pepoy**

Colors
Liquid! Graphics

Letters
Tom Orzechowski

Cover
Andy Park

Assistant Edtiors
**Cory Sedlmeier
& Sean Ryan**

Editor
**Mike Marts
& Stephanie Moore**

Collections Editor
Jeff Youngquist

Assistant Editor
Jennifer Grünwald

Book Designer
Carrie Beadle

Creative Director
Tom Marvelli

Editor in Chief
Joe Quesada

Publisher
Dan Buckley

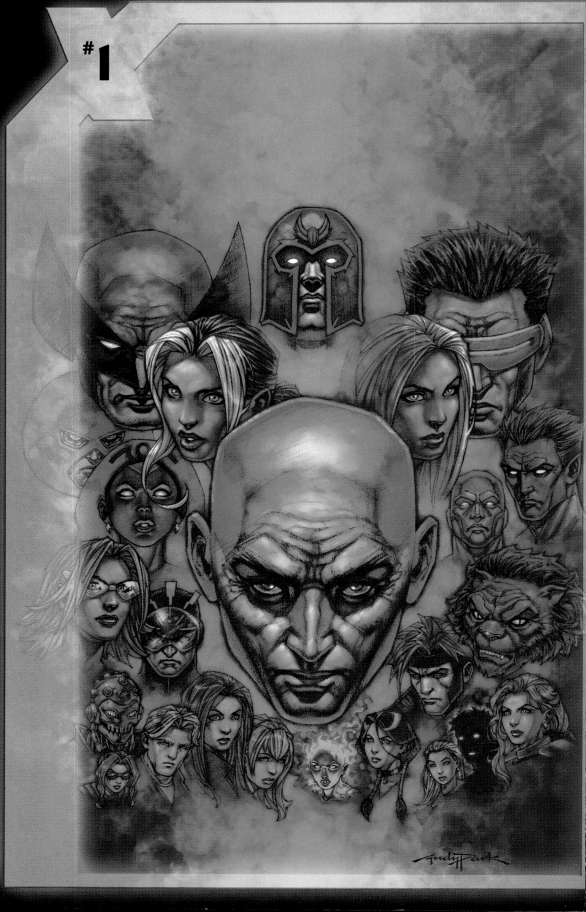

MY NAME IS *CHARLES XAVIER*.

I AM A *MUTANT*.

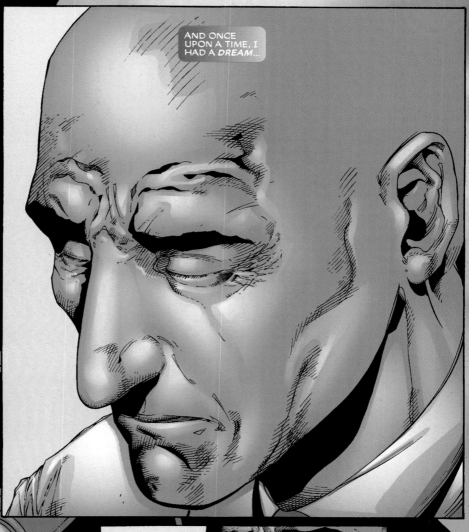

AND ONCE UPON A TIME, I HAD A *DREAM*...

...OF A WORLD WHERE ALL EARTH'S CHILDREN, BOTH MUTANT AND BASELINE HUMAN, MIGHT LIVE TOGETHER IN *PEACE*.

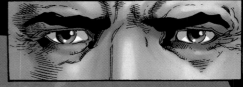

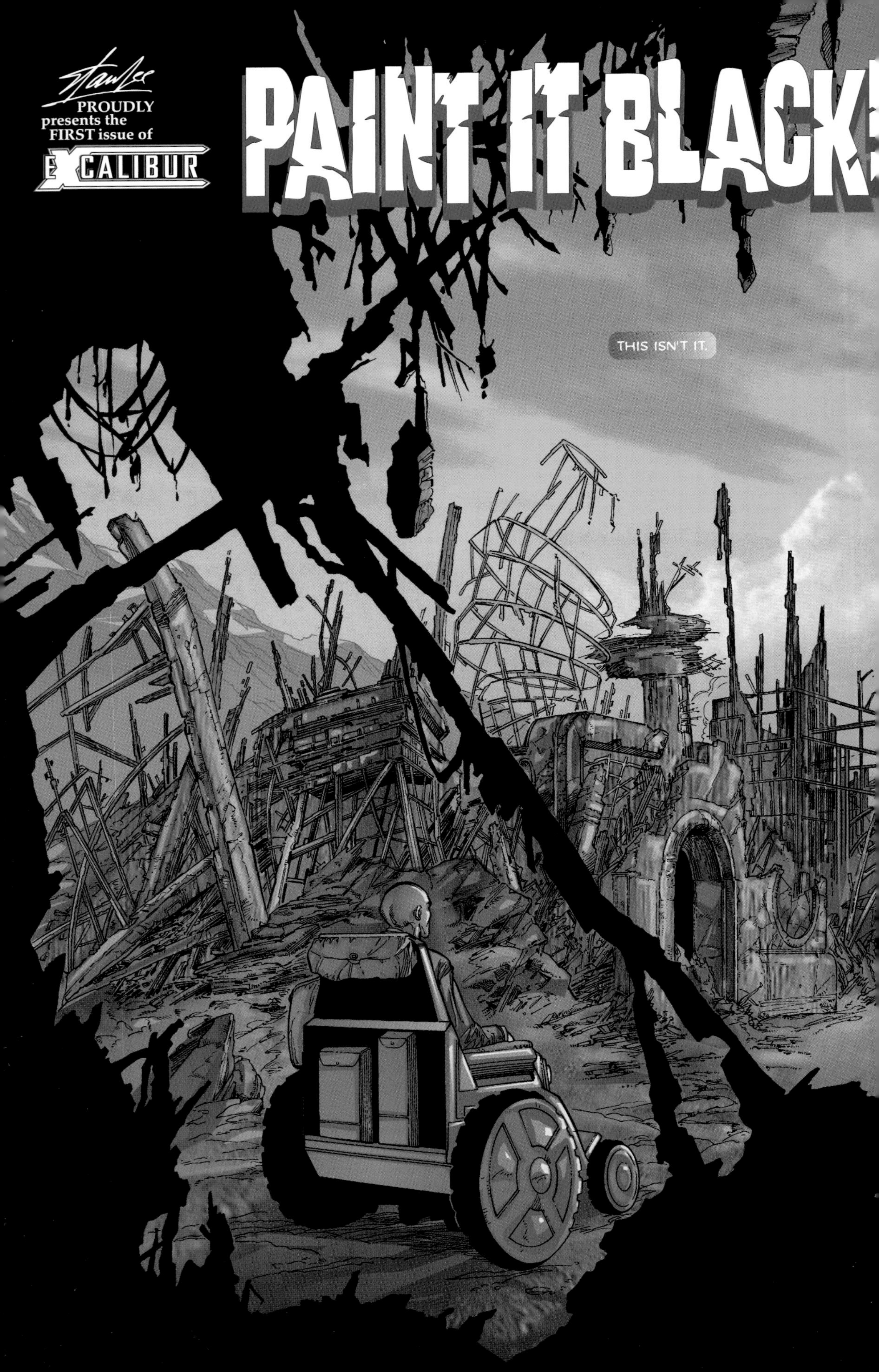
Stan Lee
PROUDLY
presents the
FIRST issue of
EXCALIBUR
PAINT IT BLACK!
THIS ISN'T IT.

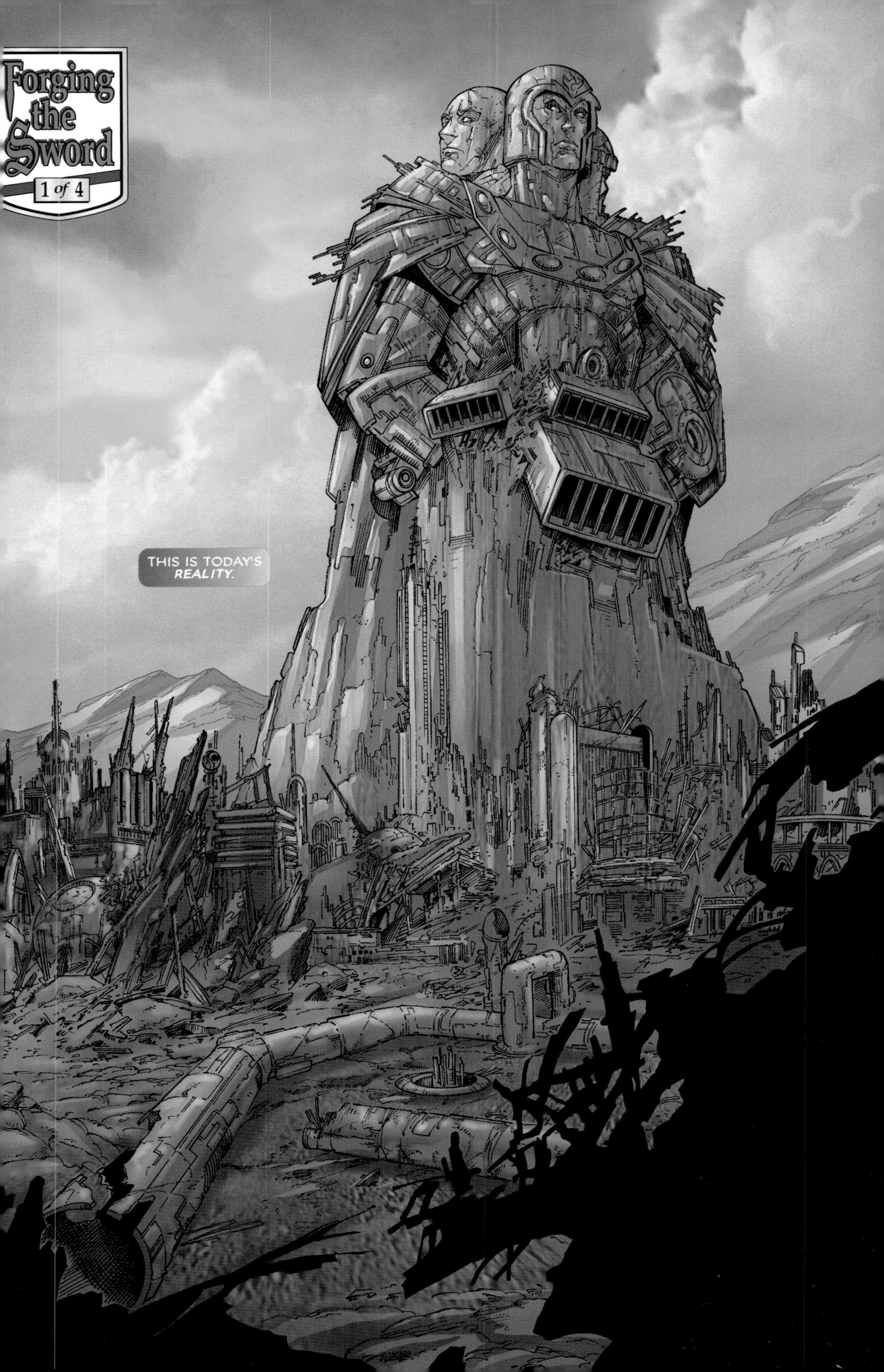
Forging the Sword
1 of 4
THIS IS TODAY'S REALITY.

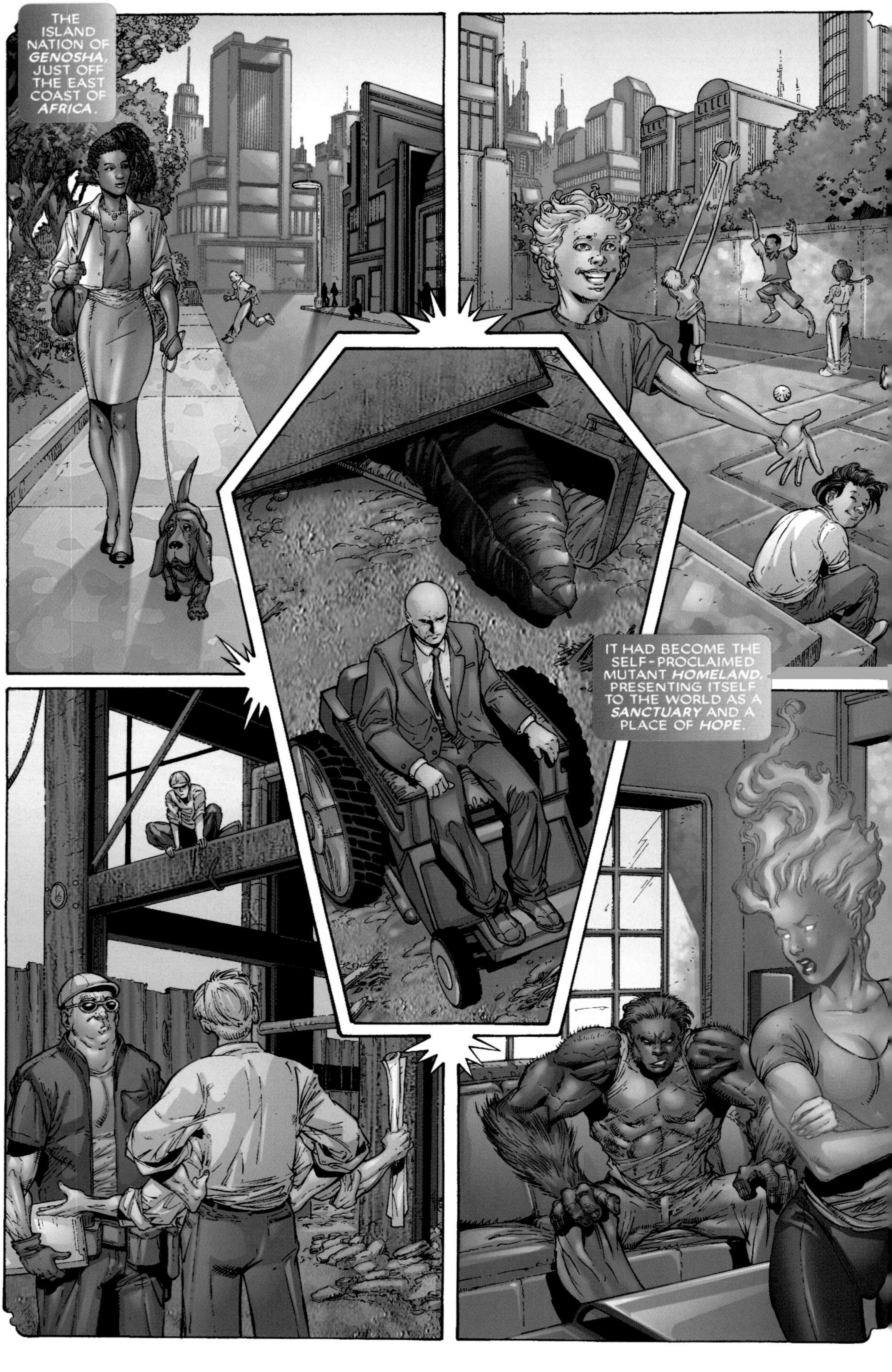
THE ISLAND NATION OF *GENOSHA*, JUST OFF THE EAST COAST OF *AFRICA*.
IT HAD BECOME THE SELF-PROCLAIMED MUTANT *HOMELAND*, PRESENTING ITSELF TO THE WORLD AS A *SANCTUARY* AND A PLACE OF *HOPE*.

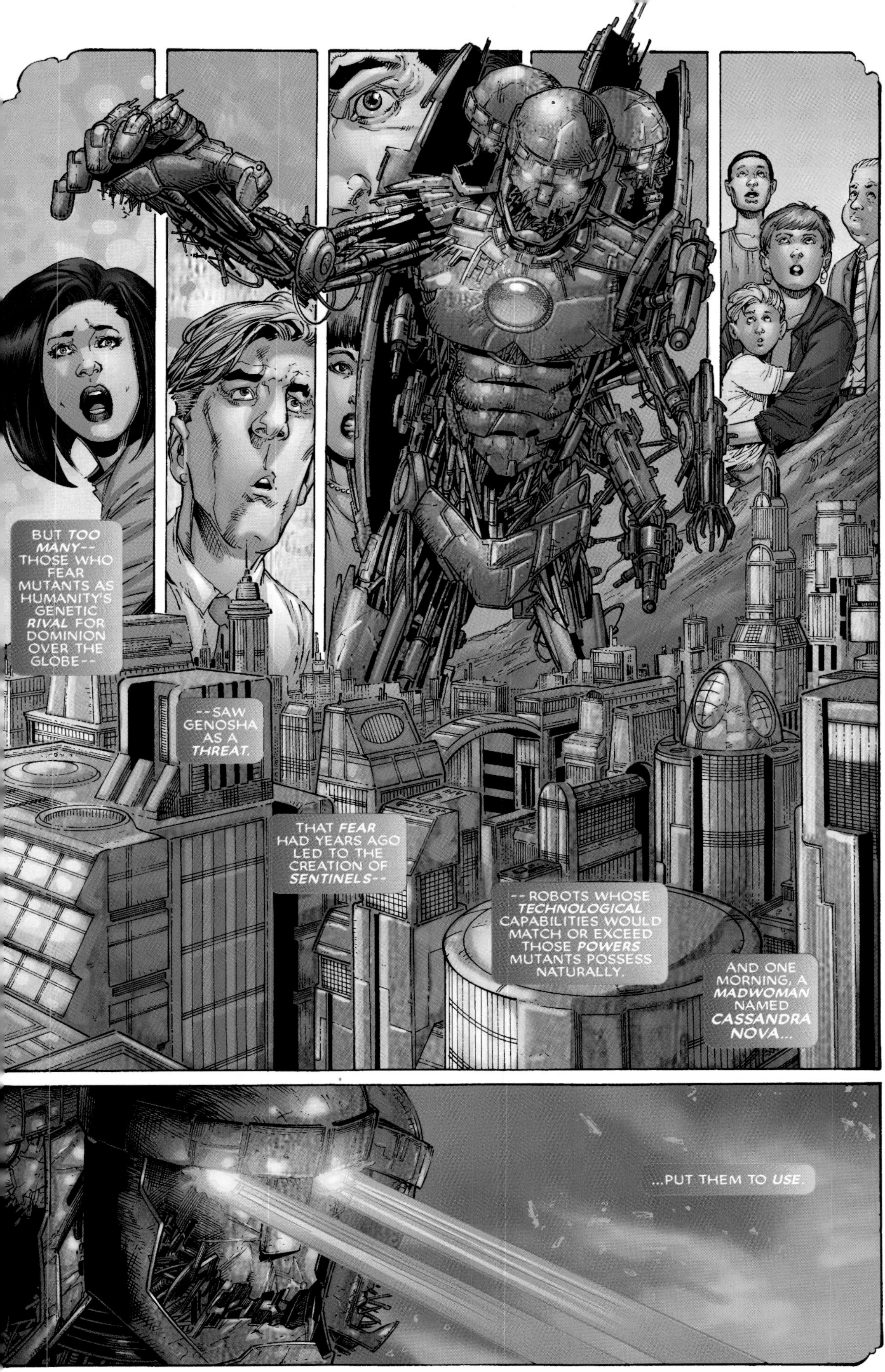
BUT TOO MANY-- THOSE WHO FEAR MUTANTS AS HUMANITY'S GENETIC RIVAL FOR DOMINION OVER THE GLOBE--
--SAW GENOSHA AS A THREAT.
THAT FEAR HAD YEARS AGO LED TO THE CREATION OF SENTINELS--
--ROBOTS WHOSE TECHNOLOGICAL CAPABILITIES WOULD MATCH OR EXCEED THOSE POWERS MUTANTS POSSESS NATURALLY.
AND ONE MORNING, A MADWOMAN NAMED CASSANDRA NOVA...
...PUT THEM TO USE.

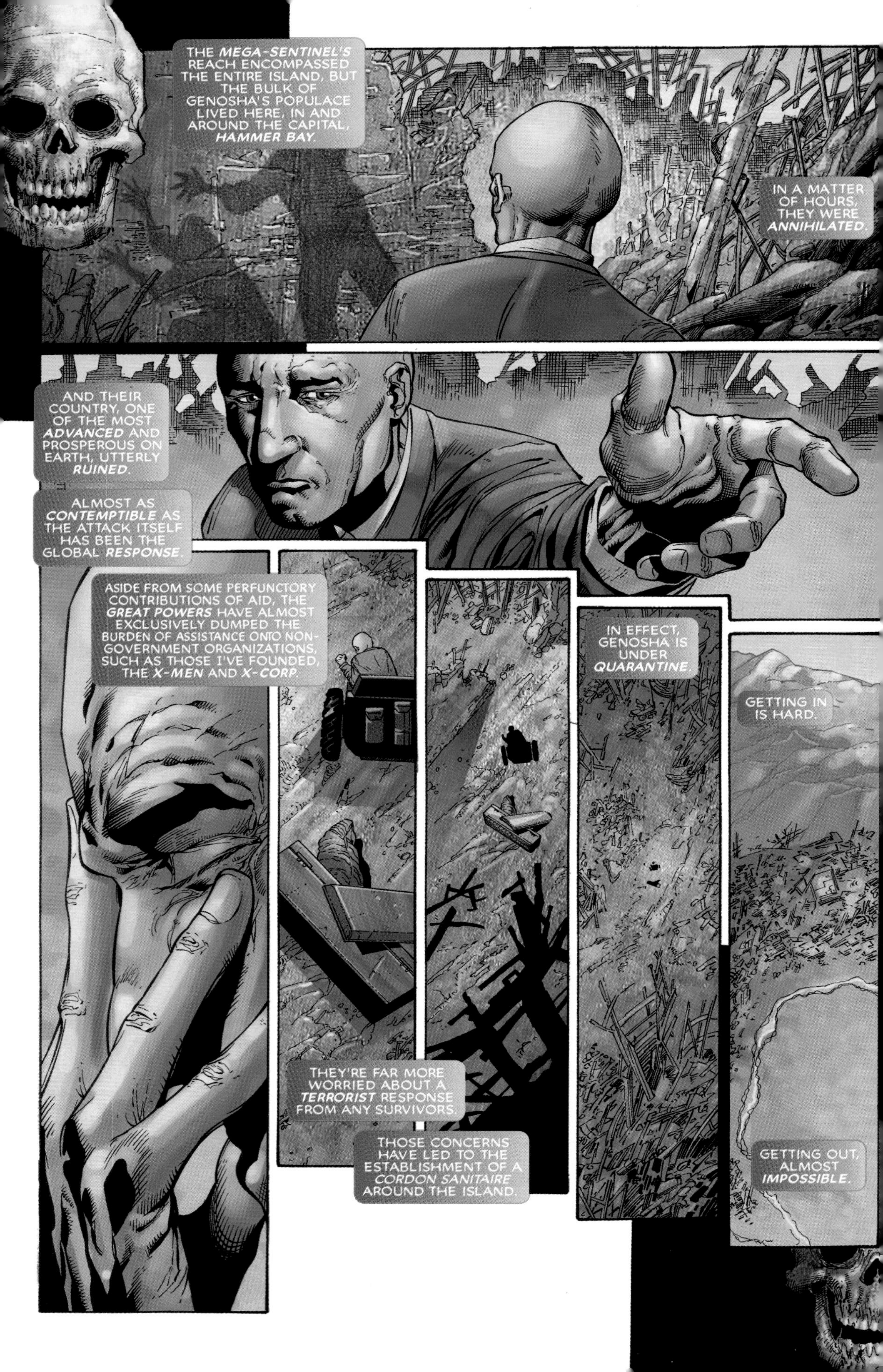
THE MEGA-SENTINEL'S REACH ENCOMPASSED THE ENTIRE ISLAND, BUT THE BULK OF GENOSHA'S POPULACE LIVED HERE, IN AND AROUND THE CAPITAL, HAMMER BAY.
IN A MATTER OF HOURS, THEY WERE ANNIHILATED.
AND THEIR COUNTRY, ONE OF THE MOST ADVANCED AND PROSPEROUS ON EARTH, UTTERLY RUINED.
ALMOST AS CONTEMPTIBLE AS THE ATTACK ITSELF HAS BEEN THE GLOBAL RESPONSE.
ASIDE FROM SOME PERFUNCTORY CONTRIBUTIONS OF AID, THE GREAT POWERS HAVE ALMOST EXCLUSIVELY DUMPED THE BURDEN OF ASSISTANCE ONTO NON-GOVERNMENT ORGANIZATIONS, SUCH AS THOSE I'VE FOUNDED, THE X-MEN AND X-CORP.
THEY'RE FAR MORE WORRIED ABOUT A TERRORIST RESPONSE FROM ANY SURVIVORS.
THOSE CONCERNS HAVE LED TO THE ESTABLISHMENT OF A CORDON SANITAIRE AROUND THE ISLAND.
IN EFFECT, GENOSHA IS UNDER QUARANTINE.
GETTING IN IS HARD.
GETTING OUT, ALMOST IMPOSSIBLE.

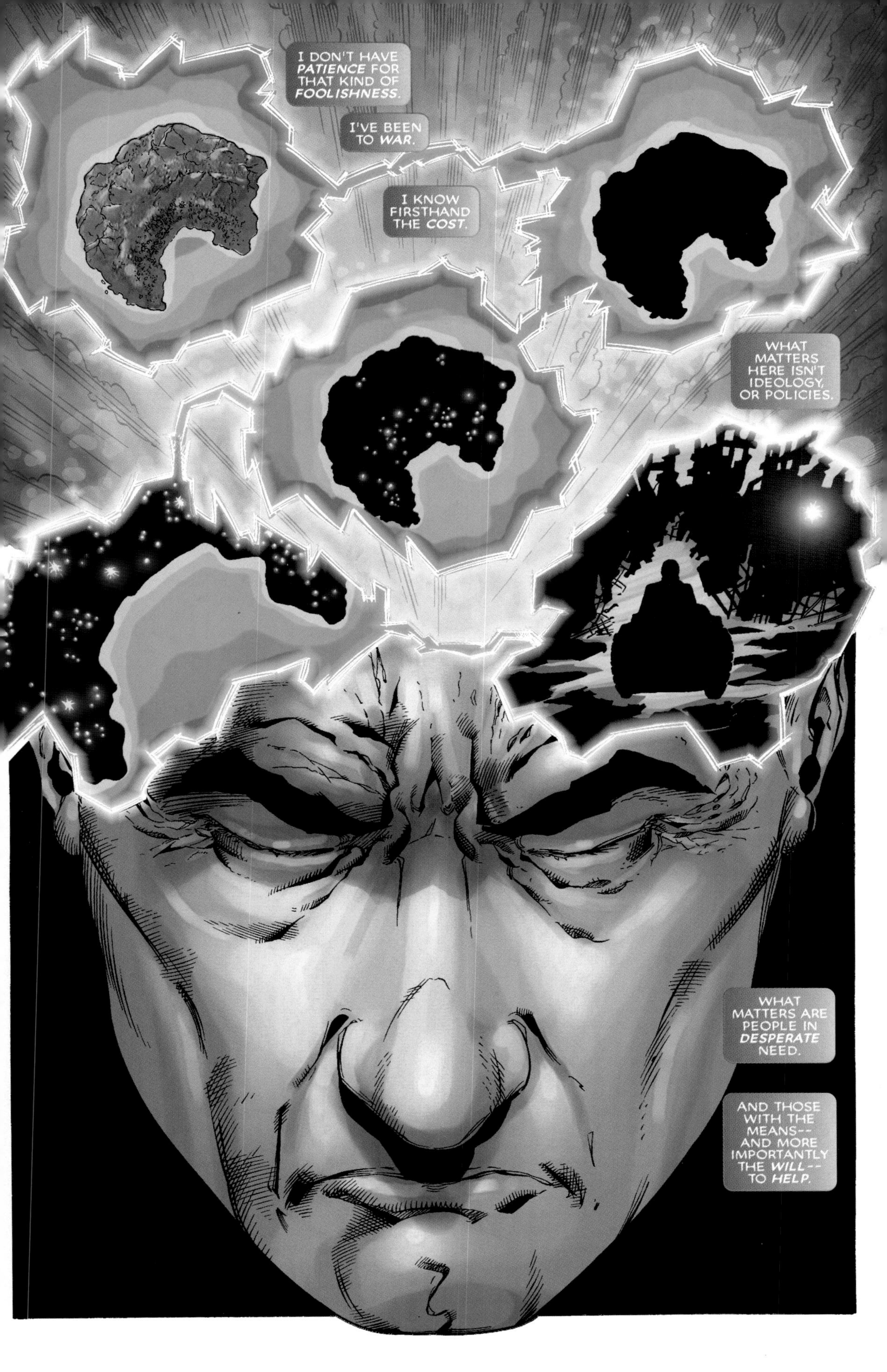
I DON'T HAVE PATIENCE FOR THAT KIND OF FOOLISHNESS.
I'VE BEEN TO WAR.
I KNOW FIRSTHAND THE COST.
WHAT MATTERS HERE ISN'T IDEOLOGY, OR POLICIES.
WHAT MATTERS ARE PEOPLE IN DESPERATE NEED.
AND THOSE WITH THE MEANS-- AND MORE IMPORTANTLY THE WILL-- TO HELP.

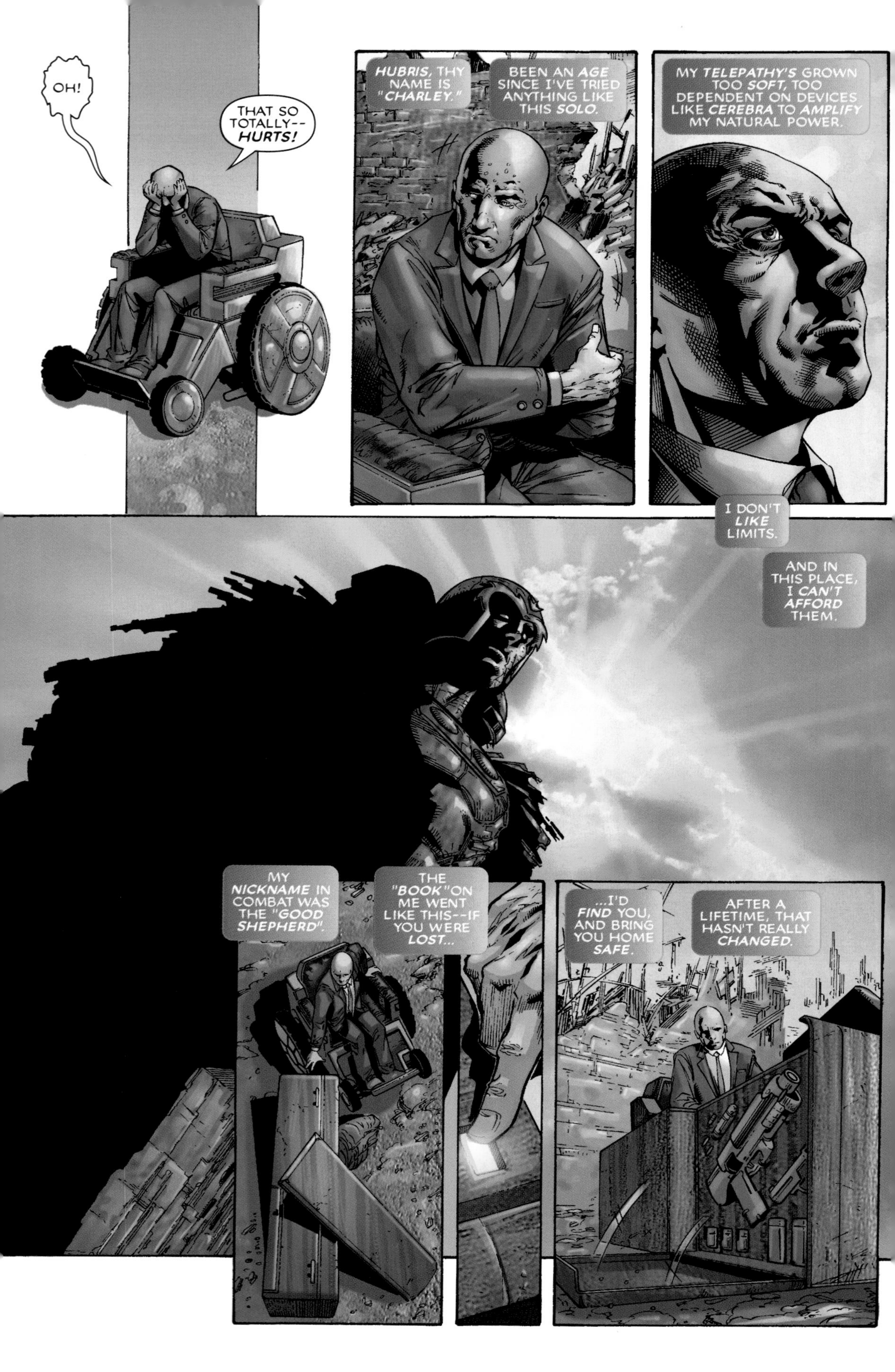
OH!
THAT SO TOTALLY-- HURTS!
HUBRIS, THY NAME IS "CHARLEY."
BEEN AN AGE SINCE I'VE TRIED ANYTHING LIKE THIS SOLO.
MY TELEPATHY'S GROWN TOO SOFT, TOO DEPENDENT ON DEVICES LIKE CEREBRA TO AMPLIFY MY NATURAL POWER.
I DON'T LIKE LIMITS.
AND IN THIS PLACE, I CAN'T AFFORD THEM.
MY NICKNAME IN COMBAT WAS THE "GOOD SHEPHERD".
THE "BOOK" ON ME WENT LIKE THIS--IF YOU WERE LOST...
...I'D FIND YOU, AND BRING YOU HOME SAFE.
AFTER A LIFETIME, THAT HASN'T REALLY CHANGED.

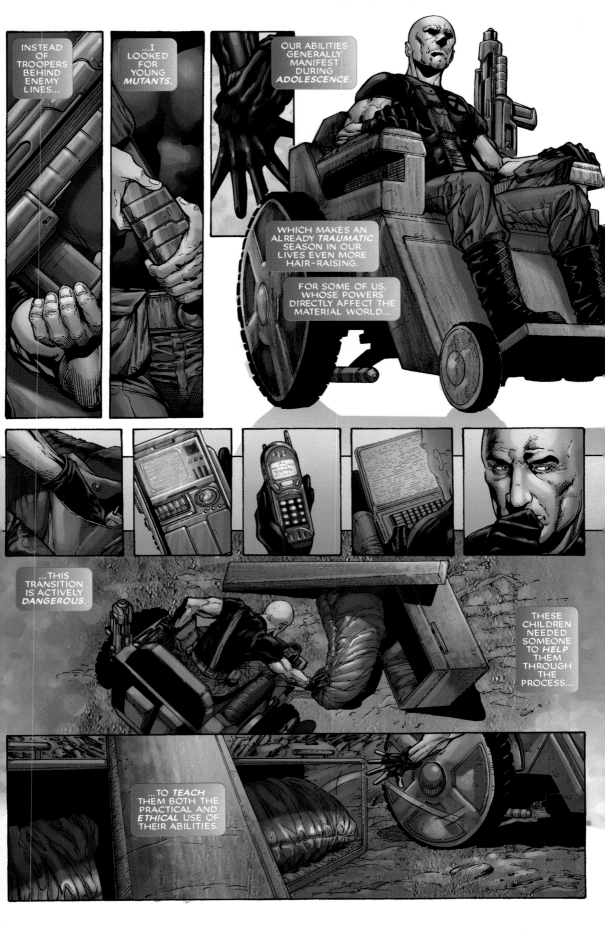

INSTEAD OF TROOPERS BEHIND ENEMY LINES...

...I LOOKED FOR YOUNG *MUTANTS.*

OUR ABILITIES GENERALLY MANIFEST DURING *ADOLESCENCE.*

WHICH MAKES AN ALREADY *TRAUMATIC* SEASON IN OUR LIVES EVEN MORE HAIR-RAISING.

FOR SOME OF US, WHOSE POWERS DIRECTLY AFFECT THE MATERIAL WORLD...

...THIS TRANSITION IS ACTIVELY *DANGEROUS.*

THESE CHILDREN NEEDED SOMEONE TO *HELP* THEM THROUGH THE PROCESS...

...TO *TEACH* THEM BOTH THE PRACTICAL AND *ETHICAL* USE OF THEIR ABILITIES.

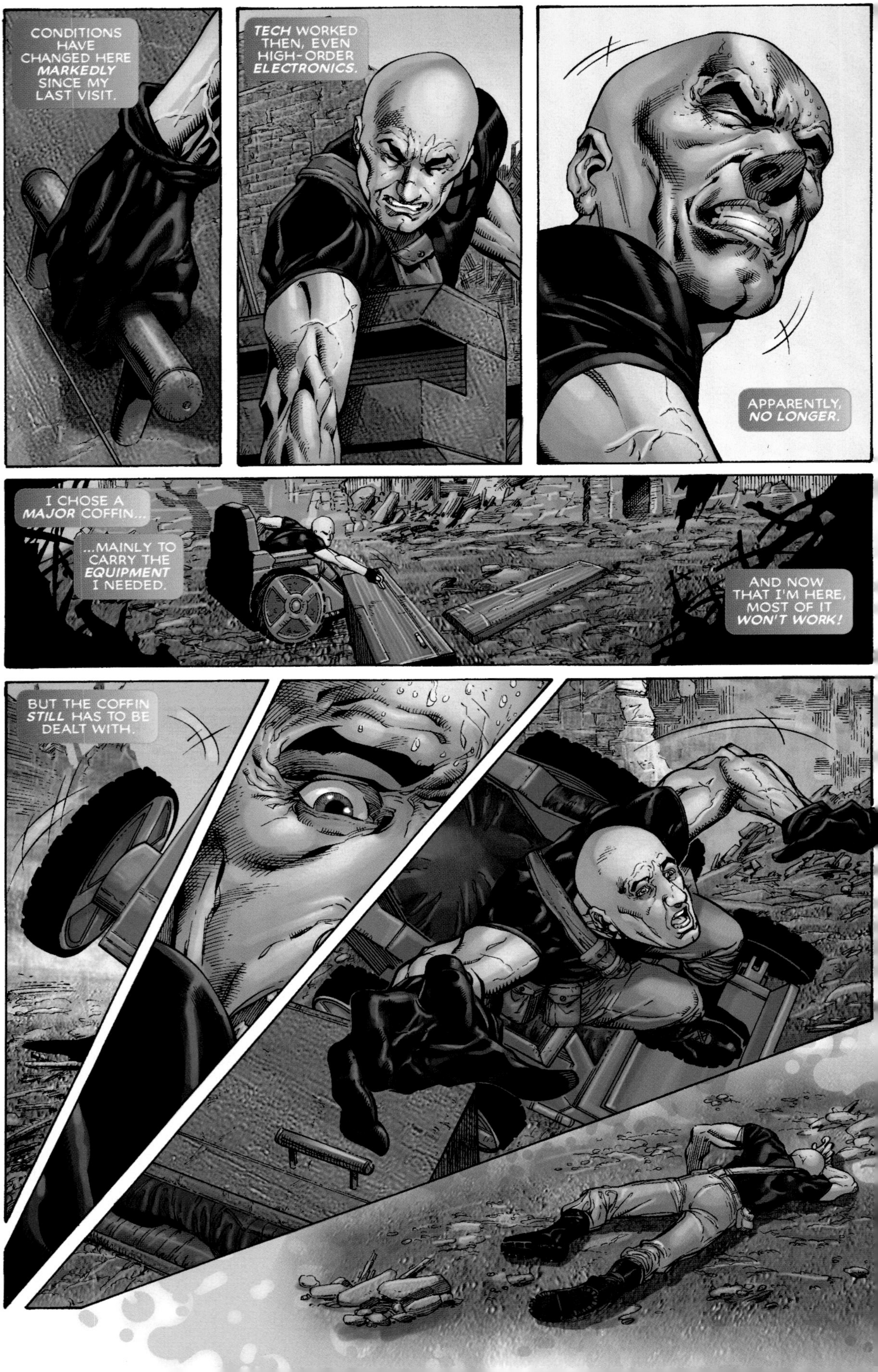
CONDITIONS HAVE CHANGED HERE MARKEDLY SINCE MY LAST VISIT.
TECH WORKED THEN, EVEN HIGH-ORDER ELECTRONICS.
APPARENTLY, NO LONGER.
I CHOSE A MAJOR COFFIN...
...MAINLY TO CARRY THE EQUIPMENT I NEEDED.
AND NOW THAT I'M HERE, MOST OF IT WON'T WORK!
BUT THE COFFIN STILL HAS TO BE DEALT WITH.

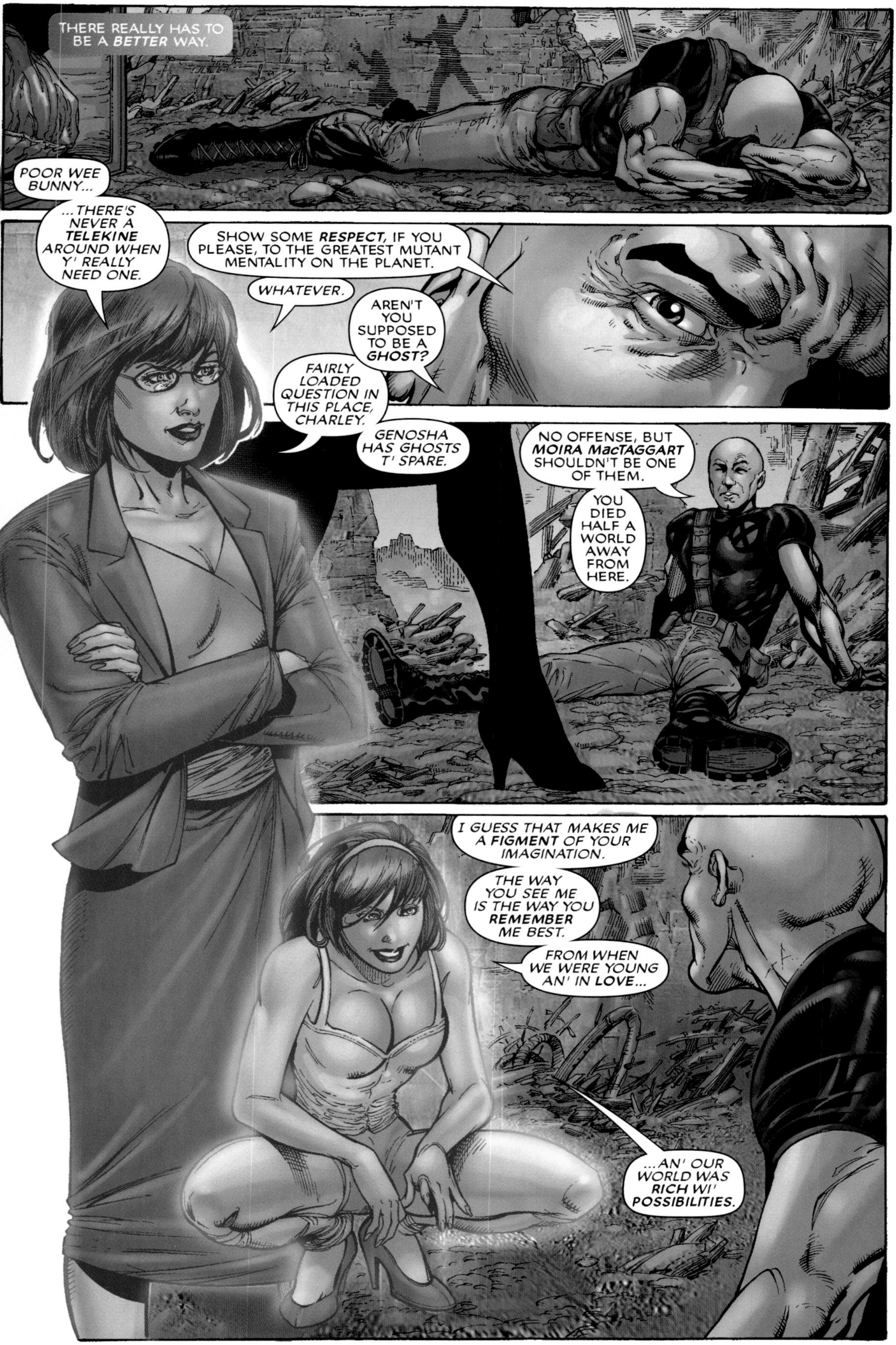
THERE REALLY HAS TO BE A BETTER WAY.
POOR WEE BUNNY...
...THERE'S NEVER A TELEKINE AROUND WHEN Y' REALLY NEED ONE.
SHOW SOME RESPECT, IF YOU PLEASE, TO THE GREATEST MUTANT MENTALITY ON THE PLANET.
WHATEVER.
AREN'T YOU SUPPOSED TO BE A GHOST?
FAIRLY LOADED QUESTION IN THIS PLACE, CHARLEY.
GENOSHA HAS GHOSTS T' SPARE.
NO OFFENSE, BUT MOIRA MacTAGGART SHOULDN'T BE ONE OF THEM.
YOU DIED HALF A WORLD AWAY FROM HERE.
I GUESS THAT MAKES ME A FIGMENT OF YOUR IMAGINATION.
THE WAY YOU SEE ME IS THE WAY YOU REMEMBER ME BEST.
FROM WHEN WE WERE YOUNG AN' IN LOVE...
...AN' OUR WORLD WAS RICH WI' POSSIBILITIES.

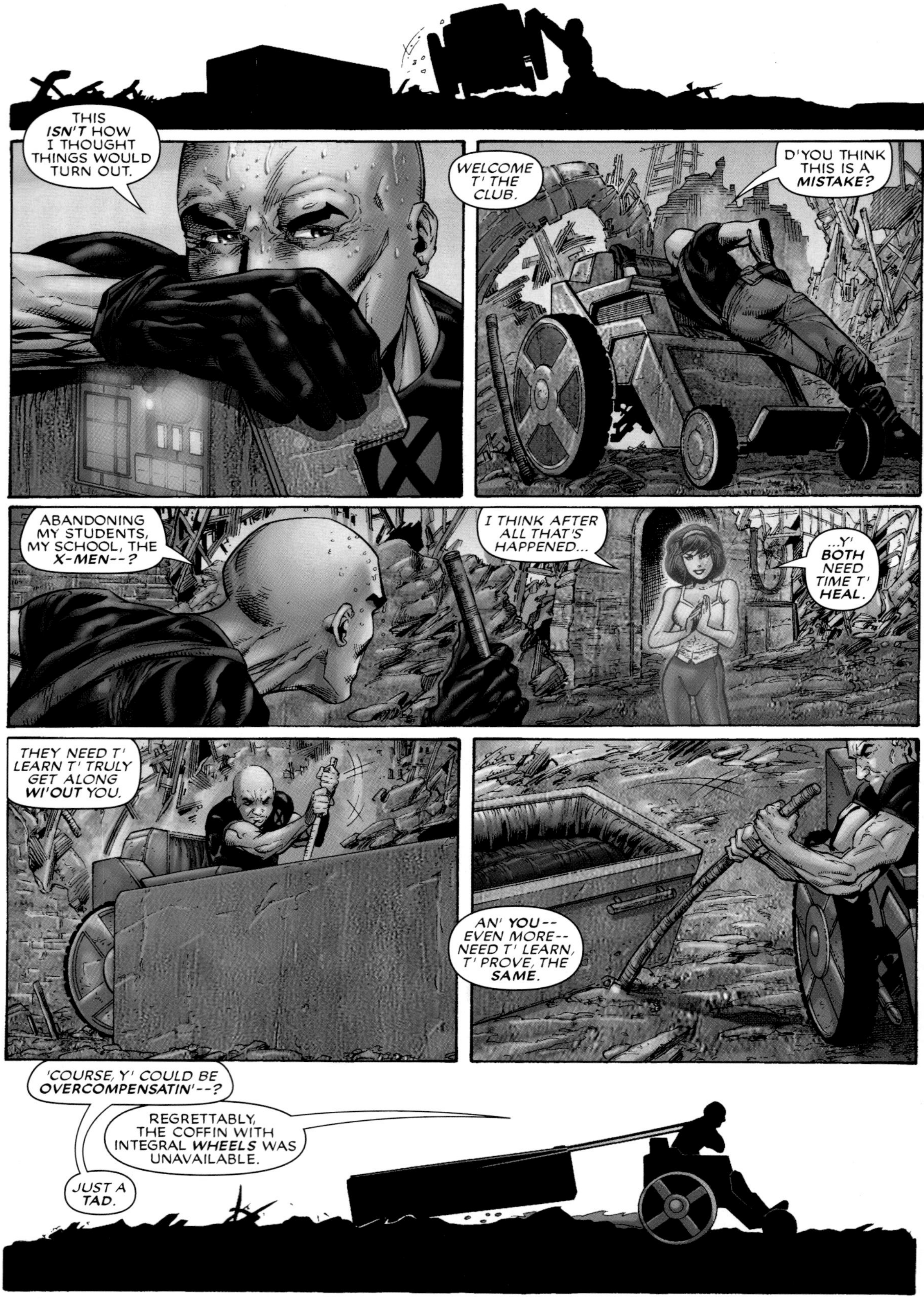
THIS ISN'T HOW I THOUGHT THINGS WOULD TURN OUT.
WELCOME T' THE CLUB.
D'YOU THINK THIS IS A MISTAKE?
ABANDONING MY STUDENTS, MY SCHOOL, THE X-MEN--?
I THINK AFTER ALL THAT'S HAPPENED...
...Y' BOTH NEED TIME T' HEAL.
THEY NEED T' LEARN T' TRULY GET ALONG WI'OUT YOU.
AN' YOU-- EVEN MORE-- NEED T' LEARN, T' PROVE, THE SAME.
'COURSE, Y' COULD BE OVERCOMPENSATIN'--?
REGRETTABLY, THE COFFIN WITH INTEGRAL WHEELS WAS UNAVAILABLE.
JUST A TAD.

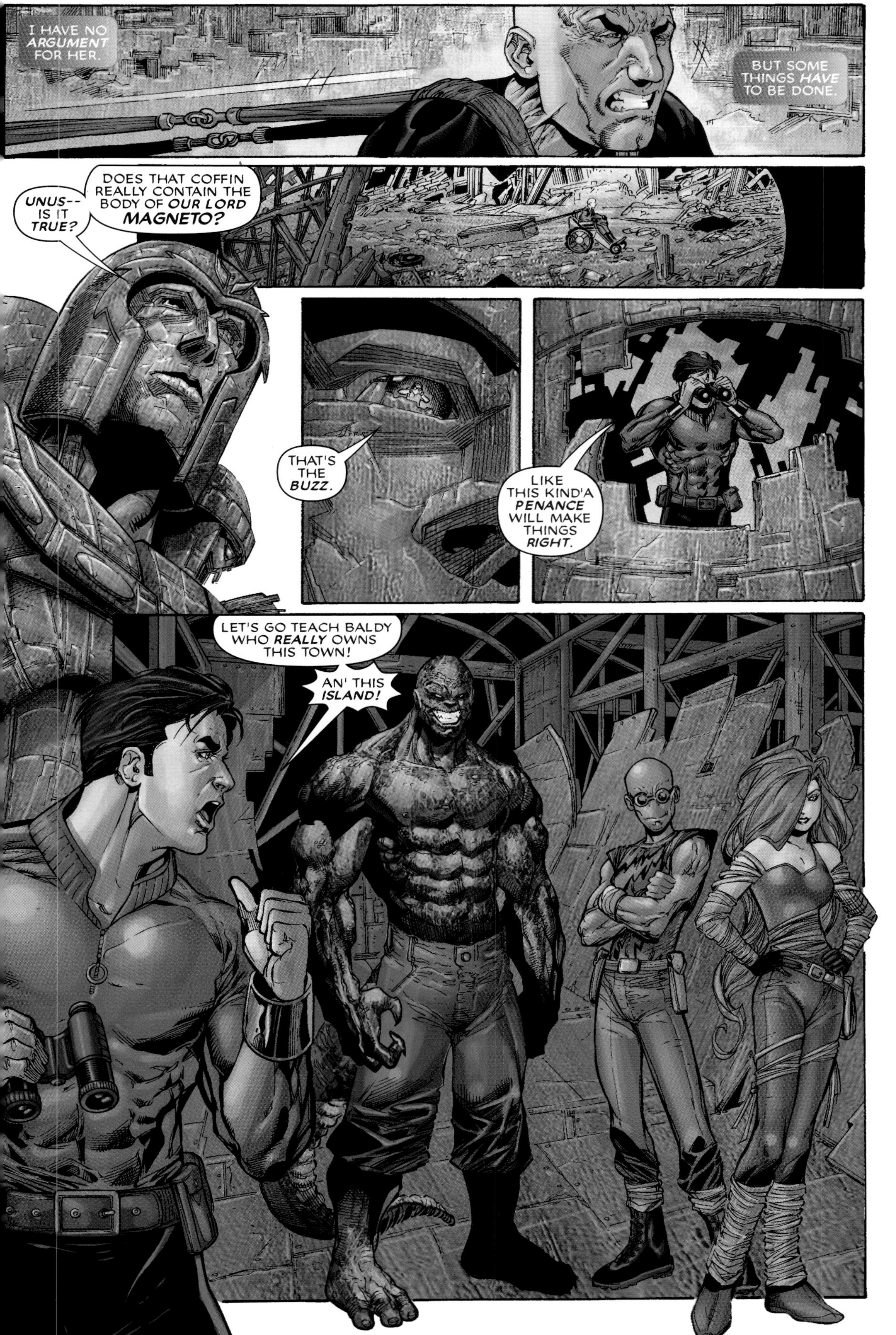
I HAVE NO *ARGUMENT* FOR HER.
BUT SOME THINGS *HAVE* TO BE DONE.
UNUS-- IS IT *TRUE?*
DOES THAT COFFIN REALLY CONTAIN THE BODY OF *OUR LORD MAGNETO?*
THAT'S THE *BUZZ*.
LIKE THIS KIND'A *PENANCE* WILL MAKE THINGS *RIGHT*.
LET'S GO TEACH BALDY WHO *REALLY* OWNS THIS TOWN!
AN' THIS *ISLAND!*

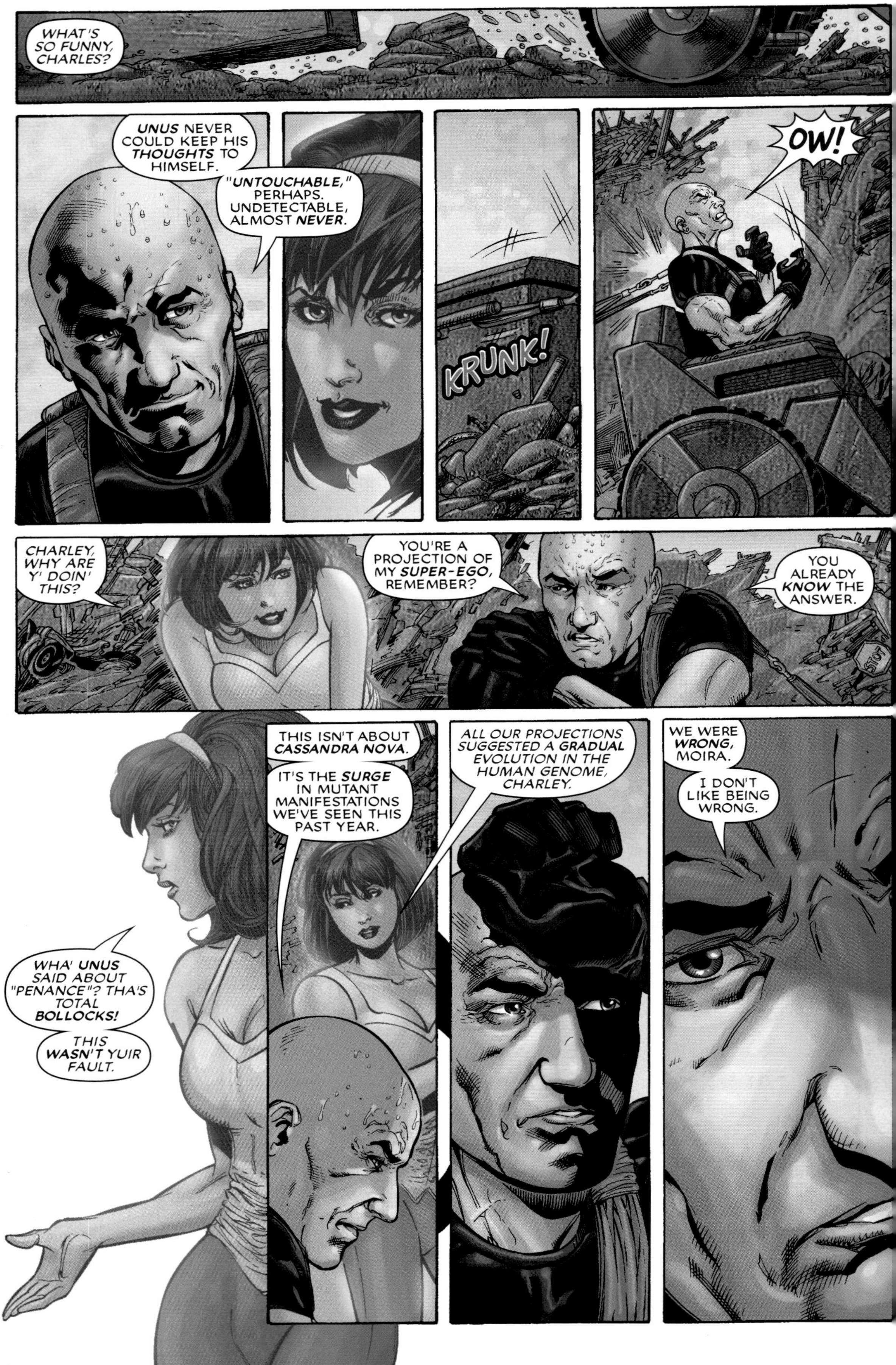
WHAT'S SO FUNNY, CHARLES?
UNUS NEVER COULD KEEP HIS THOUGHTS TO HIMSELF.
"UNTOUCHABLE," PERHAPS. UNDETECTABLE, ALMOST NEVER.
KRUNK!
OW!
CHARLEY, WHY ARE Y' DOIN' THIS?
YOU'RE A PROJECTION OF MY SUPER-EGO, REMEMBER?
YOU ALREADY KNOW THE ANSWER.
STOP
WHA' UNUS SAID ABOUT "PENANCE"? THA'S TOTAL BOLLOCKS!
THIS WASN'T YUIR FAULT.
THIS ISN'T ABOUT CASSANDRA NOVA.
IT'S THE SURGE IN MUTANT MANIFESTATIONS WE'VE SEEN THIS PAST YEAR.
ALL OUR PROJECTIONS SUGGESTED A GRADUAL EVOLUTION IN THE HUMAN GENOME, CHARLEY.
WE WERE WRONG, MOIRA.
I DON'T LIKE BEING WRONG.

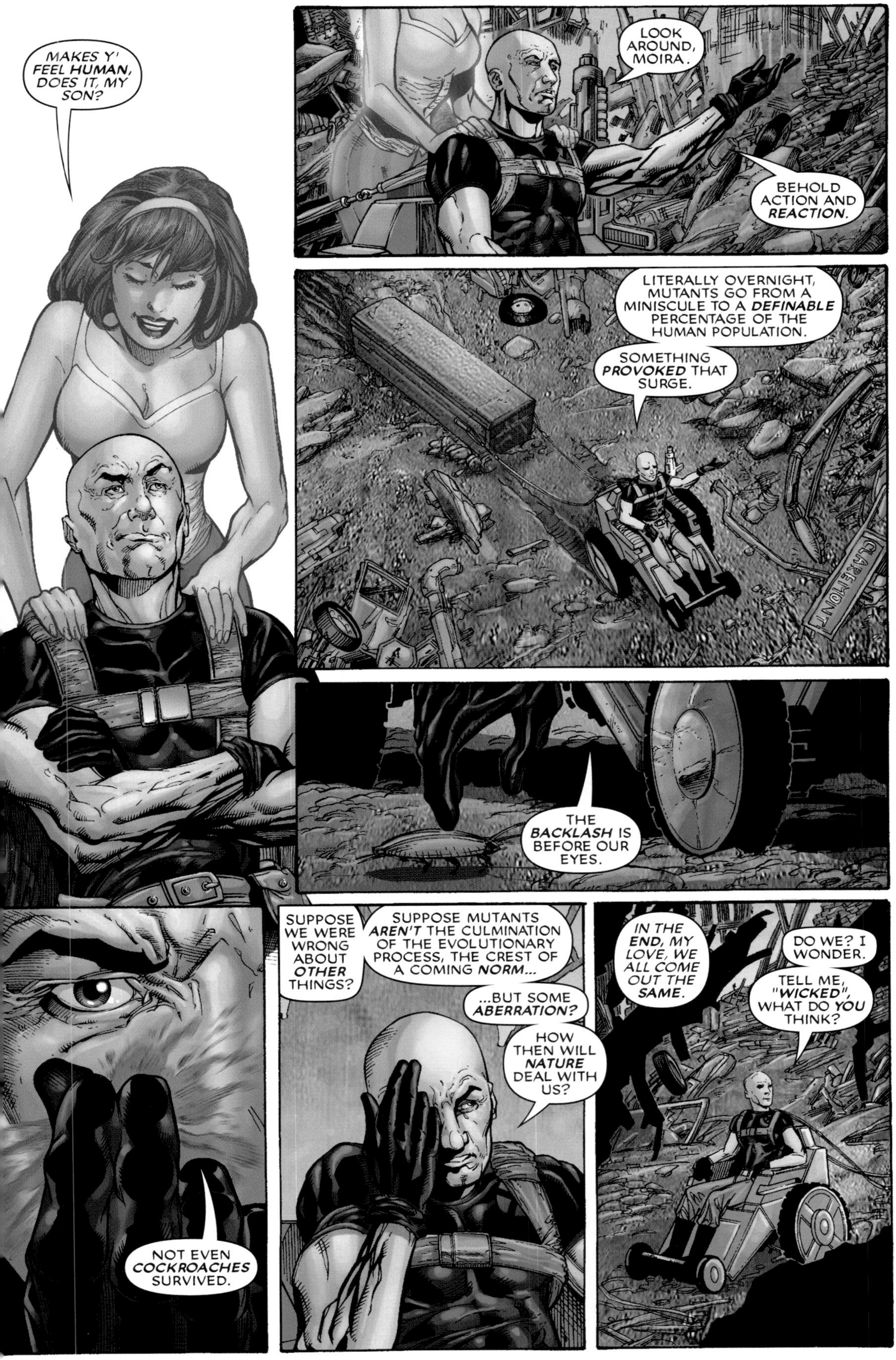

MAKES Y' FEEL HUMAN, DOES IT, MY SON?
LOOK AROUND, MOIRA.
BEHOLD ACTION AND REACTION.
LITERALLY OVERNIGHT, MUTANTS GO FROM A MINISCULE TO A DEFINABLE PERCENTAGE OF THE HUMAN POPULATION.
SOMETHING PROVOKED THAT SURGE.
CLAREMONT
THE BACKLASH IS BEFORE OUR EYES.
NOT EVEN COCKROACHES SURVIVED.
SUPPOSE WE WERE WRONG ABOUT OTHER THINGS?
SUPPOSE MUTANTS AREN'T THE CULMINATION OF THE EVOLUTIONARY PROCESS, THE CREST OF A COMING NORM...
...BUT SOME ABERRATION?
HOW THEN WILL NATURE DEAL WITH US?
IN THE END, MY LOVE, WE ALL COME OUT THE SAME.
DO WE? I WONDER.
TELL ME, "WICKED", WHAT DO YOU THINK?

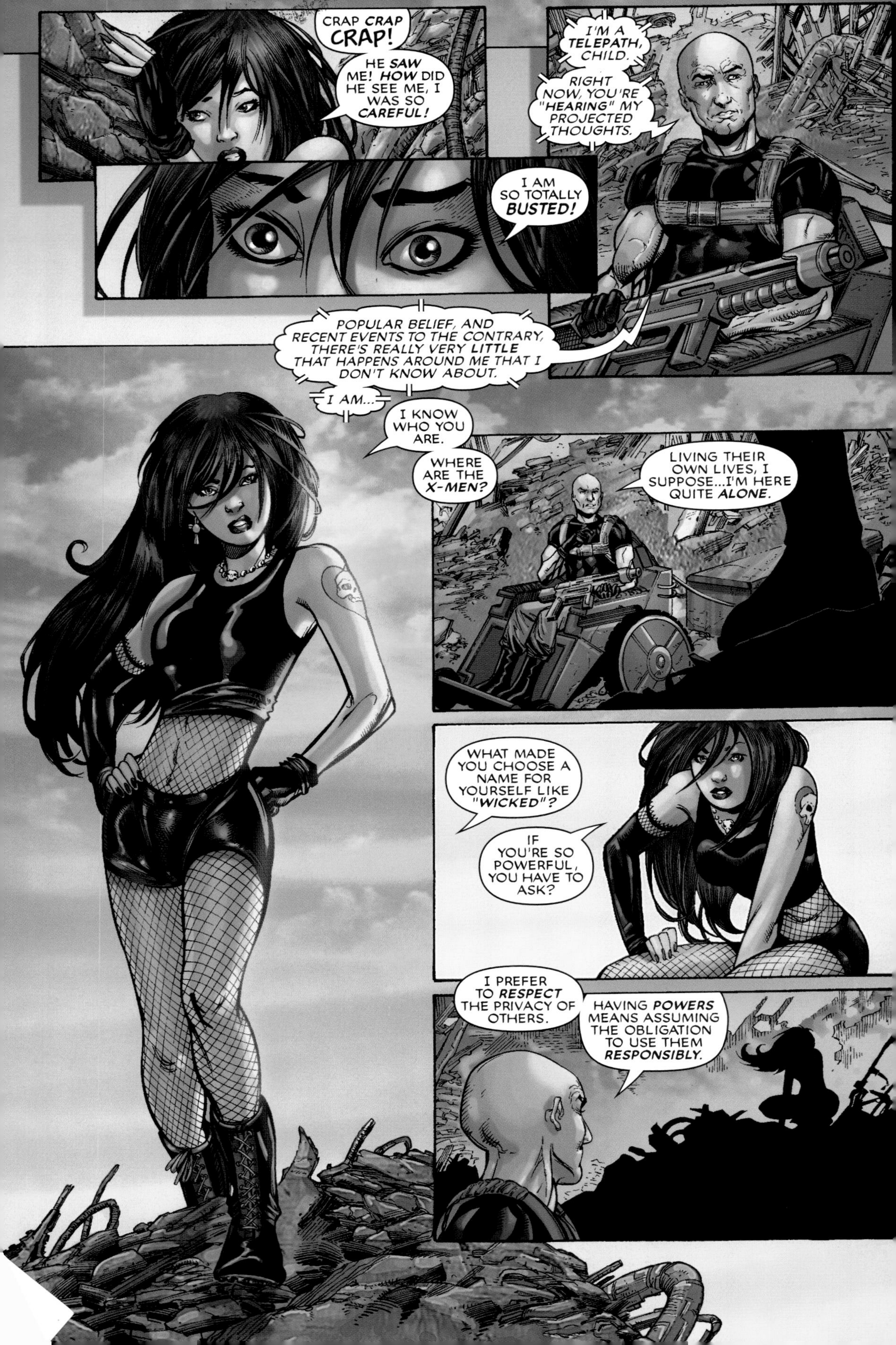

CRAP CRAP CRAP!
HE SAW ME! HOW DID HE SEE ME, I WAS SO CAREFUL!
I AM SO TOTALLY BUSTED!
I'M A TELEPATH, CHILD.
RIGHT NOW, YOU'RE "HEARING" MY PROJECTED THOUGHTS.
POPULAR BELIEF, AND RECENT EVENTS TO THE CONTRARY, THERE'S REALLY VERY LITTLE THAT HAPPENS AROUND ME THAT I DON'T KNOW ABOUT.
I AM...
I KNOW WHO YOU ARE.
WHERE ARE THE X-MEN?
LIVING THEIR OWN LIVES, I SUPPOSE...I'M HERE QUITE ALONE.
WHAT MADE YOU CHOOSE A NAME FOR YOURSELF LIKE "WICKED"?
IF YOU'RE SO POWERFUL, YOU HAVE TO ASK?
I PREFER TO RESPECT THE PRIVACY OF OTHERS.
HAVING POWERS MEANS ASSUMING THE OBLIGATION TO USE THEM RESPONSIBLY.

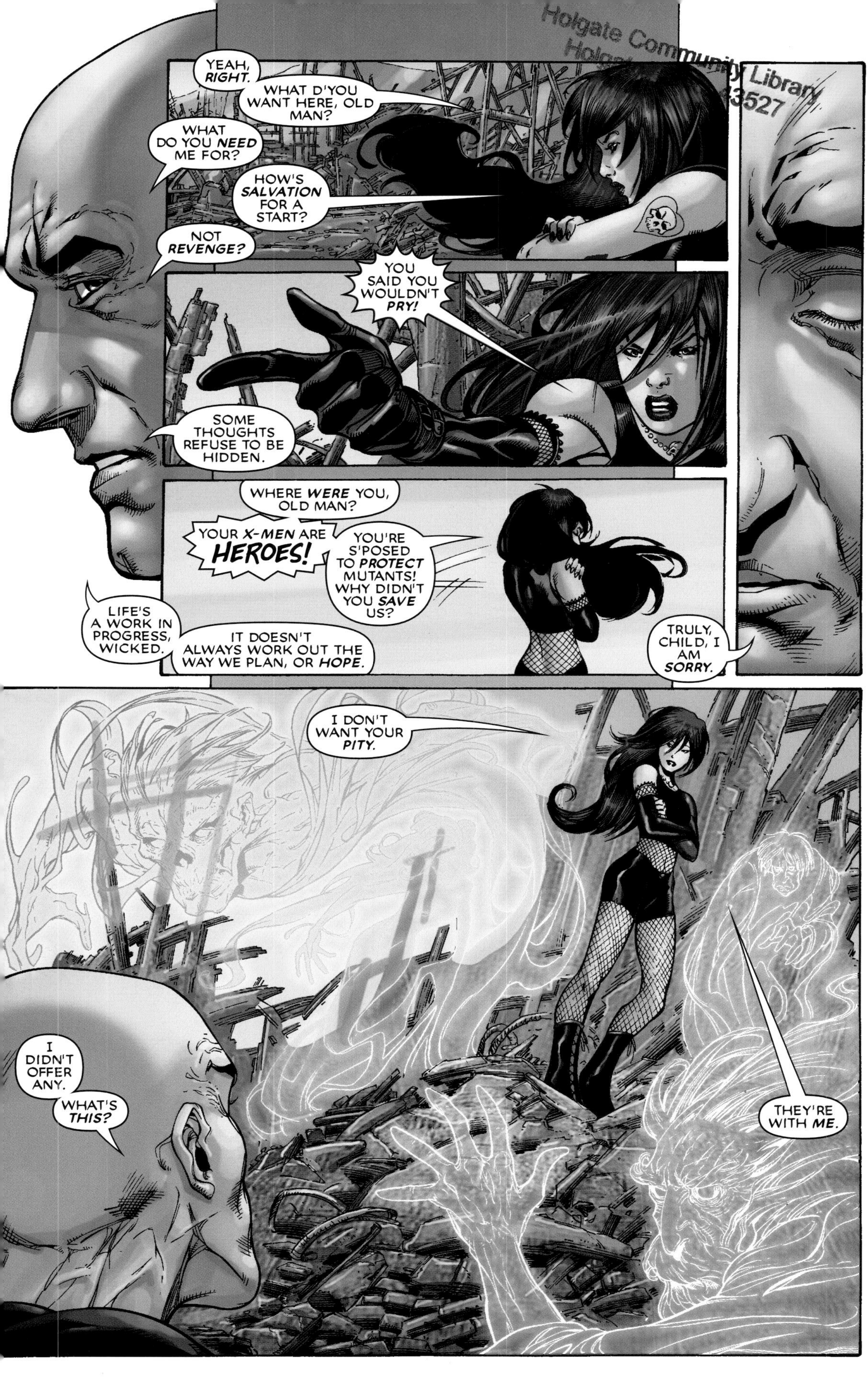
YEAH, RIGHT.
WHAT D'YOU WANT HERE, OLD MAN?
WHAT DO YOU NEED ME FOR?
HOW'S SALVATION FOR A START?
NOT REVENGE?
YOU SAID YOU WOULDN'T PRY!
SOME THOUGHTS REFUSE TO BE HIDDEN.
WHERE WERE YOU, OLD MAN?
YOUR X-MEN ARE HEROES!
YOU'RE S'POSED TO PROTECT MUTANTS! WHY DIDN'T YOU SAVE US?
LIFE'S A WORK IN PROGRESS, WICKED.
IT DOESN'T ALWAYS WORK OUT THE WAY WE PLAN, OR HOPE.
TRULY, CHILD, I AM SORRY.
I DON'T WANT YOUR PITY.
I DIDN'T OFFER ANY.
WHAT'S THIS?
THEY'RE WITH ME.

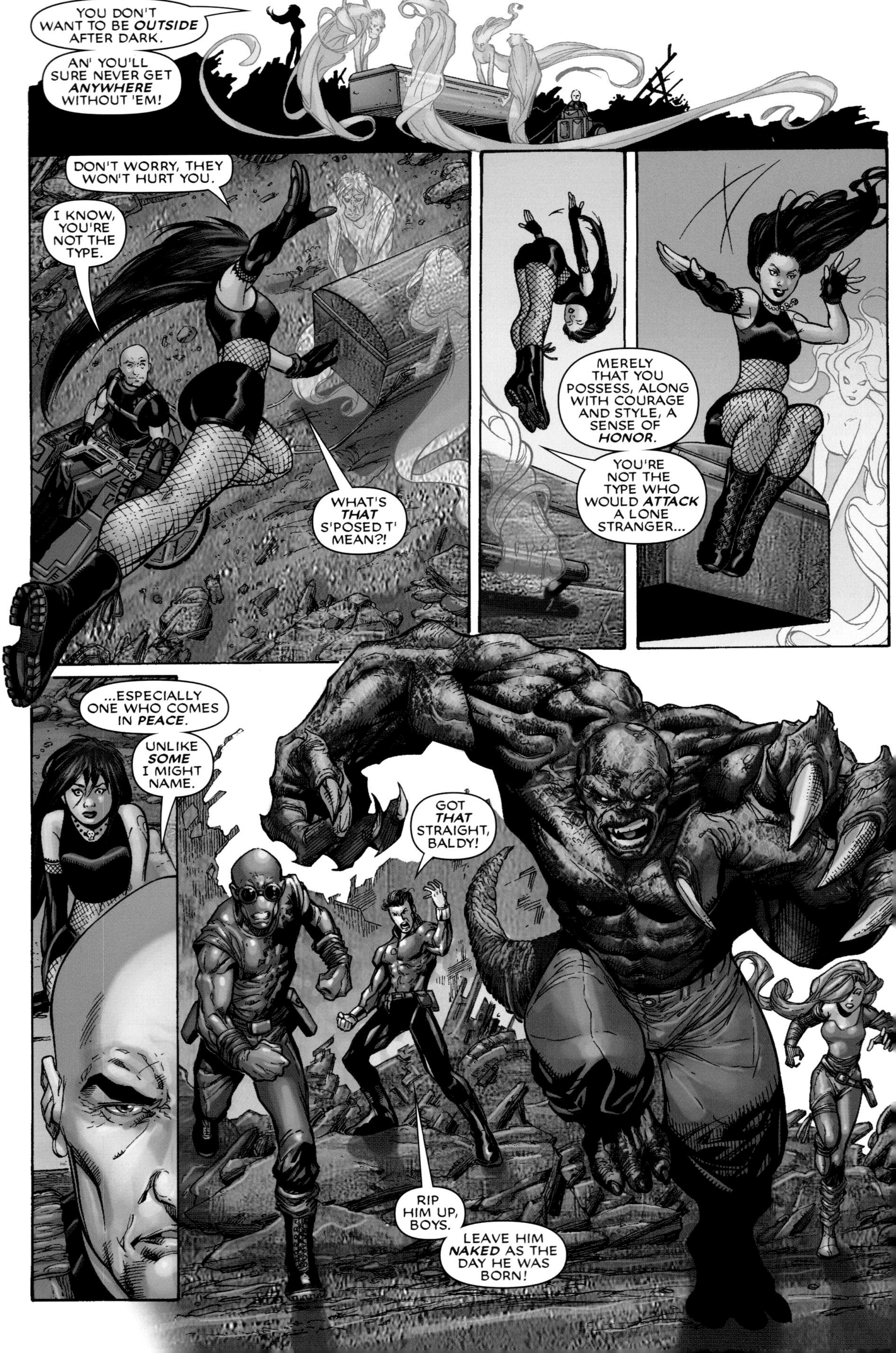
YOU DON'T WANT TO BE *OUTSIDE* AFTER DARK.
AN' YOU'LL SURE NEVER GET ***ANYWHERE*** WITHOUT 'EM!
DON'T WORRY, THEY WON'T HURT YOU.
I KNOW, YOU'RE NOT THE TYPE.
WHAT'S ***THAT*** S'POSED T' MEAN?!
MERELY THAT YOU POSSESS, ALONG WITH COURAGE AND STYLE, A SENSE OF ***HONOR***.
YOU'RE NOT THE TYPE WHO WOULD ***ATTACK*** A LONE STRANGER...
...ESPECIALLY ONE WHO COMES IN *PEACE*.
UNLIKE ***SOME*** I MIGHT NAME.
GOT ***THAT*** STRAIGHT, BALDY!
RIP HIM UP, BOYS.
LEAVE HIM ***NAKED*** AS THE DAY HE WAS BORN!

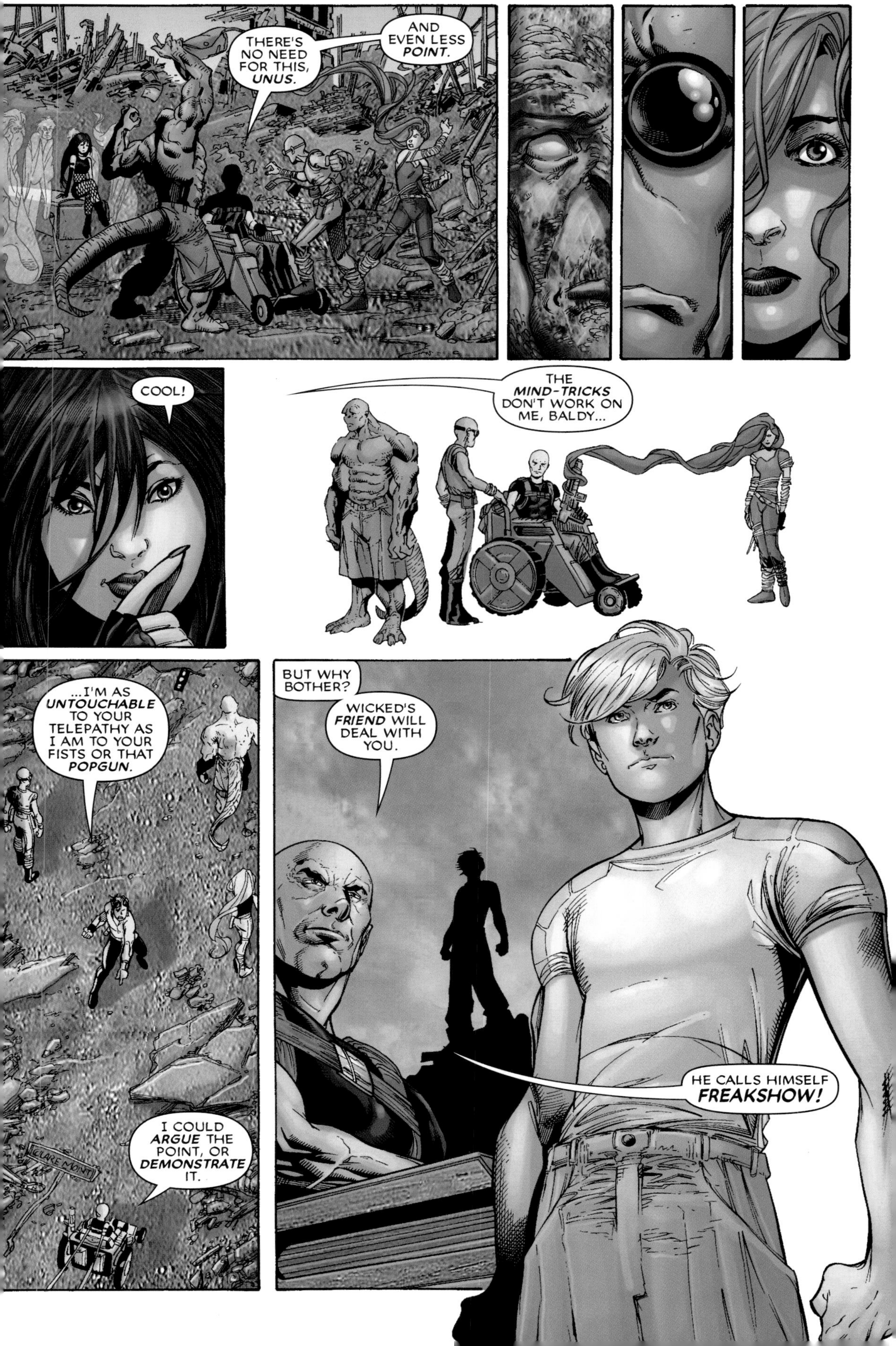
THERE'S NO NEED FOR THIS, UNUS.
AND EVEN LESS POINT.
COOL!
THE MIND-TRICKS DON'T WORK ON ME, BALDY...
...I'M AS UNTOUCHABLE TO YOUR TELEPATHY AS I AM TO YOUR FISTS OR THAT POPGUN.
I COULD ARGUE THE POINT, OR DEMONSTRATE IT.
BUT WHY BOTHER?
WICKED'S FRIEND WILL DEAL WITH YOU.
HE CALLS HIMSELF FREAKSHOW!

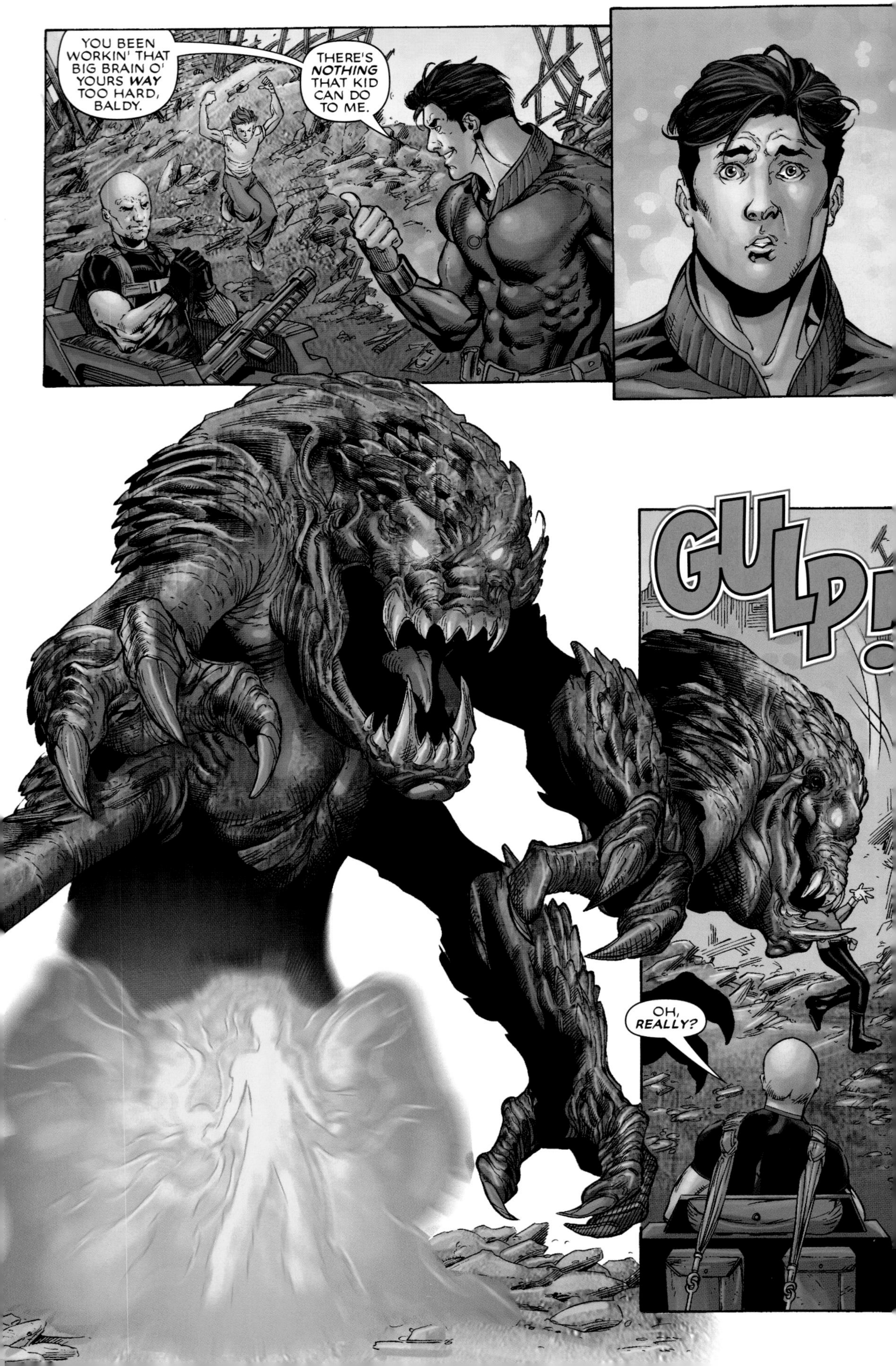
YOU BEEN WORKIN' THAT BIG BRAIN O' YOURS WAY TOO HARD, BALDY.
THERE'S NOTHING THAT KID CAN DO TO ME.
GULP!
OH, REALLY?

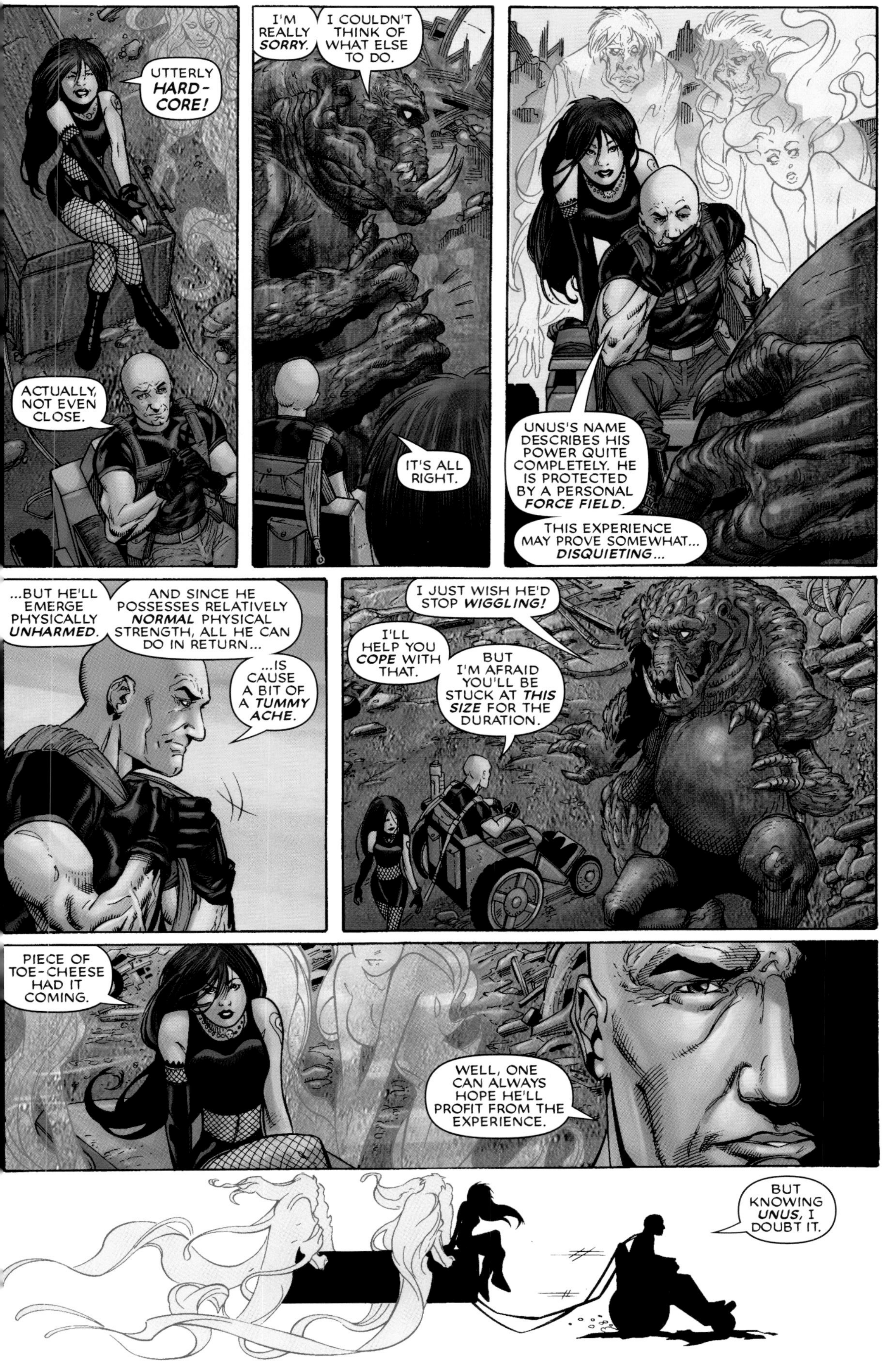
UTTERLY HARD-CORE!
ACTUALLY, NOT EVEN CLOSE.
I'M REALLY SORRY.
I COULDN'T THINK OF WHAT ELSE TO DO.
IT'S ALL RIGHT.
UNUS'S NAME DESCRIBES HIS POWER QUITE COMPLETELY. HE IS PROTECTED BY A PERSONAL FORCE FIELD.
THIS EXPERIENCE MAY PROVE SOMEWHAT... DISQUIETING...
AND SINCE HE POSSESSES RELATIVELY NORMAL PHYSICAL STRENGTH, ALL HE CAN DO IN RETURN...
...IS CAUSE A BIT OF A TUMMY ACHE.
...BUT HE'LL EMERGE PHYSICALLY UNHARMED.
I JUST WISH HE'D STOP WIGGLING!
I'LL HELP YOU COPE WITH THAT.
BUT I'M AFRAID YOU'LL BE STUCK AT THIS SIZE FOR THE DURATION.
PIECE OF TOE-CHEESE HAD IT COMING.
WELL, ONE CAN ALWAYS HOPE HE'LL PROFIT FROM THE EXPERIENCE.
BUT KNOWING UNUS, I DOUBT IT.

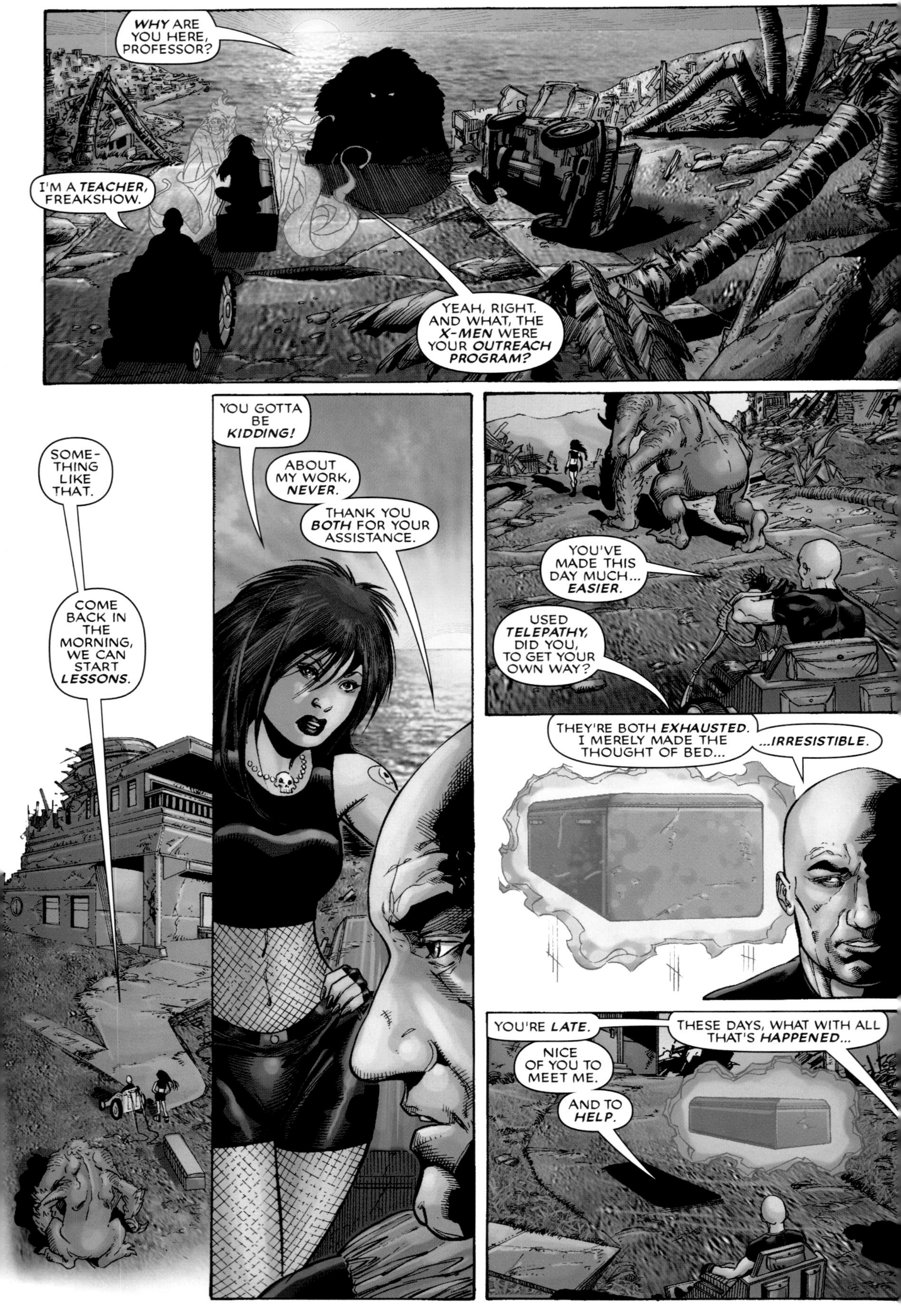

WHY ARE YOU HERE, PROFESSOR?
I'M A TEACHER, FREAKSHOW.
YEAH, RIGHT. AND WHAT, THE X-MEN WERE YOUR OUTREACH PROGRAM?
SOME-THING LIKE THAT.
COME BACK IN THE MORNING, WE CAN START LESSONS.
YOU GOTTA BE KIDDING!
ABOUT MY WORK, NEVER.
THANK YOU BOTH FOR YOUR ASSISTANCE.
YOU'VE MADE THIS DAY MUCH... EASIER.
USED TELEPATHY, DID YOU, TO GET YOUR OWN WAY?
THEY'RE BOTH EXHAUSTED. I MERELY MADE THE THOUGHT OF BED...
...IRRESISTIBLE.
YOU'RE LATE.
NICE OF YOU TO MEET ME.
AND TO HELP.
THESE DAYS, WHAT WITH ALL THAT'S HAPPENED...

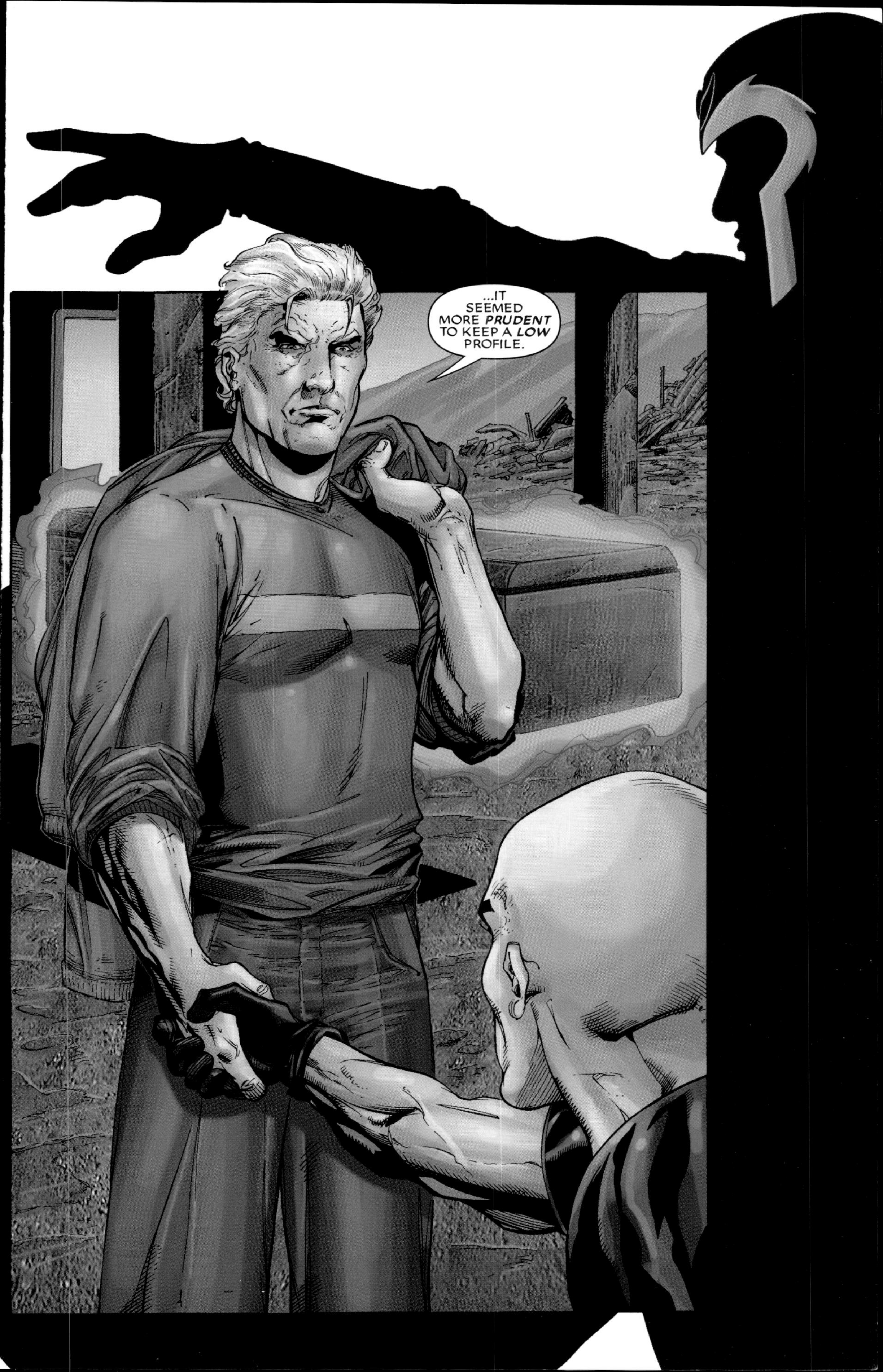
...IT SEEMED MORE PRUDENT TO KEEP A LOW PROFILE.

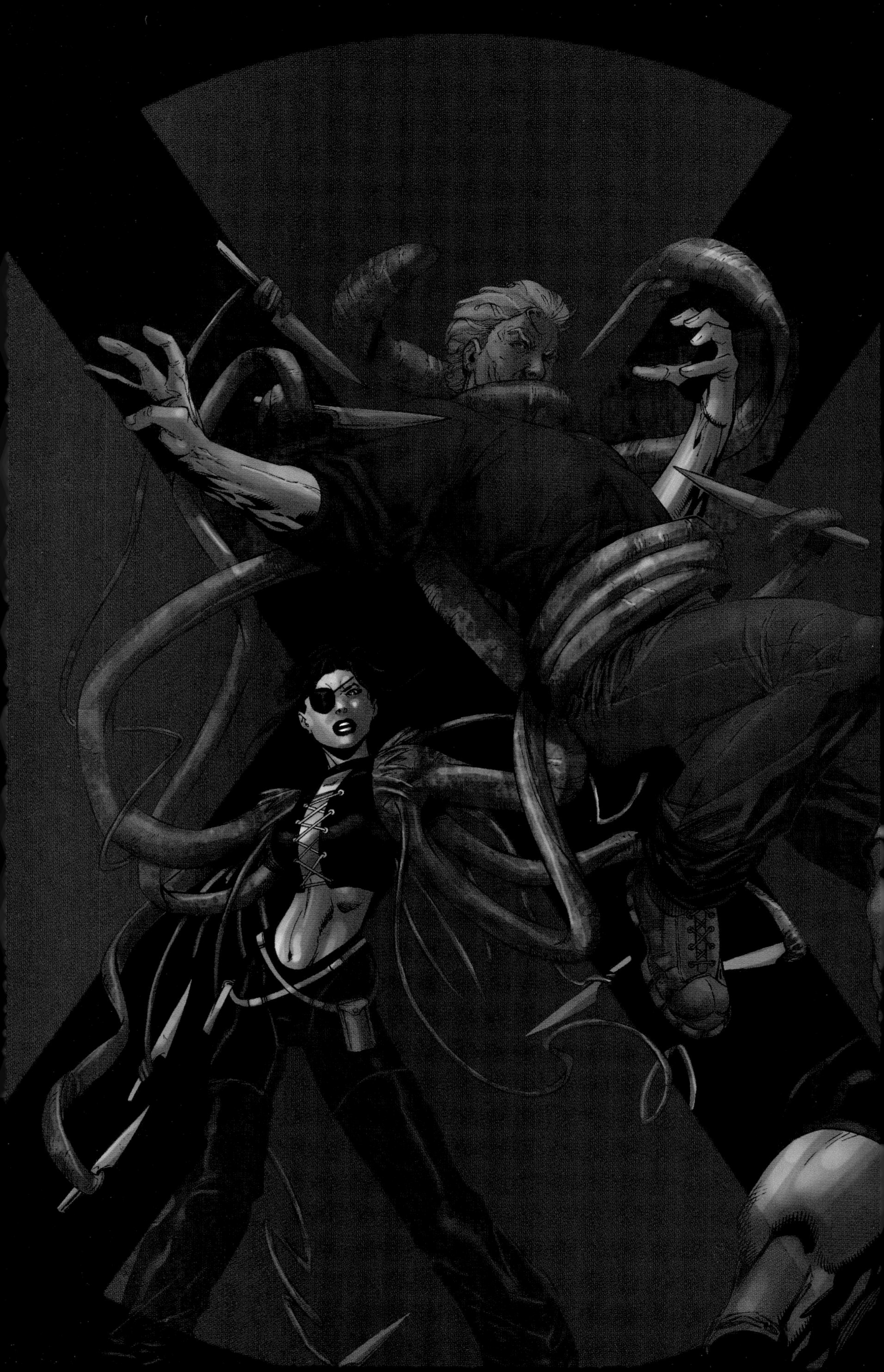

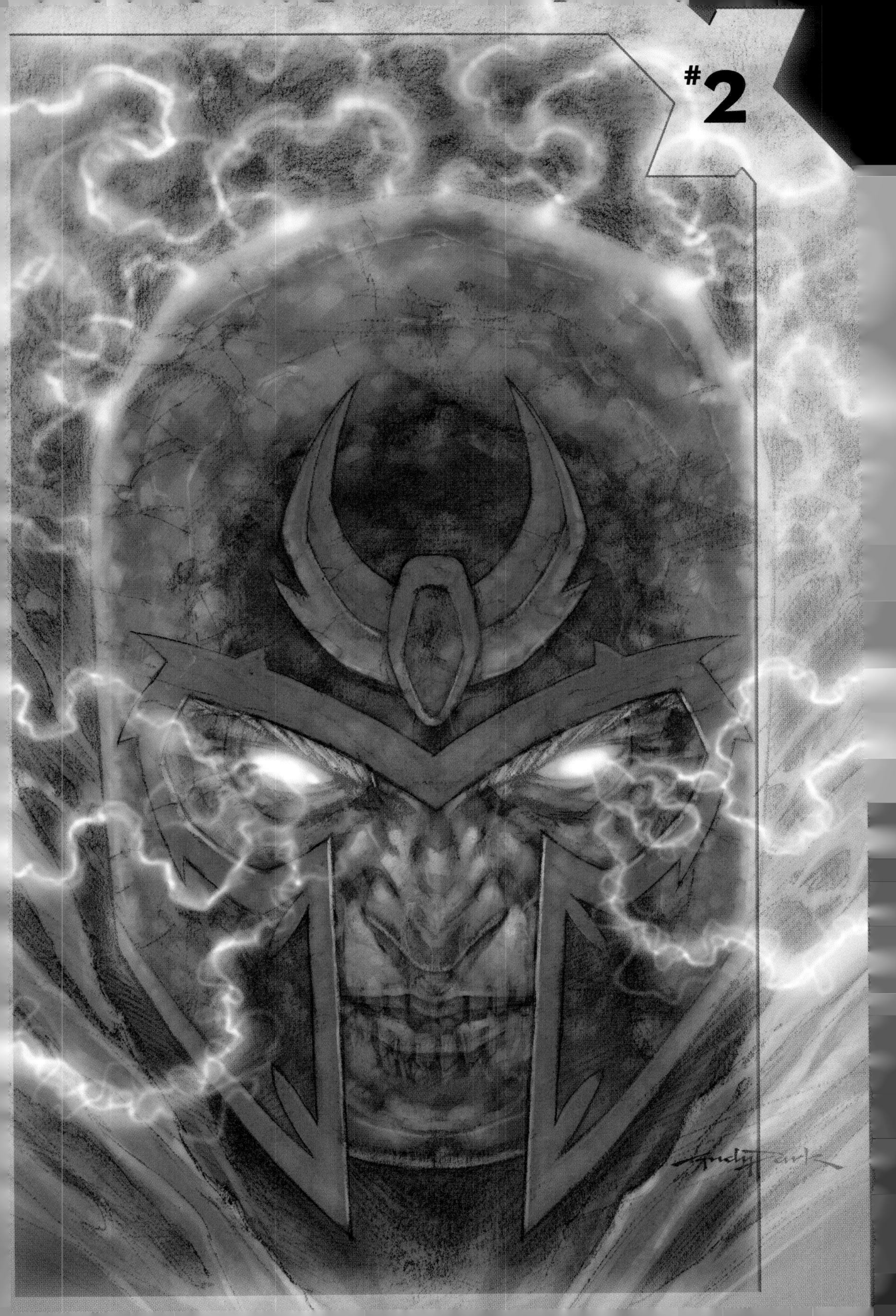
#2

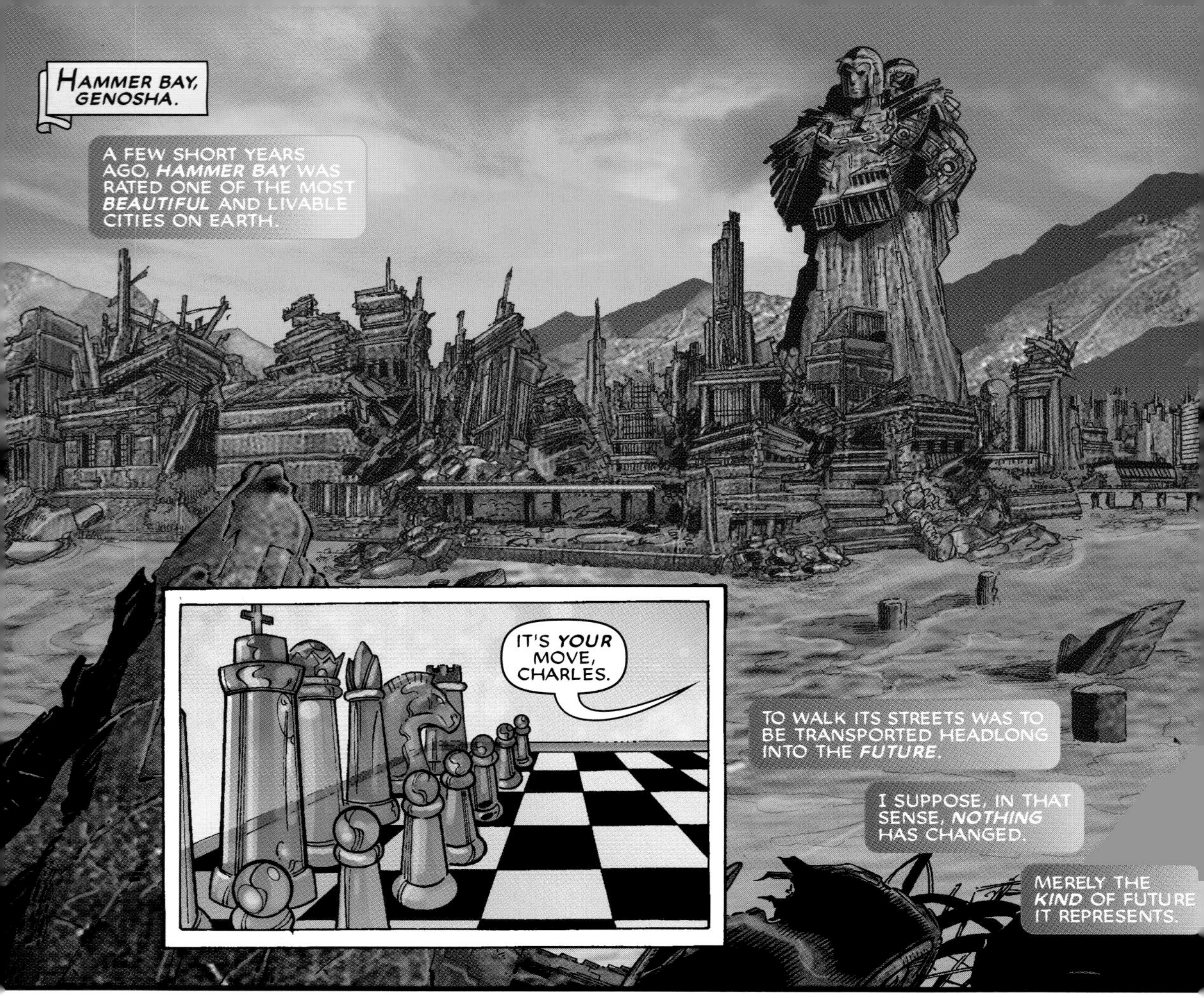
HAMMER BAY, GENOSHA.
A FEW SHORT YEARS AGO, HAMMER BAY WAS RATED ONE OF THE MOST BEAUTIFUL AND LIVABLE CITIES ON EARTH.
IT'S YOUR MOVE, CHARLES.
TO WALK ITS STREETS WAS TO BE TRANSPORTED HEADLONG INTO THE FUTURE.
I SUPPOSE, IN THAT SENSE, NOTHING HAS CHANGED.
MERELY THE KIND OF FUTURE IT REPRESENTS.

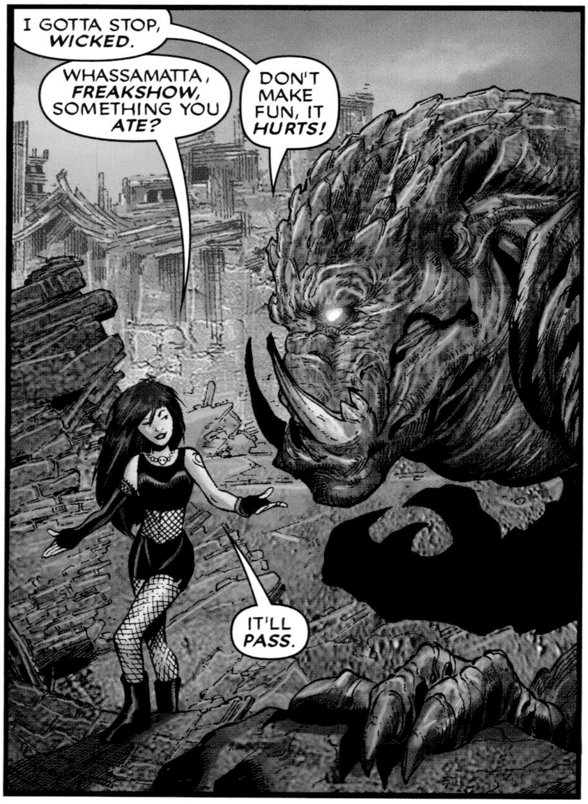
I GOTTA STOP, WICKED.
WHASSAMATTA, FREAKSHOW, SOMETHING YOU ATE?
DON'T MAKE FUN, IT HURTS!
IT'LL PASS.

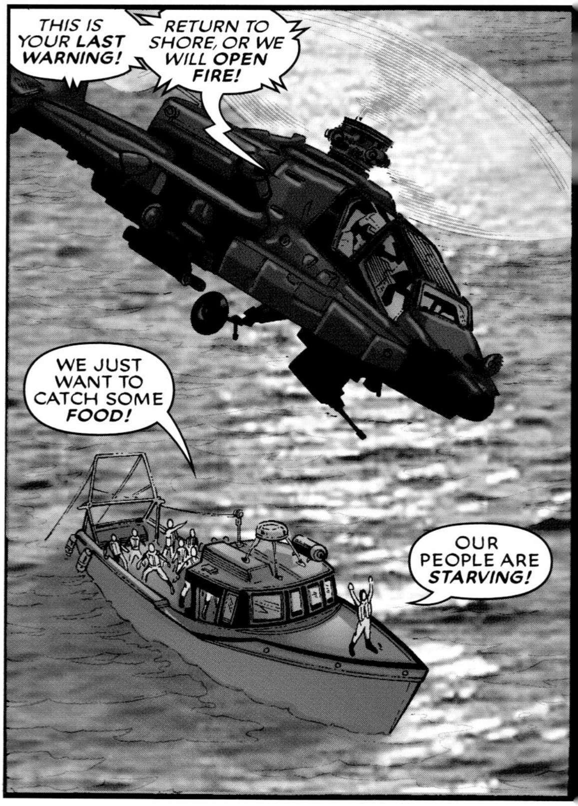
THIS IS YOUR LAST WARNING!
RETURN TO SHORE, OR WE WILL OPEN FIRE!
WE JUST WANT TO CATCH SOME FOOD!
OUR PEOPLE ARE STARVING!

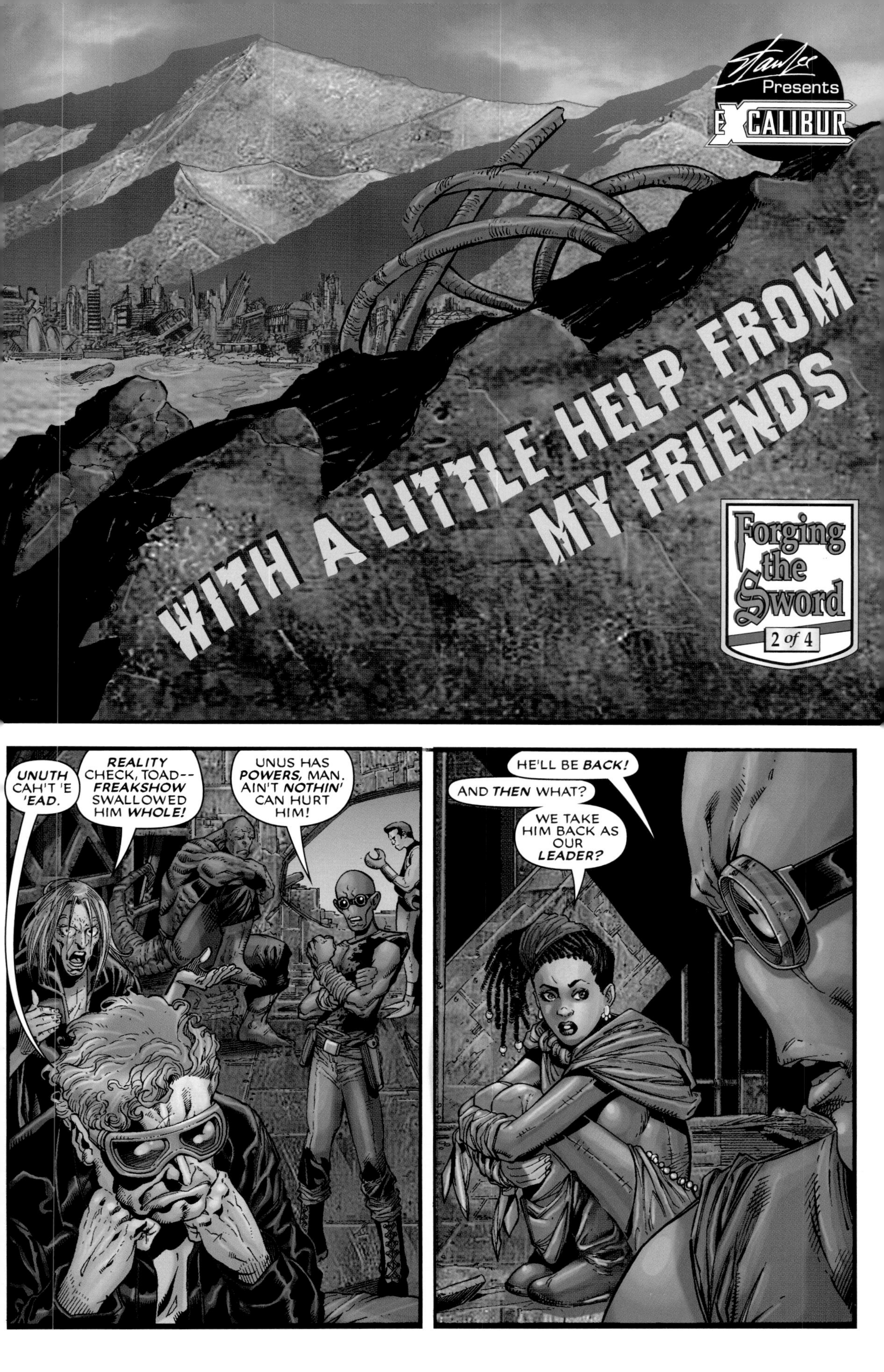
Stan Lee Presents
EXCALIBUR
WITH A LITTLE HELP FROM MY FRIENDS
Forging the Sword
2 of 4
UNUTH CAH'T 'E 'EAD.
REALITY CHECK, TOAD-- FREAKSHOW SWALLOWED HIM WHOLE!
UNUS HAS POWERS, MAN. AIN'T NOTHIN' CAN HURT HIM!
HE'LL BE BACK!
AND THEN WHAT?
WE TAKE HIM BACK AS OUR LEADER?

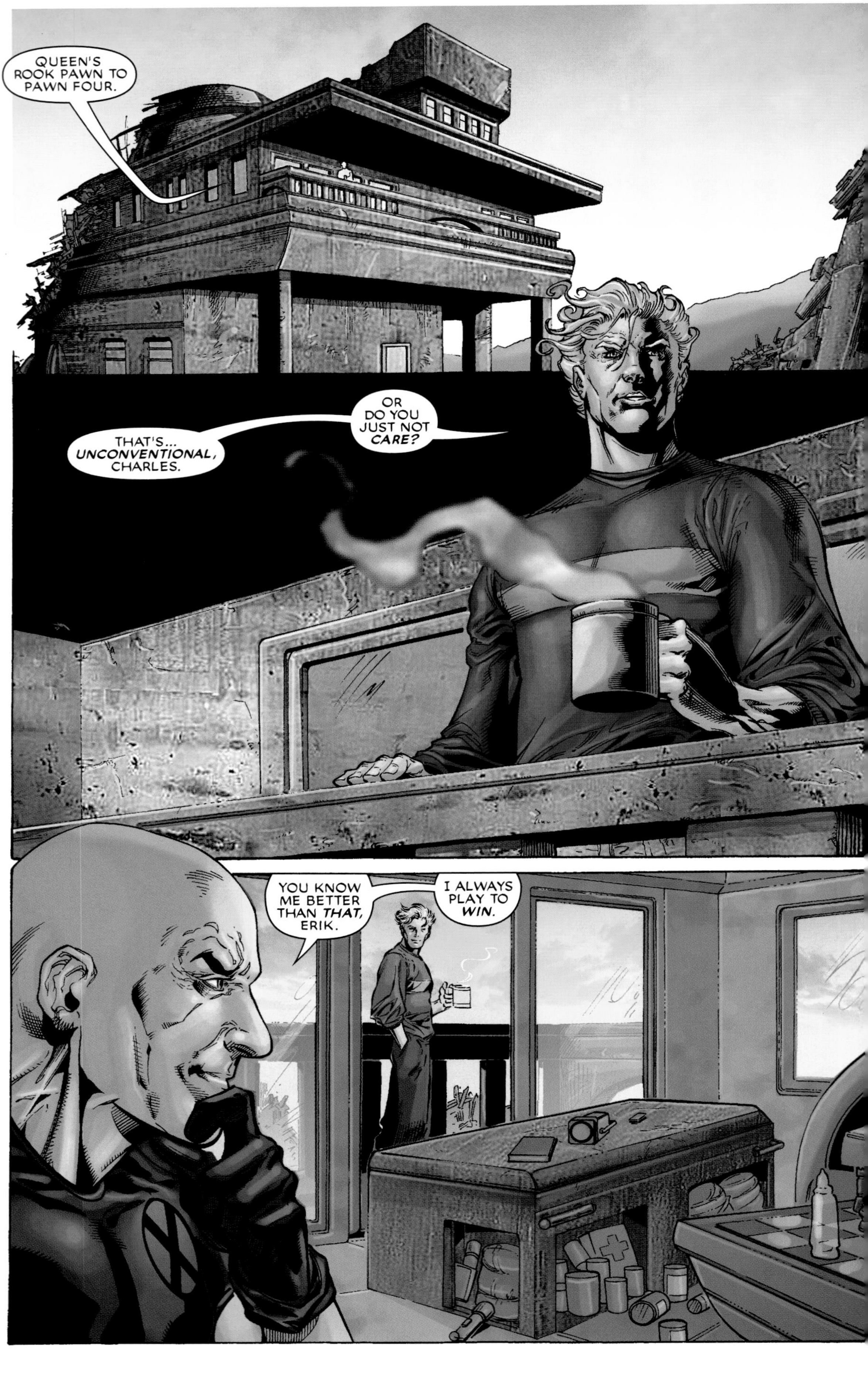
QUEEN'S ROOK PAWN TO PAWN FOUR.
THAT'S... *UNCONVENTIONAL*, CHARLES.
OR DO YOU JUST NOT *CARE?*
YOU KNOW ME BETTER THAN *THAT,* ERIK.
I ALWAYS PLAY TO *WIN*.

I'M SORRY I COULDN'T HAVE BROUGHT MORE *SUPPLIES*.

BUT THIS IS THE *LIMIT* OF WHAT I COULD SAFELY *SMUGGLE IN*.

I'VE ALWAYS BEEN IMPRESSED BY YOUR *RESOURCEFULNESS*.

I WASN'T ALWAYS A *TEACHER*.

WE BOTH HAVE *SHADOWS* ON OUR SOULS.

ANY IDEA WHO *THIS* IS IN THE COFFIN?

NOK!

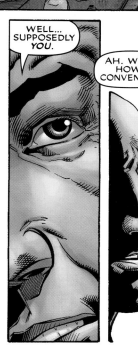

WELL... SUPPOSEDLY *YOU*.

AH. WELL. HOW... CONVENIENT.

YOUR IMPOSTER TOLD ME HIS SECONDARY MUTATION WAS TO ALWAYS COME BACK FROM THE *DEAD*.

HMPH. PREVIOUSLY THE NIGH-*EXCLUSIVE* PROVINCE OF MS. *JEAN GREY*.

WHOEVER HE WAS, HE *KILLED* JEAN.

JUST FOR *SPITE*.

I--I DIDN'T KNOW.

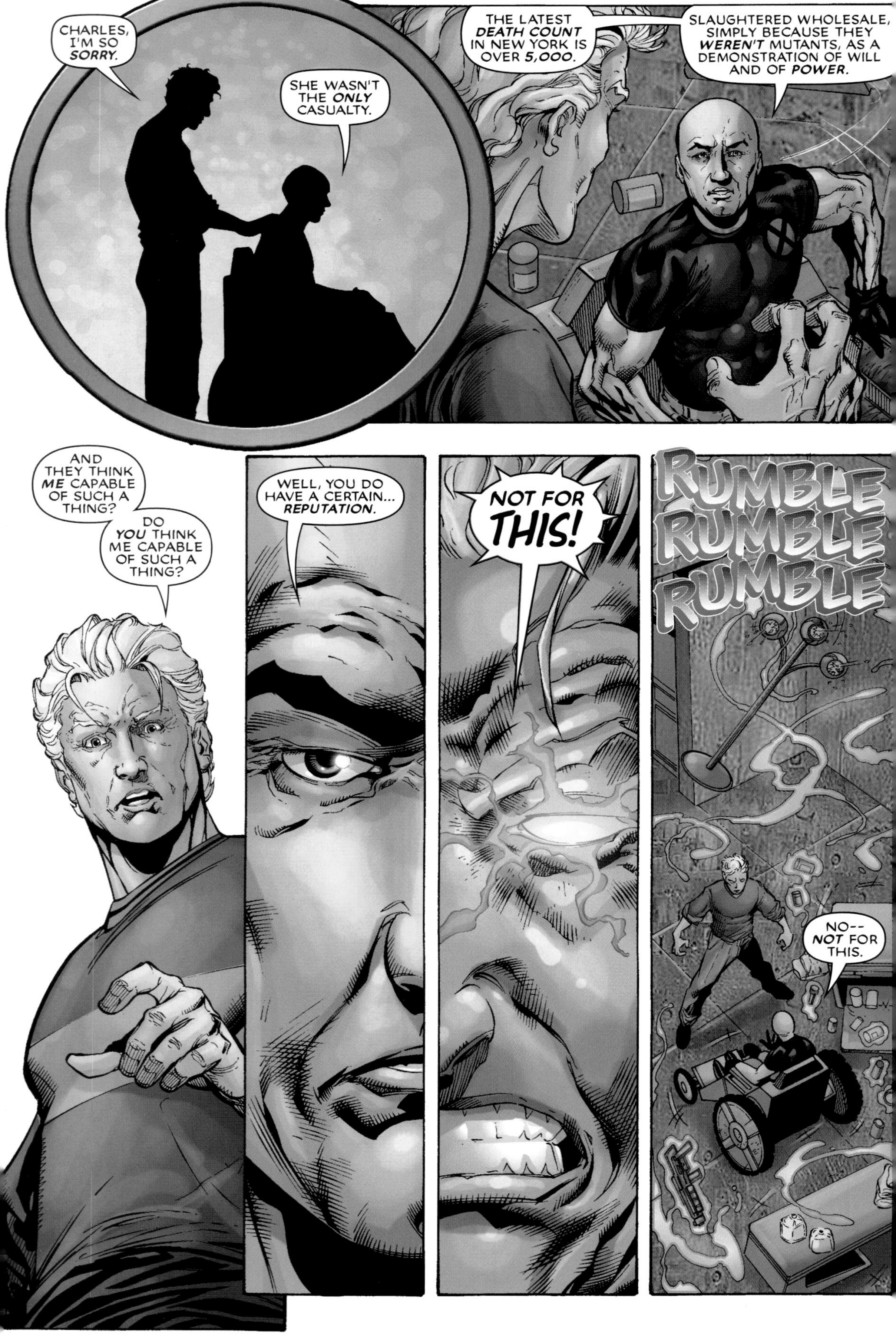
CHARLES, I'M SO SORRY.
SHE WASN'T THE ONLY CASUALTY.
THE LATEST DEATH COUNT IN NEW YORK IS OVER 5,000.
SLAUGHTERED WHOLESALE, SIMPLY BECAUSE THEY WEREN'T MUTANTS, AS A DEMONSTRATION OF WILL AND OF POWER.
AND THEY THINK ME CAPABLE OF SUCH A THING?
DO YOU THINK ME CAPABLE OF SUCH A THING?
WELL, YOU DO HAVE A CERTAIN... REPUTATION.
NOT FOR THIS!
RUMBLE RUMBLE RUMBLE
NO-- NOT FOR THIS.

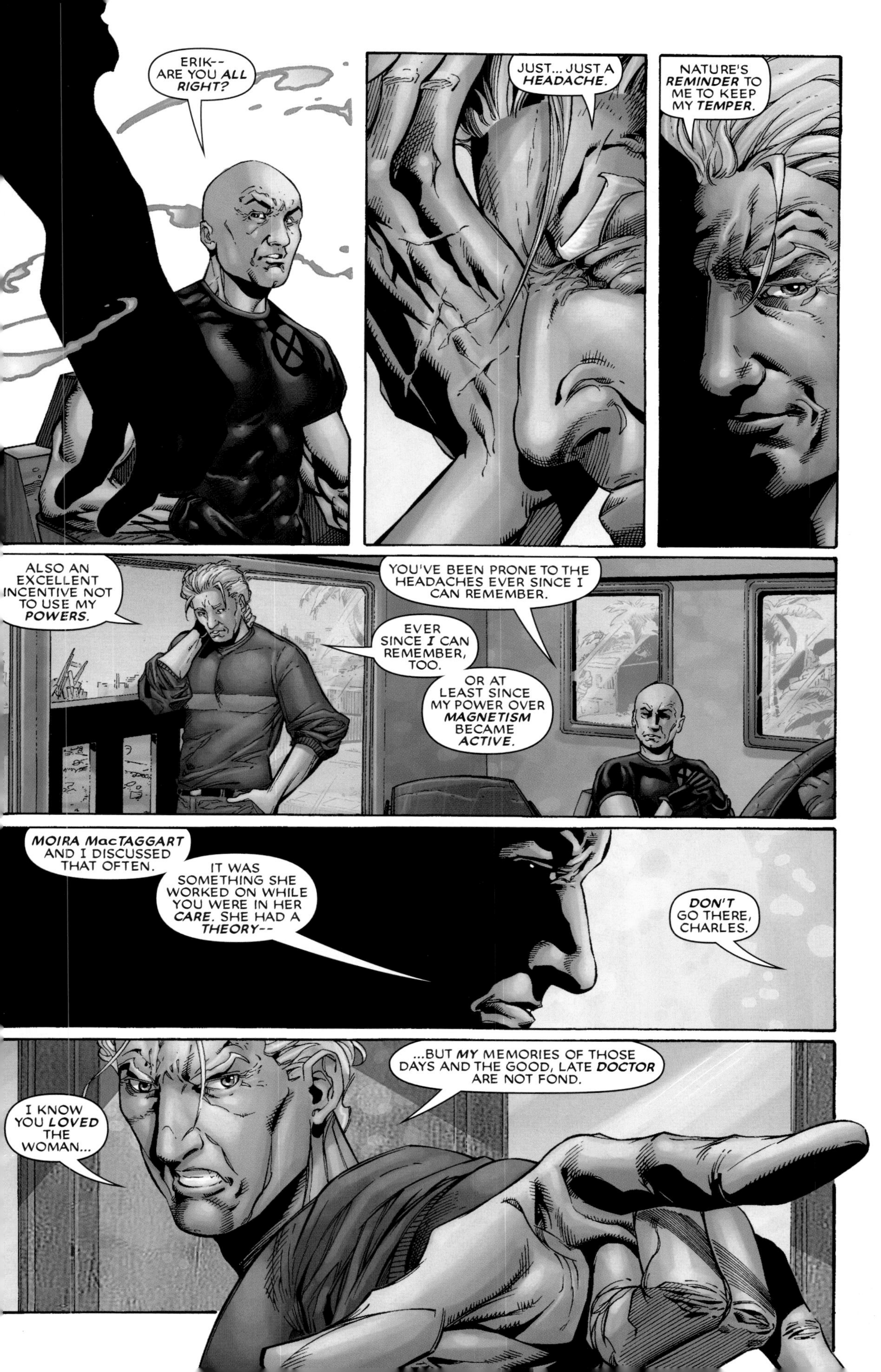
ERIK-- ARE YOU ALL RIGHT?
JUST... JUST A HEADACHE.
NATURE'S REMINDER TO ME TO KEEP MY TEMPER.
ALSO AN EXCELLENT INCENTIVE NOT TO USE MY POWERS.
YOU'VE BEEN PRONE TO THE HEADACHES EVER SINCE I CAN REMEMBER.
EVER SINCE I CAN REMEMBER, TOO.
OR AT LEAST SINCE MY POWER OVER MAGNETISM BECAME ACTIVE.
MOIRA MacTAGGART AND I DISCUSSED THAT OFTEN.
IT WAS SOMETHING SHE WORKED ON WHILE YOU WERE IN HER CARE. SHE HAD A THEORY--
DON'T GO THERE, CHARLES.
I KNOW YOU LOVED THE WOMAN...
...BUT MY MEMORIES OF THOSE DAYS AND THE GOOD, LATE DOCTOR ARE NOT FOND.

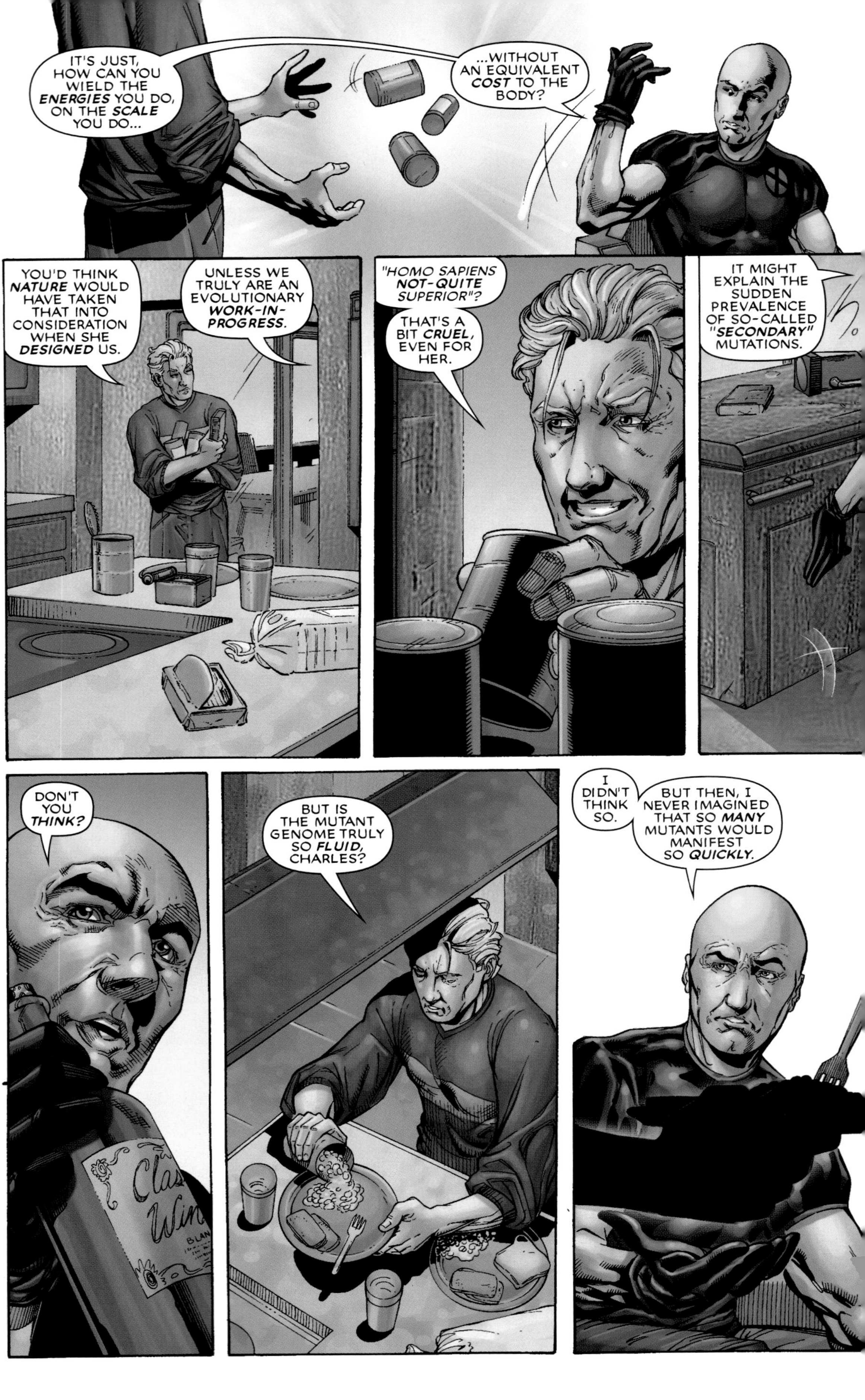
IT'S JUST, HOW CAN YOU WIELD THE ENERGIES YOU DO, ON THE SCALE YOU DO...
...WITHOUT AN EQUIVALENT COST TO THE BODY?
YOU'D THINK NATURE WOULD HAVE TAKEN THAT INTO CONSIDERATION WHEN SHE DESIGNED US.
UNLESS WE TRULY ARE AN EVOLUTIONARY WORK-IN-PROGRESS.
"HOMO SAPIENS NOT-QUITE SUPERIOR"?
THAT'S A BIT CRUEL, EVEN FOR HER.
IT MIGHT EXPLAIN THE SUDDEN PREVALENCE OF SO-CALLED "SECONDARY" MUTATIONS.
DON'T YOU THINK?
BUT IS THE MUTANT GENOME TRULY SO FLUID, CHARLES?
I DIDN'T THINK SO.
BUT THEN, I NEVER IMAGINED THAT SO MANY MUTANTS WOULD MANIFEST SO QUICKLY.

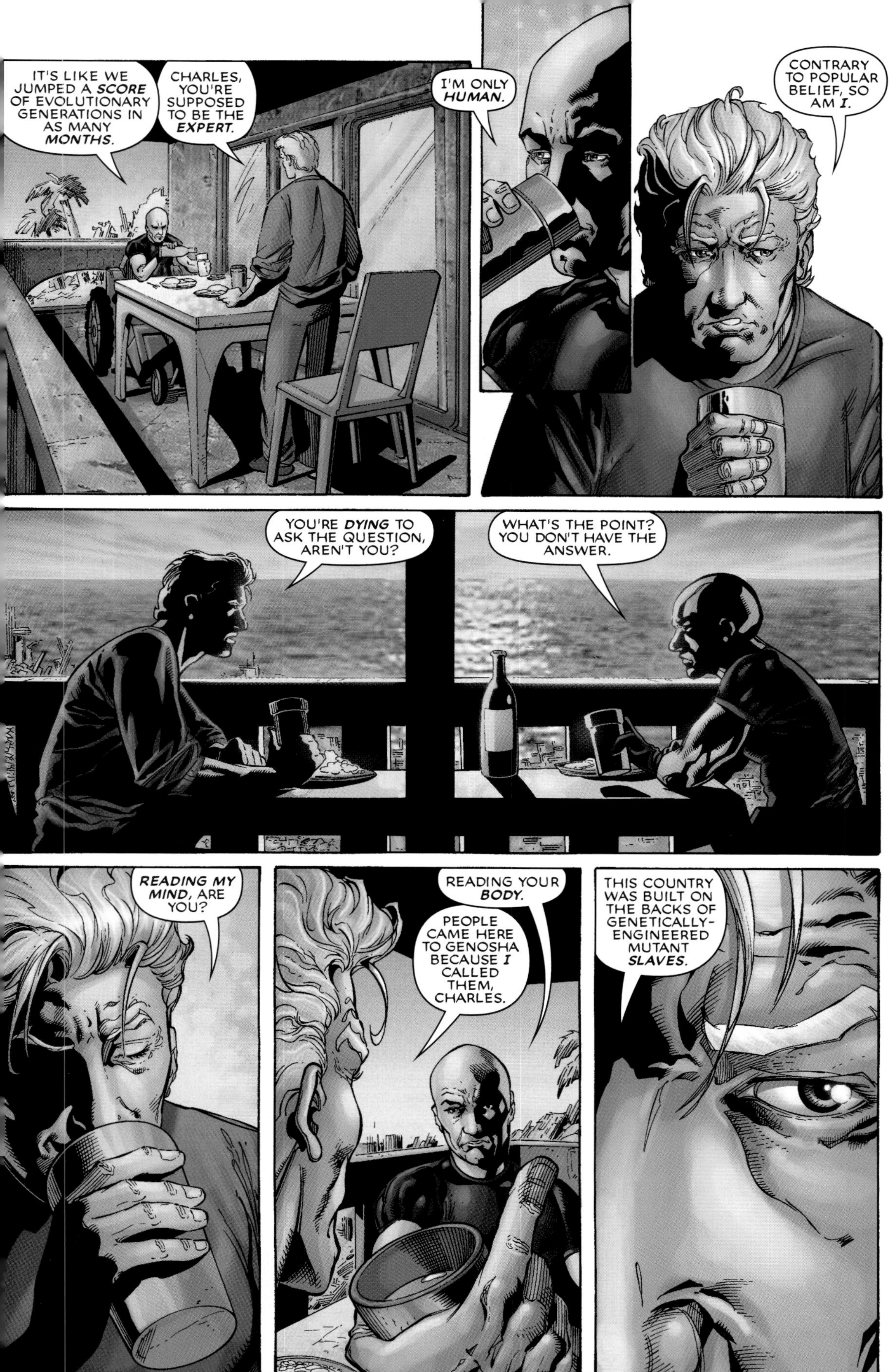
IT'S LIKE WE JUMPED A SCORE OF EVOLUTIONARY GENERATIONS IN AS MANY MONTHS.
CHARLES, YOU'RE SUPPOSED TO BE THE EXPERT.
I'M ONLY HUMAN.
CONTRARY TO POPULAR BELIEF, SO AM I.
YOU'RE DYING TO ASK THE QUESTION, AREN'T YOU?
WHAT'S THE POINT? YOU DON'T HAVE THE ANSWER.
READING MY MIND, ARE YOU?
READING YOUR BODY.
PEOPLE CAME HERE TO GENOSHA BECAUSE I CALLED THEM, CHARLES.
THIS COUNTRY WAS BUILT ON THE BACKS OF GENETICALLY-ENGINEERED MUTANT SLAVES.

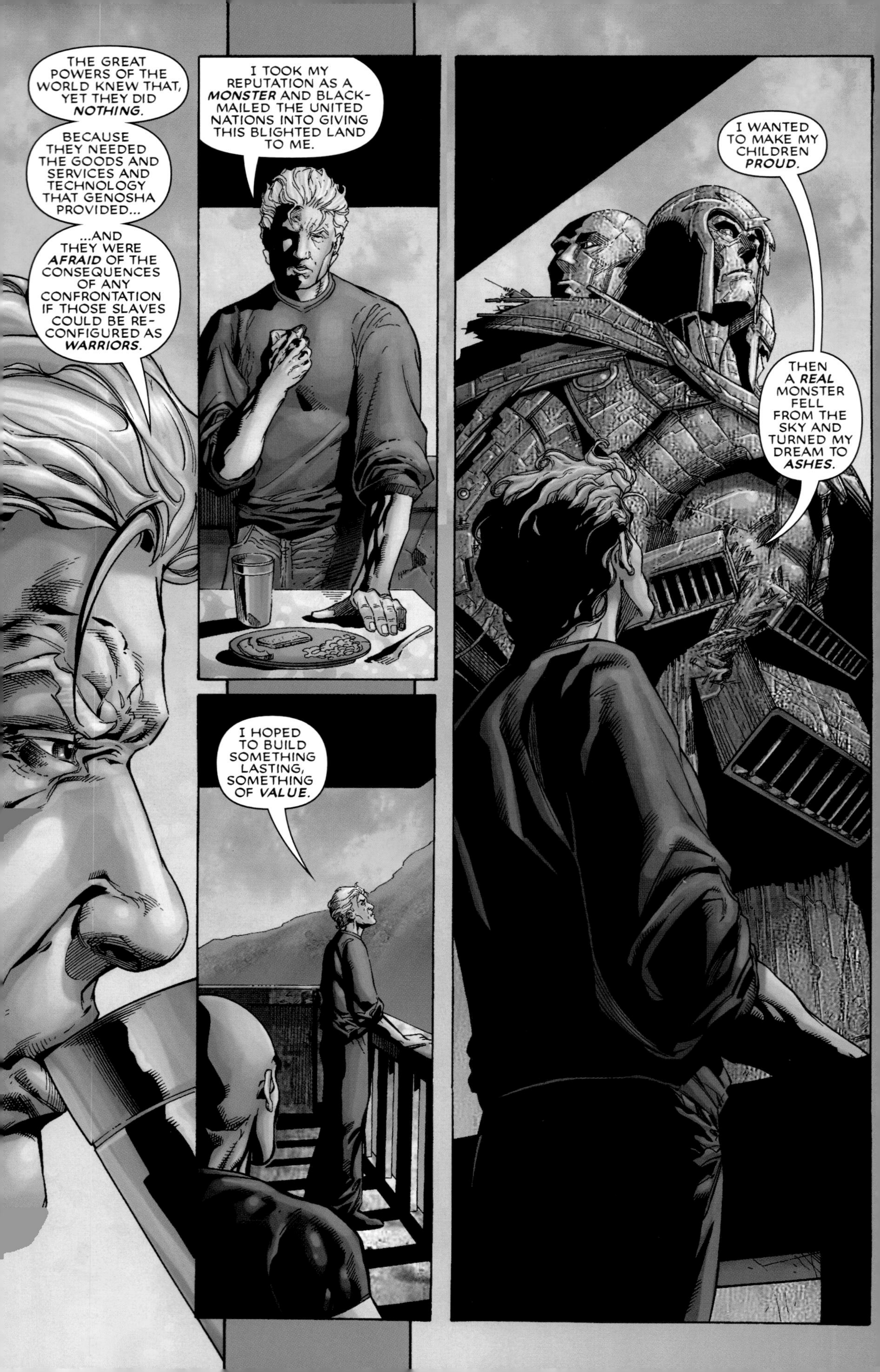
THE GREAT POWERS OF THE WORLD KNEW THAT, YET THEY DID NOTHING.
BECAUSE THEY NEEDED THE GOODS AND SERVICES AND TECHNOLOGY THAT GENOSHA PROVIDED...
...AND THEY WERE AFRAID OF THE CONSEQUENCES OF ANY CONFRONTATION IF THOSE SLAVES COULD BE RE-CONFIGURED AS WARRIORS.
I TOOK MY REPUTATION AS A MONSTER AND BLACK-MAILED THE UNITED NATIONS INTO GIVING THIS BLIGHTED LAND TO ME.
I HOPED TO BUILD SOMETHING LASTING, SOMETHING OF VALUE.
I WANTED TO MAKE MY CHILDREN PROUD.
THEN A REAL MONSTER FELL FROM THE SKY AND TURNED MY DREAM TO ASHES.

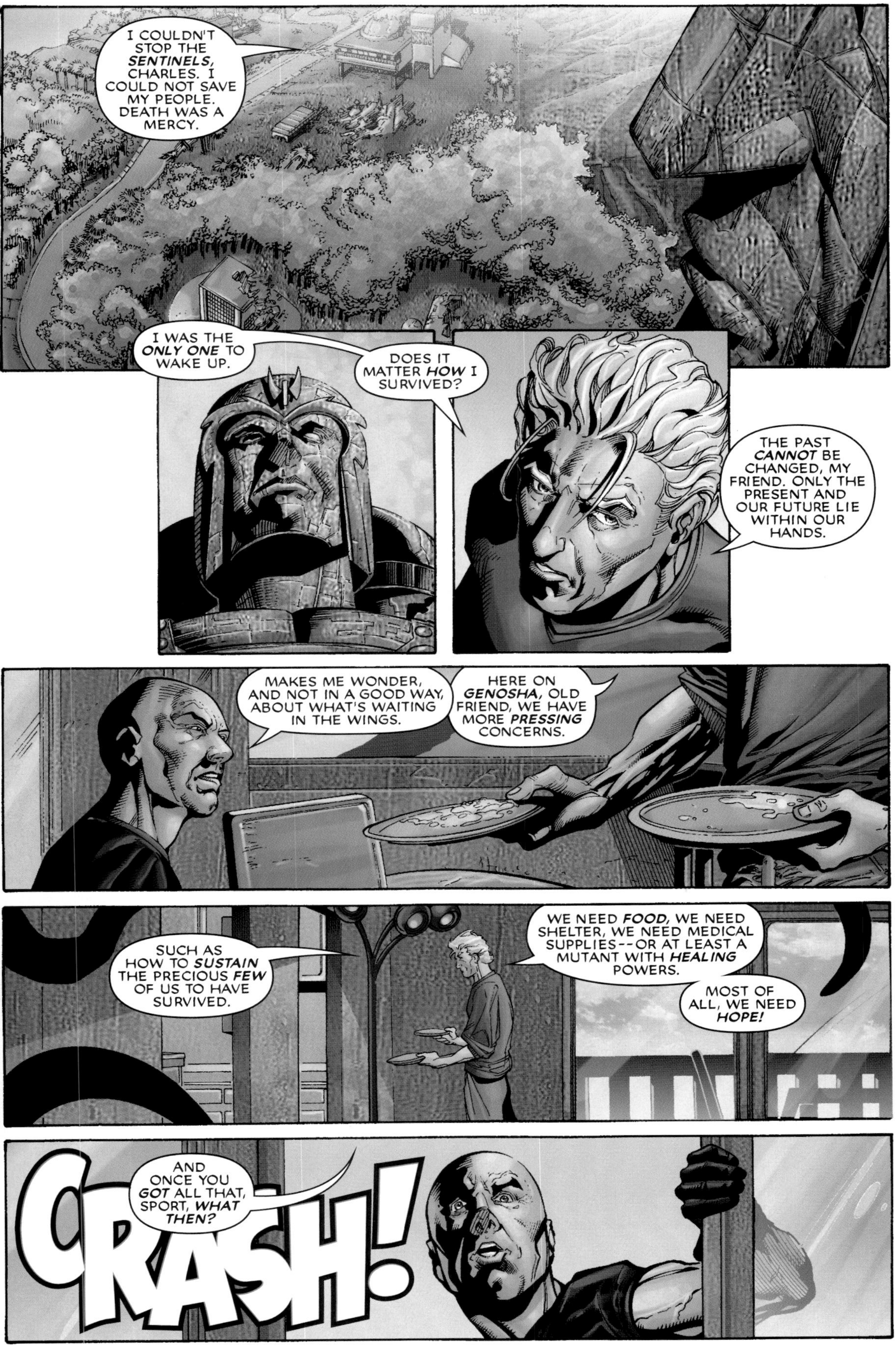
I COULDN'T STOP THE *SENTINELS,* CHARLES. I COULD NOT SAVE MY PEOPLE. DEATH WAS A MERCY.
I WAS THE *ONLY ONE* TO WAKE UP.
DOES IT MATTER *HOW* I SURVIVED?
THE PAST *CANNOT* BE CHANGED, MY FRIEND. ONLY THE PRESENT AND OUR FUTURE LIE WITHIN OUR HANDS.
MAKES ME WONDER, AND NOT IN A GOOD WAY, ABOUT WHAT'S WAITING IN THE WINGS.
HERE ON *GENOSHA,* OLD FRIEND, WE HAVE MORE *PRESSING* CONCERNS.
SUCH AS HOW TO *SUSTAIN* THE PRECIOUS *FEW* OF US TO HAVE SURVIVED.
WE NEED *FOOD,* WE NEED SHELTER, WE NEED MEDICAL SUPPLIES--OR AT LEAST A MUTANT WITH *HEALING* POWERS.
MOST OF ALL, WE NEED *HOPE!*
CRASH!
AND ONCE YOU *GOT* ALL THAT, SPORT, *WHAT THEN?*

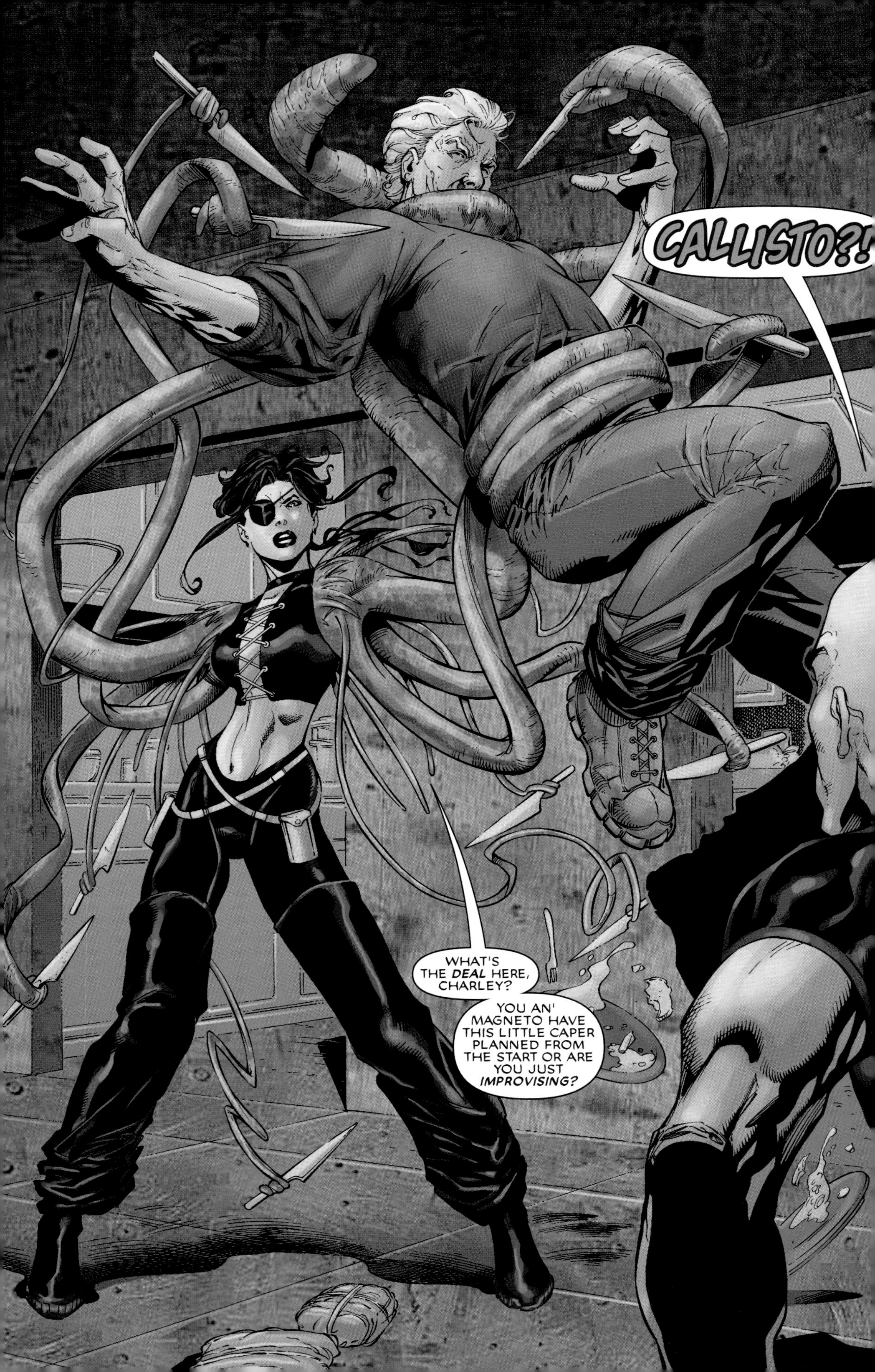
CALLISTO?!
WHAT'S THE DEAL HERE, CHARLEY?
YOU AN' MAGNETO HAVE THIS LITTLE CAPER PLANNED FROM THE START OR ARE YOU JUST IMPROVISING?

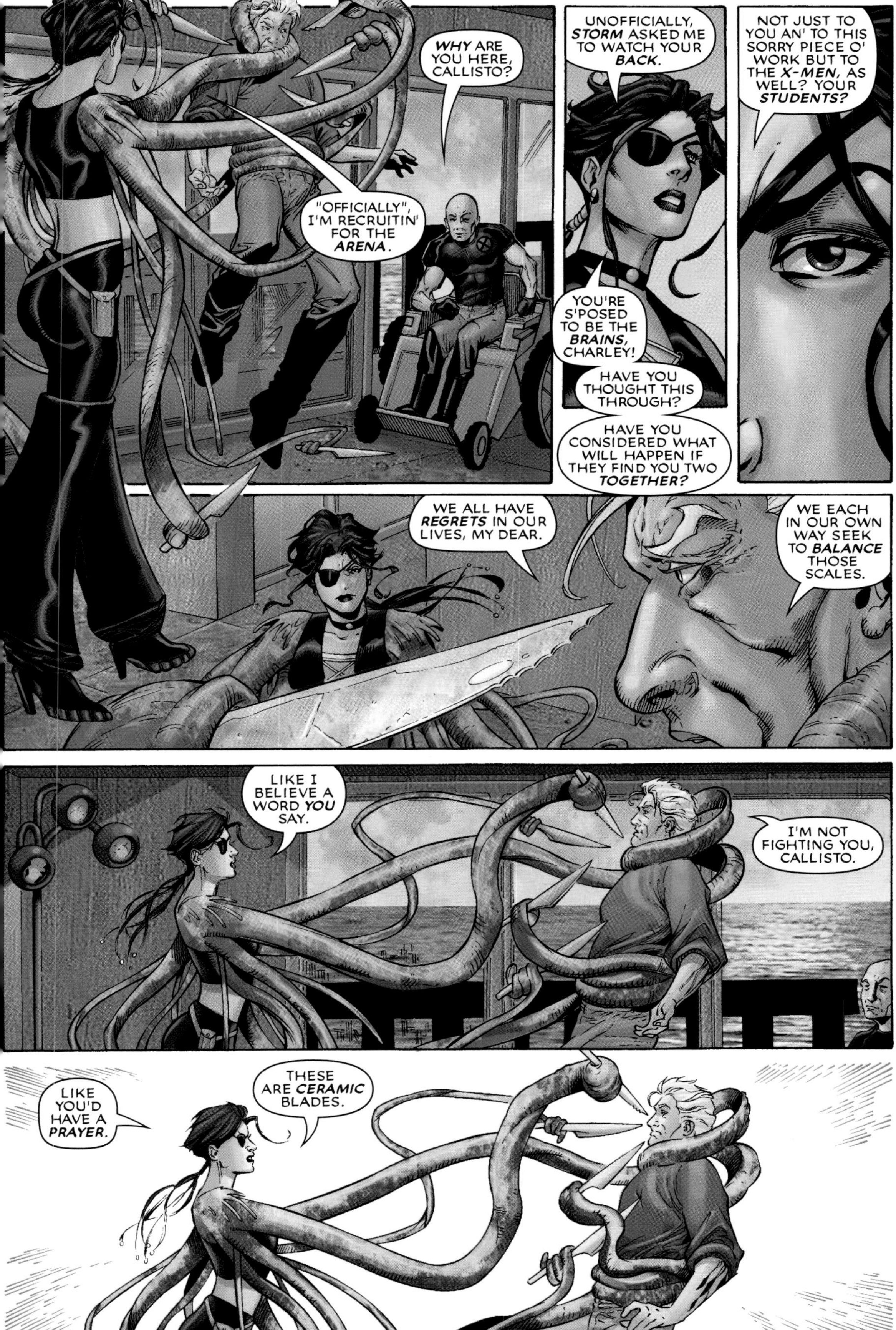
WHY ARE YOU HERE, CALLISTO?
"OFFICIALLY", I'M RECRUITIN' FOR THE ARENA.
UNOFFICIALLY, STORM ASKED ME TO WATCH YOUR BACK.
YOU'RE S'POSED TO BE THE BRAINS, CHARLEY!
HAVE YOU THOUGHT THIS THROUGH?
HAVE YOU CONSIDERED WHAT WILL HAPPEN IF THEY FIND YOU TWO TOGETHER?
NOT JUST TO YOU AN' TO THIS SORRY PIECE O' WORK BUT TO THE X-MEN, AS WELL? YOUR STUDENTS?
WE ALL HAVE REGRETS IN OUR LIVES, MY DEAR.
WE EACH IN OUR OWN WAY SEEK TO BALANCE THOSE SCALES.
LIKE I BELIEVE A WORD YOU SAY.
I'M NOT FIGHTING YOU, CALLISTO.
LIKE YOU'D HAVE A PRAYER.
THESE ARE CERAMIC BLADES.

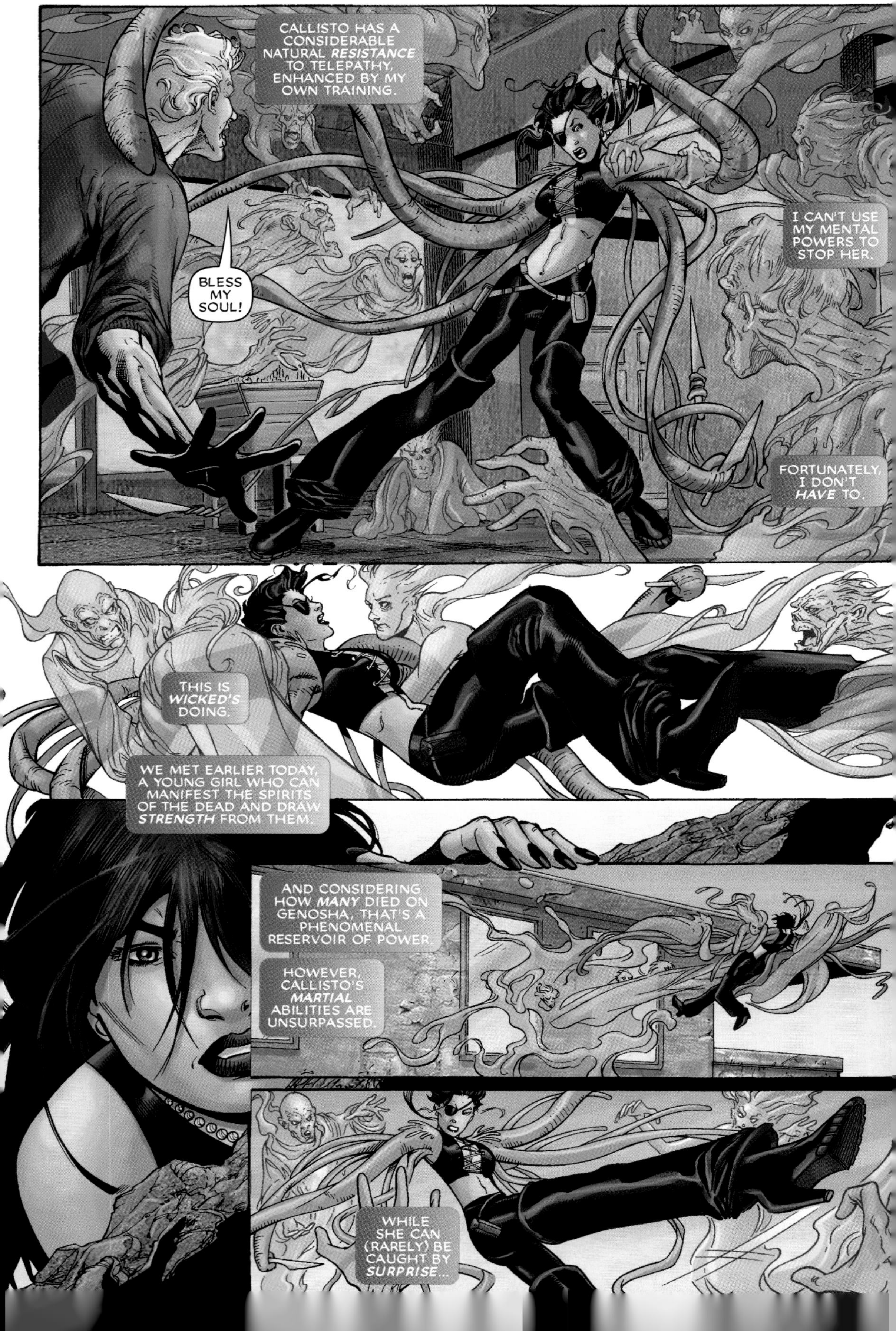
CALLISTO HAS A CONSIDERABLE NATURAL *RESISTANCE* TO TELEPATHY, ENHANCED BY MY OWN TRAINING.
BLESS MY SOUL!
I CAN'T USE MY MENTAL POWERS TO STOP HER.
FORTUNATELY, I DON'T *HAVE* TO.
THIS IS *WICKED'S* DOING.
WE MET EARLIER TODAY, A YOUNG GIRL WHO CAN MANIFEST THE SPIRITS OF THE DEAD AND DRAW *STRENGTH* FROM THEM.
AND CONSIDERING HOW *MANY* DIED ON GENOSHA, THAT'S A PHENOMENAL RESERVOIR OF POWER.
HOWEVER, CALLISTO'S *MARTIAL* ABILITIES ARE UNSURPASSED.
WHILE SHE CAN (RARELY) BE CAUGHT BY *SURPRISE*...

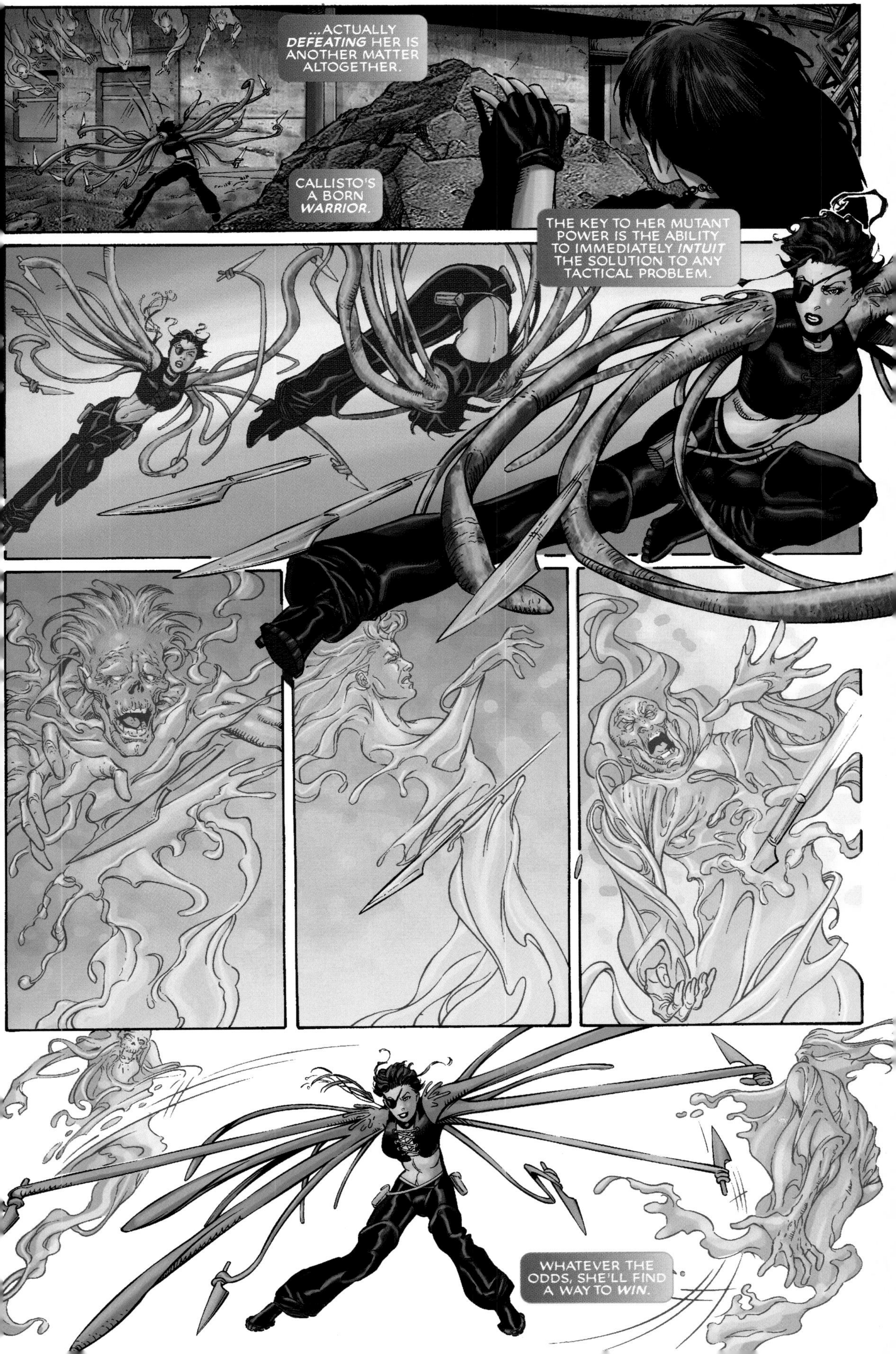
...ACTUALLY *DEFEATING* HER IS ANOTHER MATTER ALTOGETHER.
CALLISTO'S A BORN *WARRIOR*.
THE KEY TO HER MUTANT POWER IS THE ABILITY TO IMMEDIATELY *INTUIT* THE SOLUTION TO ANY TACTICAL PROBLEM.
WHATEVER THE ODDS, SHE'LL FIND A WAY TO *WIN*.

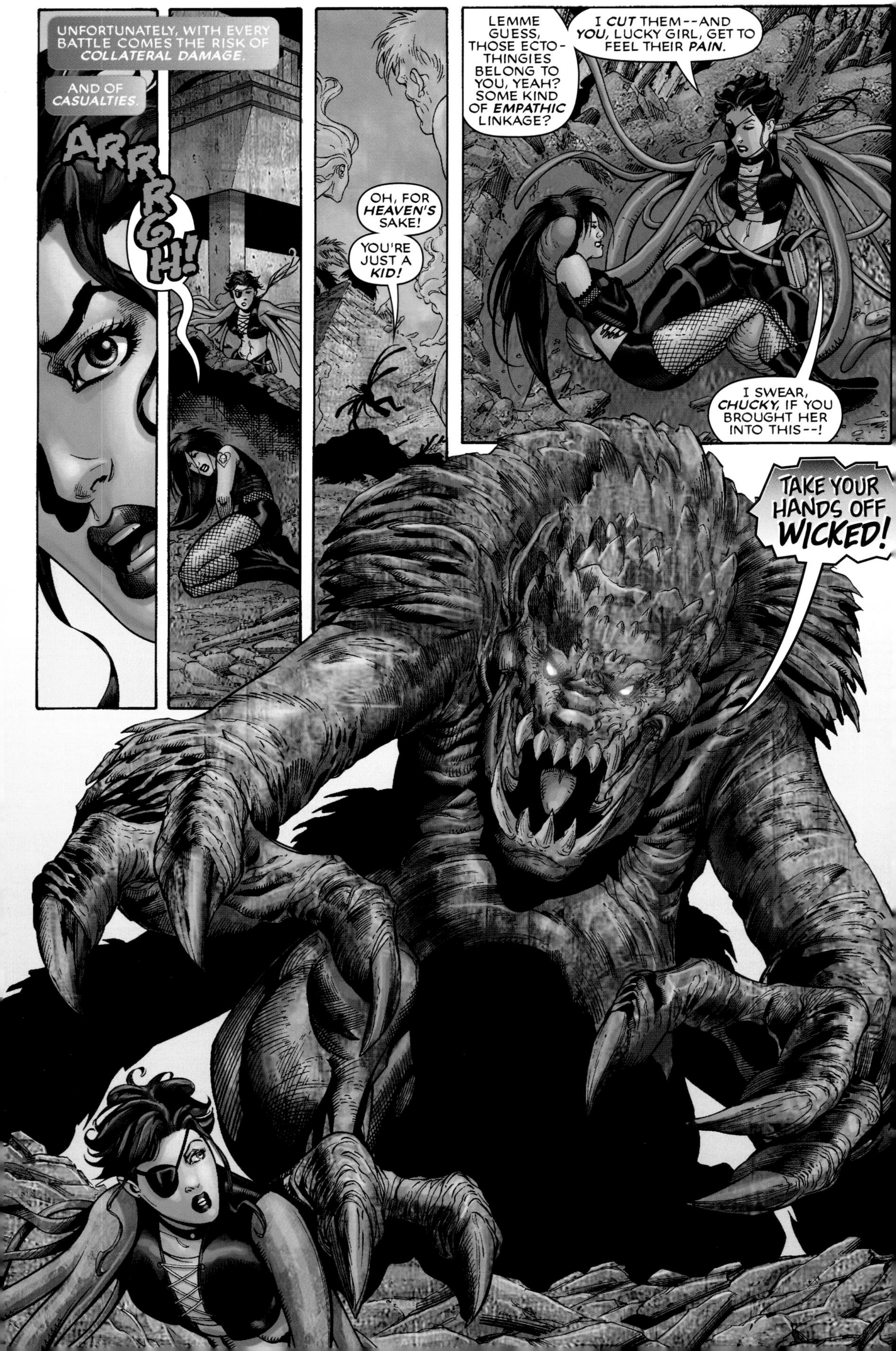
UNFORTUNATELY, WITH EVERY BATTLE COMES THE RISK OF COLLATERAL DAMAGE.
AND OF CASUALTIES.
ARRRGH!
OH, FOR HEAVEN'S SAKE!
YOU'RE JUST A KID!
LEMME GUESS, THOSE ECTO-THINGIES BELONG TO YOU, YEAH? SOME KIND OF EMPATHIC LINKAGE?
I CUT THEM--AND YOU, LUCKY GIRL, GET TO FEEL THEIR PAIN.
I SWEAR, CHUCKY, IF YOU BROUGHT HER INTO THIS--!
TAKE YOUR HANDS OFF WICKED!

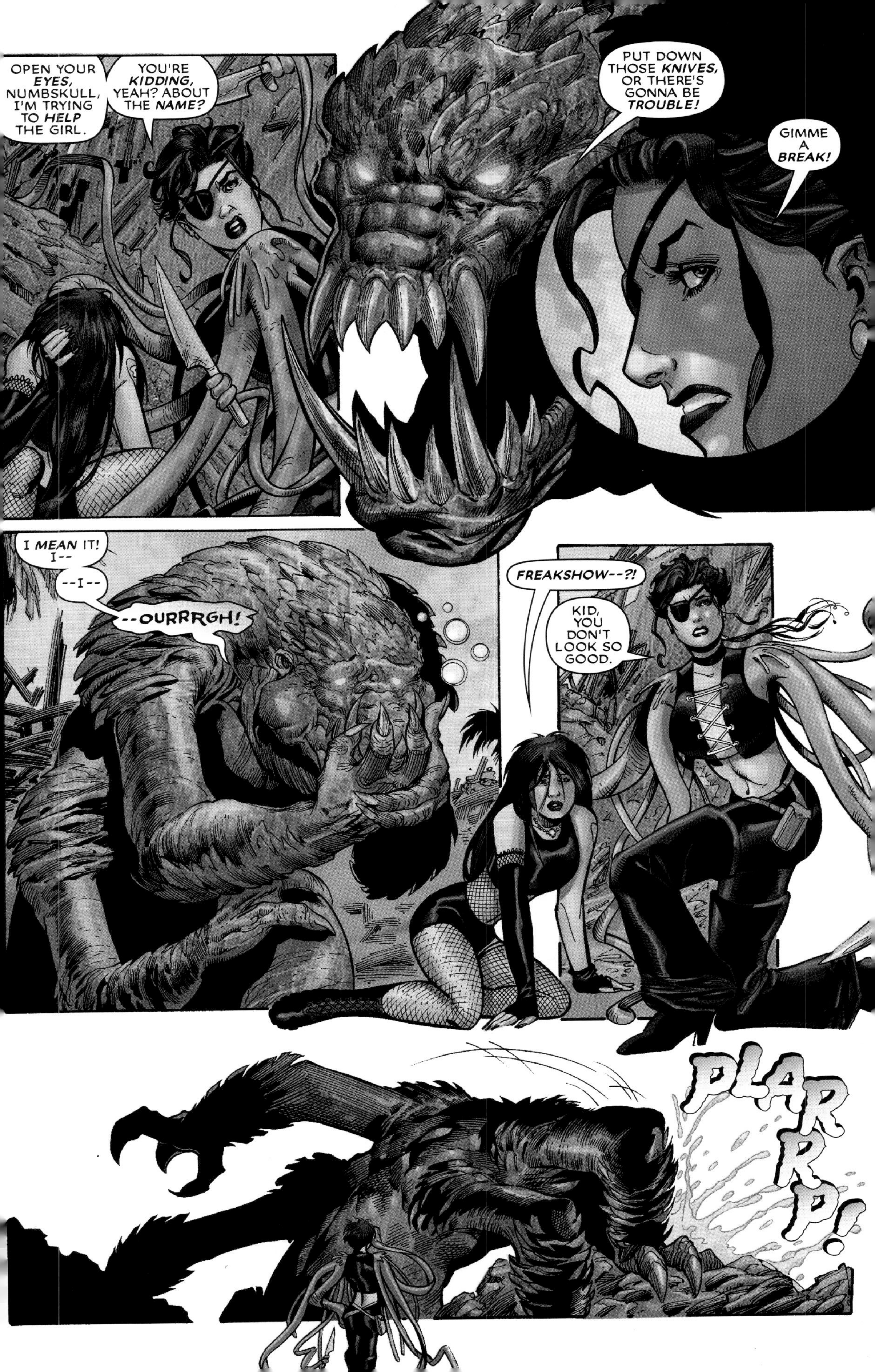
OPEN YOUR *EYES,* NUMBSKULL, I'M TRYING TO *HELP* THE GIRL.
YOU'RE *KIDDING,* YEAH? ABOUT THE *NAME?*
PUT DOWN THOSE *KNIVES,* OR THERE'S GONNA BE *TROUBLE!*
GIMME A *BREAK!*
I *MEAN* IT! I--
--I--
--OURRRGH!
FREAKSHOW--?!
KID, YOU DON'T LOOK SO GOOD.
PLARRP!

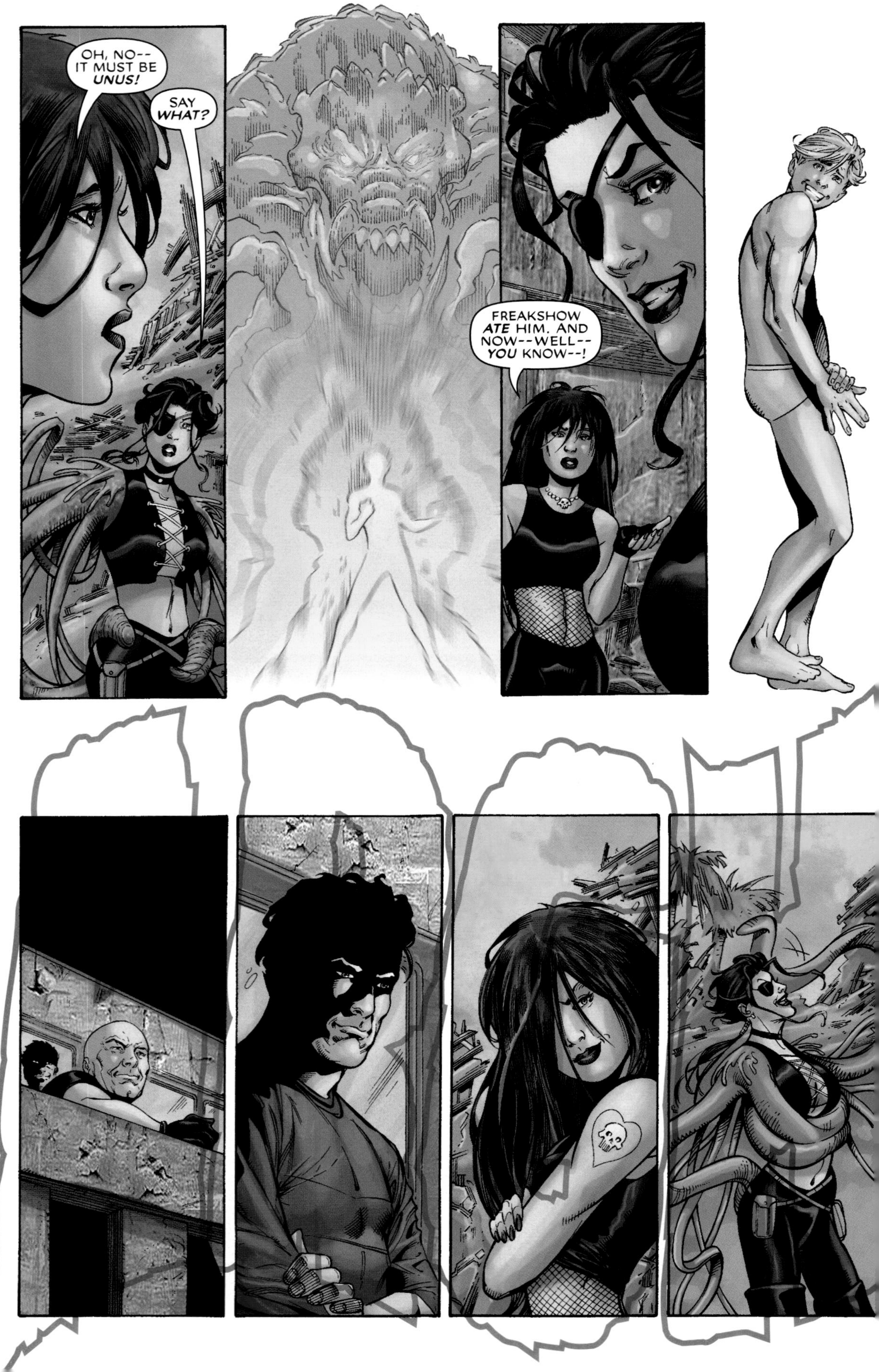
OH, NO--
IT MUST BE
UNUS!
SAY
WHAT?
FREAKSHOW
ATE HIM. AND
NOW--WELL--
YOU KNOW--!

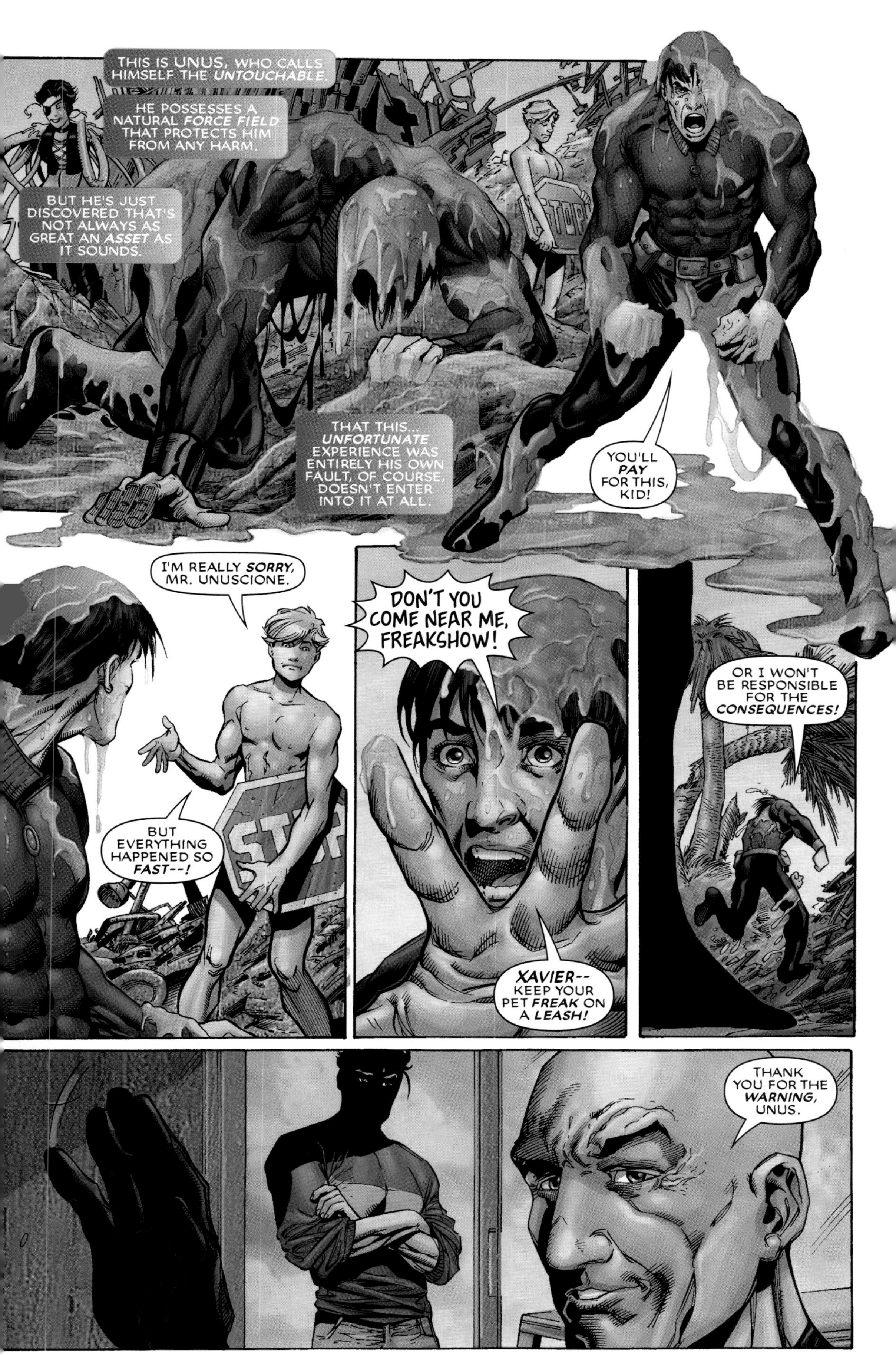

THIS IS UNUS, WHO CALLS HIMSELF THE *UNTOUCHABLE*.
HE POSSESSES A NATURAL *FORCE FIELD* THAT PROTECTS HIM FROM ANY HARM.
BUT HE'S JUST DISCOVERED THAT'S NOT ALWAYS AS GREAT AN *ASSET* AS IT SOUNDS.
THAT THIS... *UNFORTUNATE* EXPERIENCE WAS ENTIRELY HIS OWN FAULT, OF COURSE, DOESN'T ENTER INTO IT AT ALL.
YOU'LL *PAY* FOR THIS, KID!
STOP
I'M REALLY *SORRY*, MR. UNUSCIONE.
BUT EVERYTHING HAPPENED SO *FAST--!*
STOP
DON'T YOU COME NEAR ME, FREAKSHOW!
XAVIER-- KEEP YOUR PET *FREAK* ON A *LEASH!*
OR I WON'T BE RESPONSIBLE FOR THE *CONSEQUENCES!*
THANK YOU FOR THE *WARNING*, UNUS.

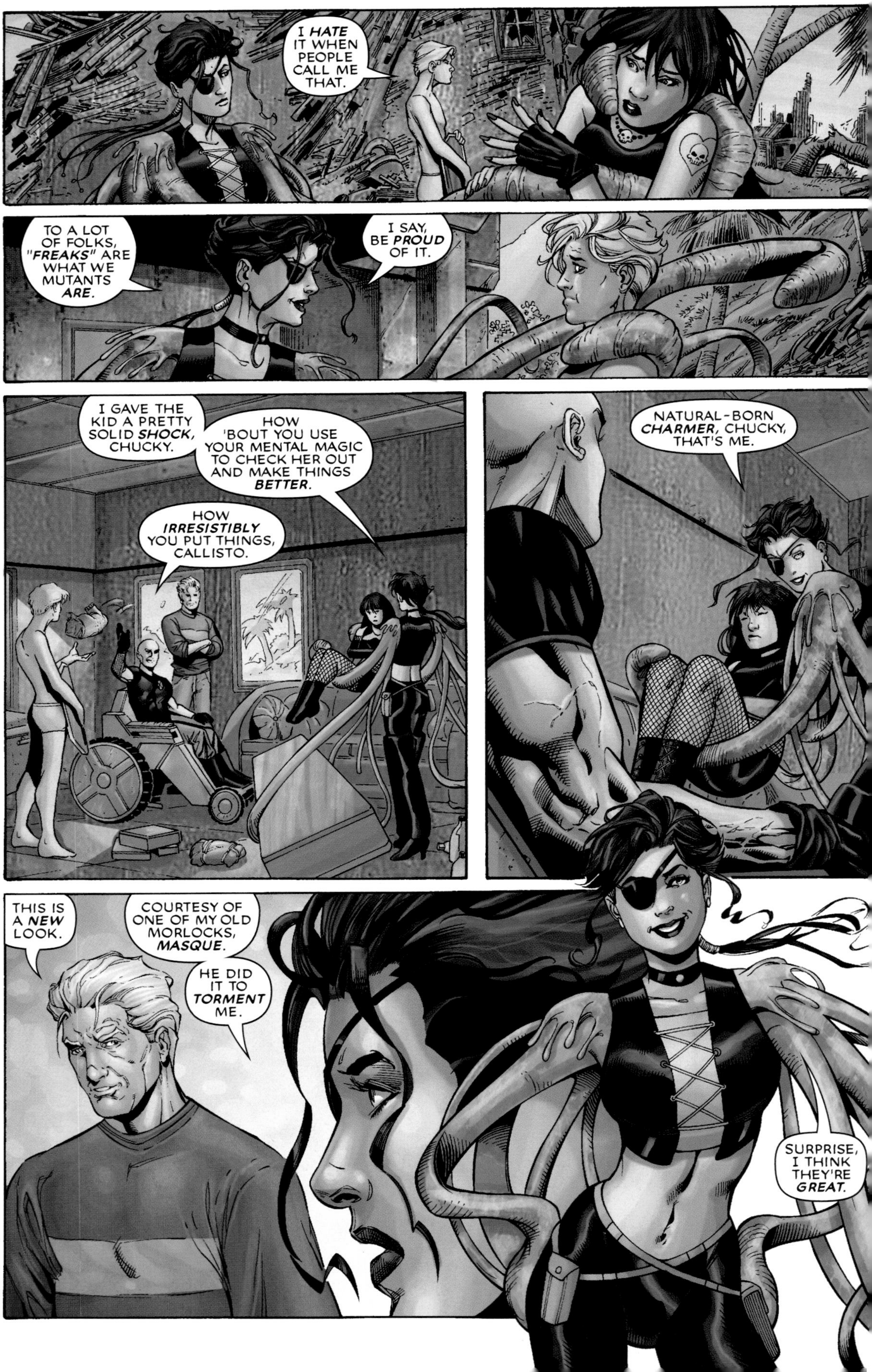
I HATE IT WHEN PEOPLE CALL ME THAT.
TO A LOT OF FOLKS, "FREAKS" ARE WHAT WE MUTANTS ARE.
I SAY, BE PROUD OF IT.
I GAVE THE KID A PRETTY SOLID SHOCK, CHUCKY.
HOW 'BOUT YOU USE YOUR MENTAL MAGIC TO CHECK HER OUT AND MAKE THINGS BETTER.
HOW IRRESISTIBLY YOU PUT THINGS, CALLISTO.
NATURAL-BORN CHARMER, CHUCKY, THAT'S ME.
THIS IS A NEW LOOK.
COURTESY OF ONE OF MY OLD MORLOCKS, MASQUE.
HE DID IT TO TORMENT ME.
SURPRISE, I THINK THEY'RE GREAT.

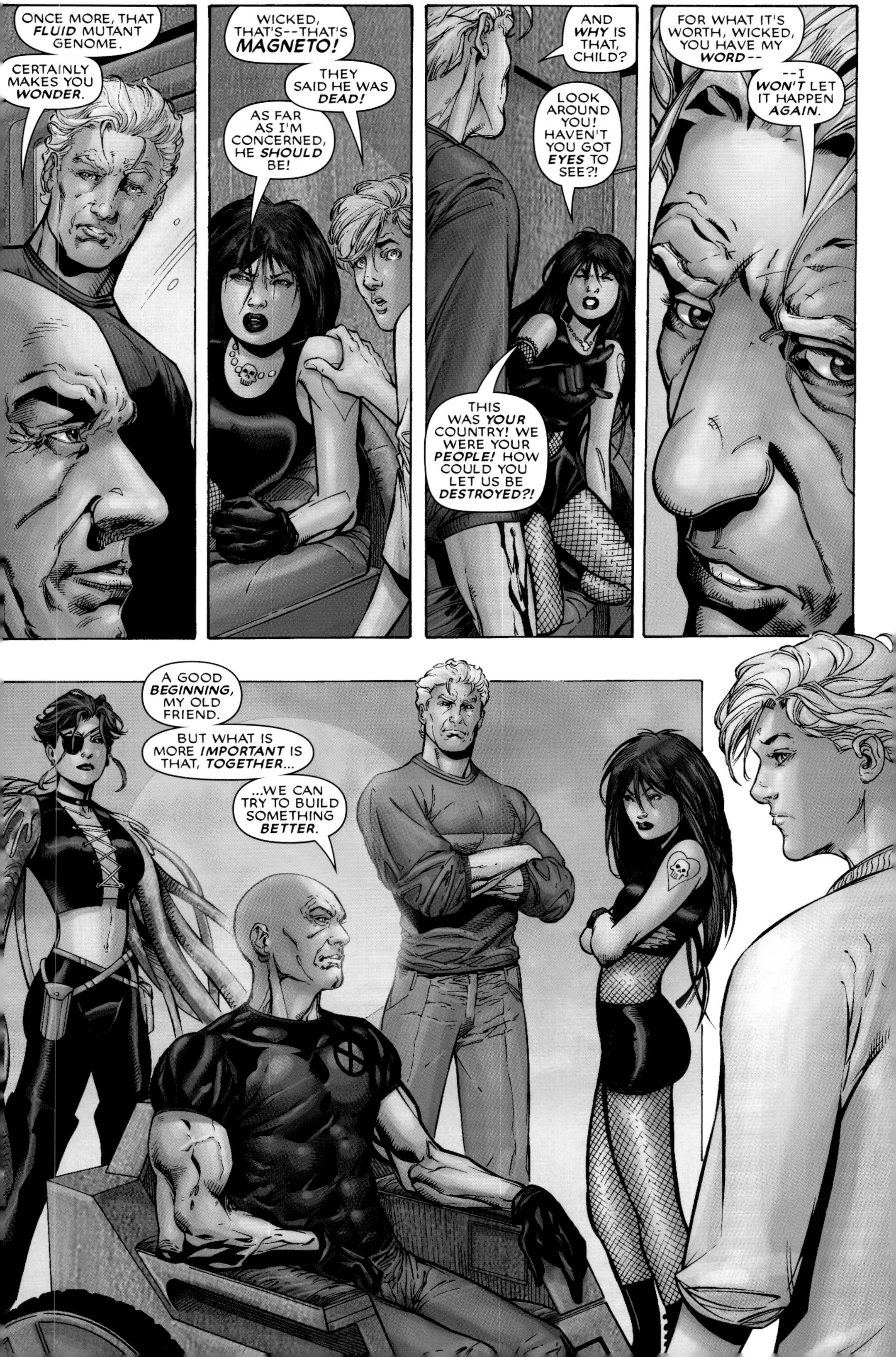
ONCE MORE, THAT FLUID MUTANT GENOME.
CERTAINLY MAKES YOU WONDER.
WICKED, THAT'S--THAT'S MAGNETO!
THEY SAID HE WAS DEAD!
AS FAR AS I'M CONCERNED, HE SHOULD BE!
AND WHY IS THAT, CHILD?
LOOK AROUND YOU! HAVEN'T YOU GOT EYES TO SEE?!
THIS WAS YOUR COUNTRY! WE WERE YOUR PEOPLE! HOW COULD YOU LET US BE DESTROYED?!
FOR WHAT IT'S WORTH, WICKED, YOU HAVE MY WORD--
--I WON'T LET IT HAPPEN AGAIN.
A GOOD BEGINNING, MY OLD FRIEND.
BUT WHAT IS MORE IMPORTANT IS THAT, TOGETHER...
...WE CAN TRY TO BUILD SOMETHING BETTER.

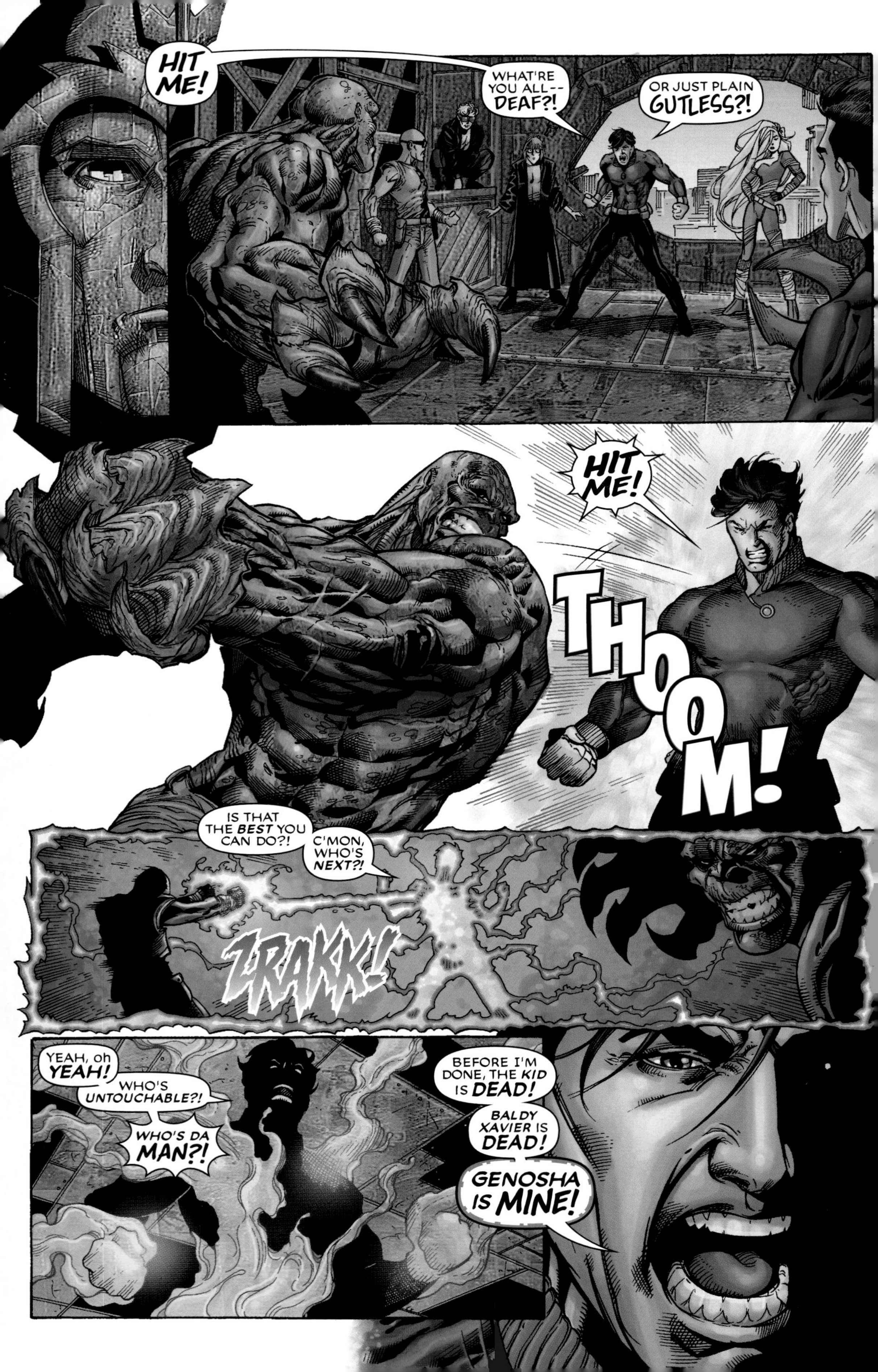
HIT ME!
WHAT'RE YOU ALL-- DEAF?!
OR JUST PLAIN GUTLESS?!
HIT ME!
THOOOM!
IS THAT THE BEST YOU CAN DO?!
C'MON, WHO'S NEXT?!
ZRAKK!
YEAH, oh YEAH!
WHO'S UNTOUCHABLE?!
WHO'S DA MAN?!
BEFORE I'M DONE, THE KID IS DEAD!
BALDY XAVIER IS DEAD!
GENOSHA IS MINE!

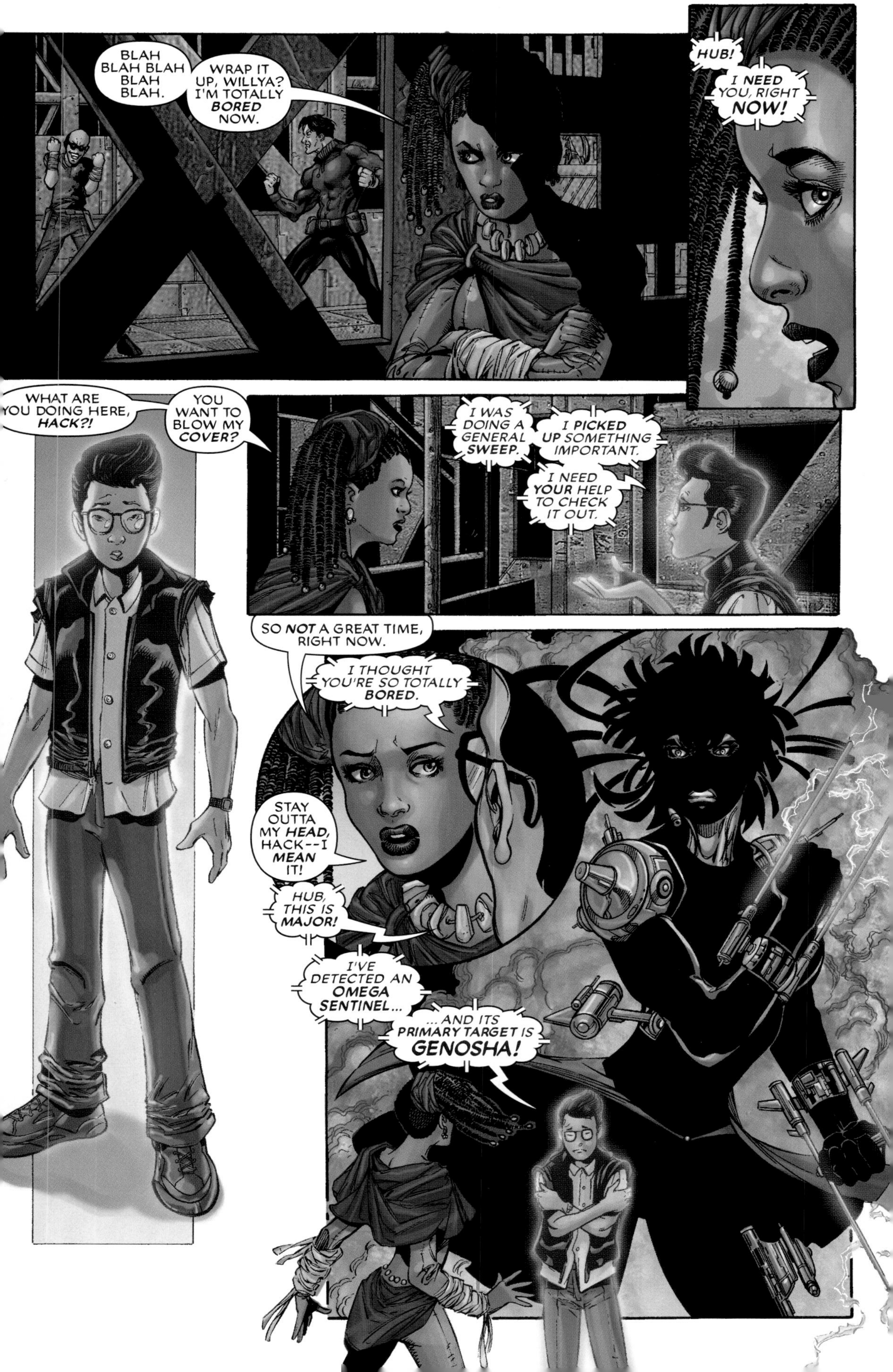
BLAH BLAH BLAH BLAH BLAH.
WRAP IT UP, WILLYA? I'M TOTALLY BORED NOW.
HUB!
I NEED YOU, RIGHT NOW!
WHAT ARE YOU DOING HERE, HACK?!
YOU WANT TO BLOW MY COVER?
I WAS DOING A GENERAL SWEEP.
I PICKED UP SOMETHING IMPORTANT.
I NEED YOUR HELP TO CHECK IT OUT.
SO NOT A GREAT TIME, RIGHT NOW.
I THOUGHT YOU'RE SO TOTALLY BORED.
STAY OUTTA MY HEAD, HACK--I MEAN IT!
HUB, THIS IS MAJOR!
I'VE DETECTED AN OMEGA SENTINEL...
...AND ITS PRIMARY TARGET IS GENOSHA!

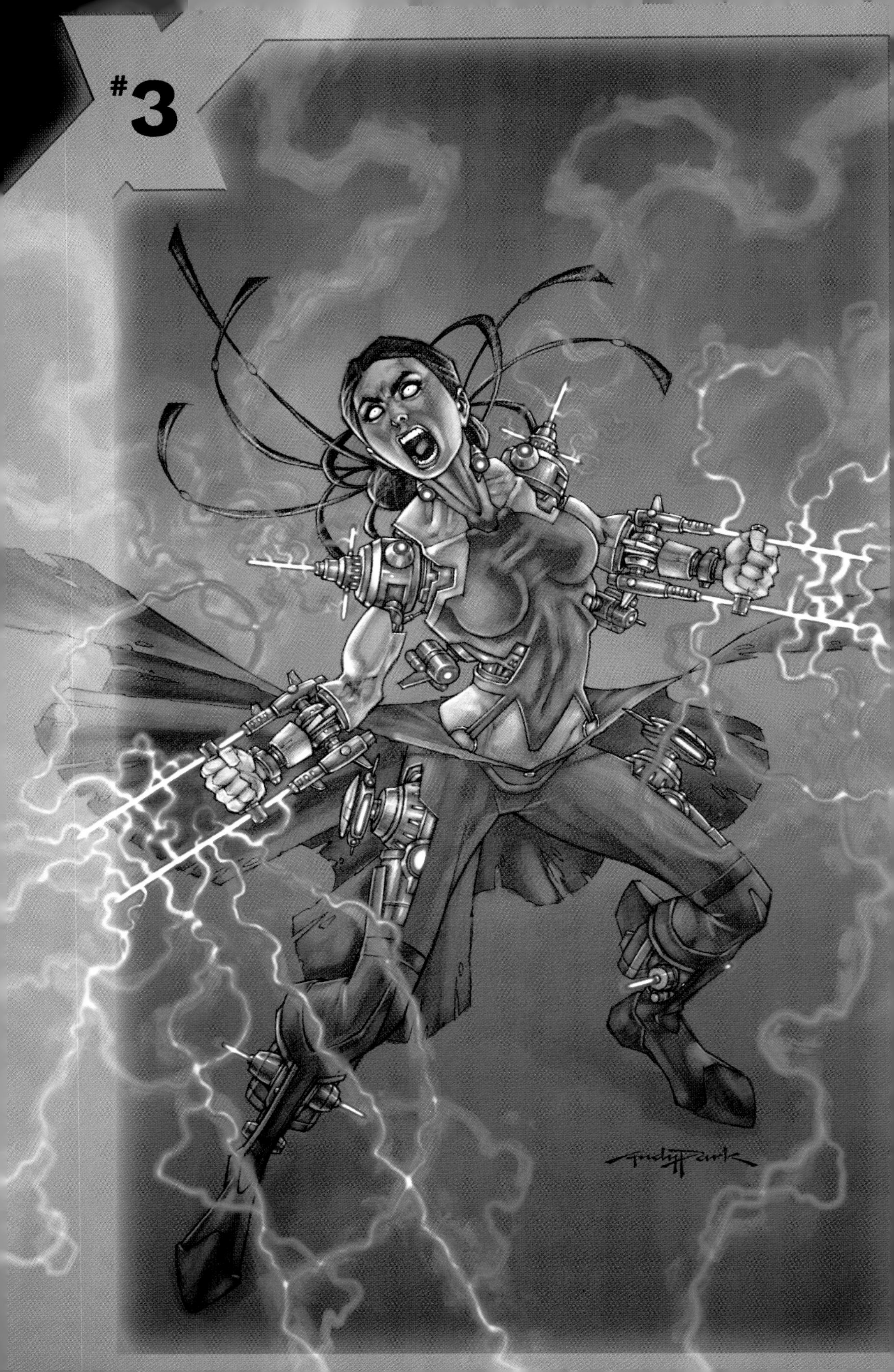
#3
AndyPark

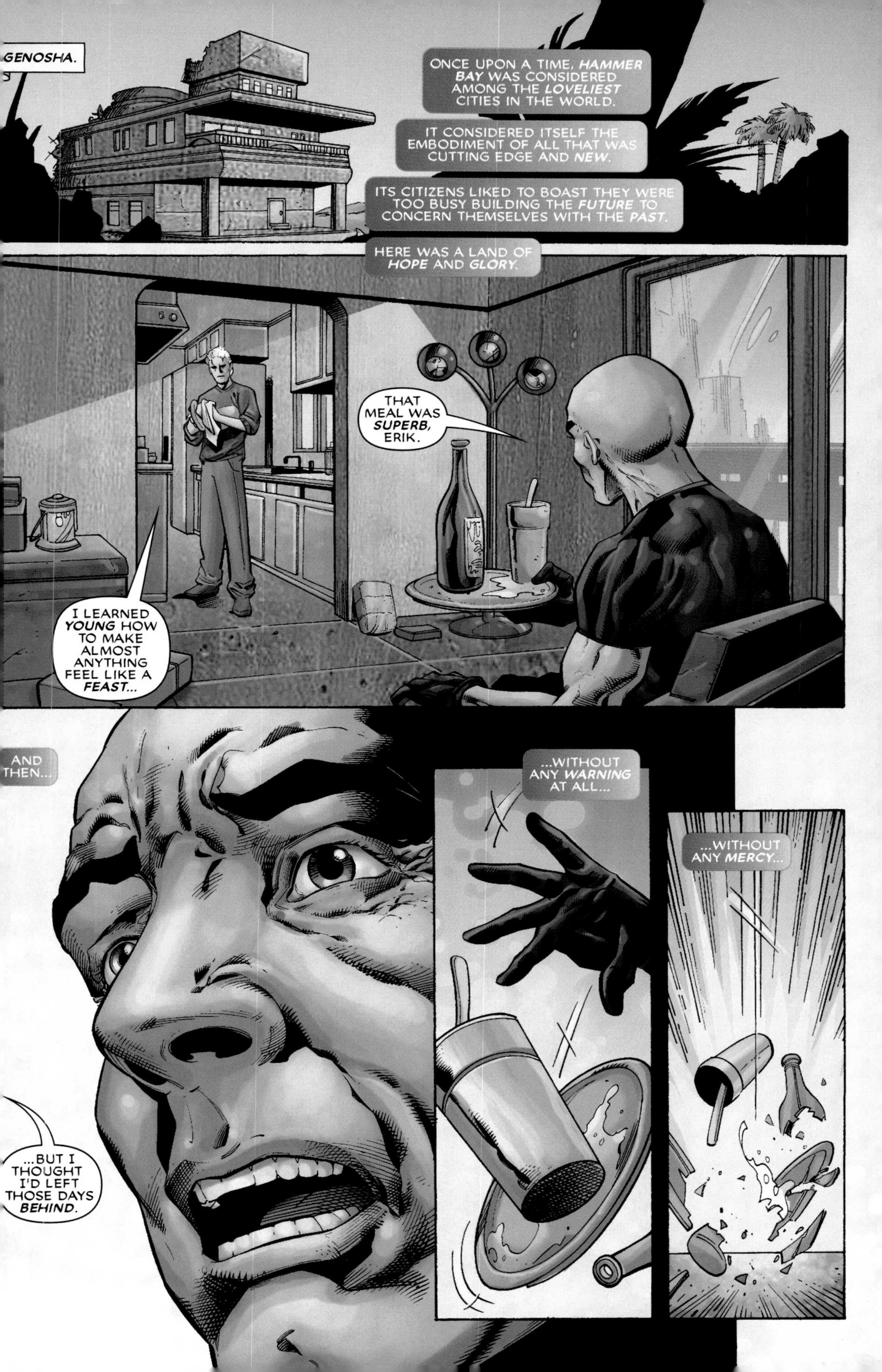
GENOSHA.
ONCE UPON A TIME, HAMMER BAY WAS CONSIDERED AMONG THE LOVELIEST CITIES IN THE WORLD.
IT CONSIDERED ITSELF THE EMBODIMENT OF ALL THAT WAS CUTTING EDGE AND NEW.
ITS CITIZENS LIKED TO BOAST THEY WERE TOO BUSY BUILDING THE FUTURE TO CONCERN THEMSELVES WITH THE PAST.
HERE WAS A LAND OF HOPE AND GLORY.
THAT MEAL WAS SUPERB, ERIK.
I LEARNED YOUNG HOW TO MAKE ALMOST ANYTHING FEEL LIKE A FEAST...
AND THEN...
...BUT I THOUGHT I'D LEFT THOSE DAYS BEHIND.
...WITHOUT ANY WARNING AT ALL...
...WITHOUT ANY MERCY...

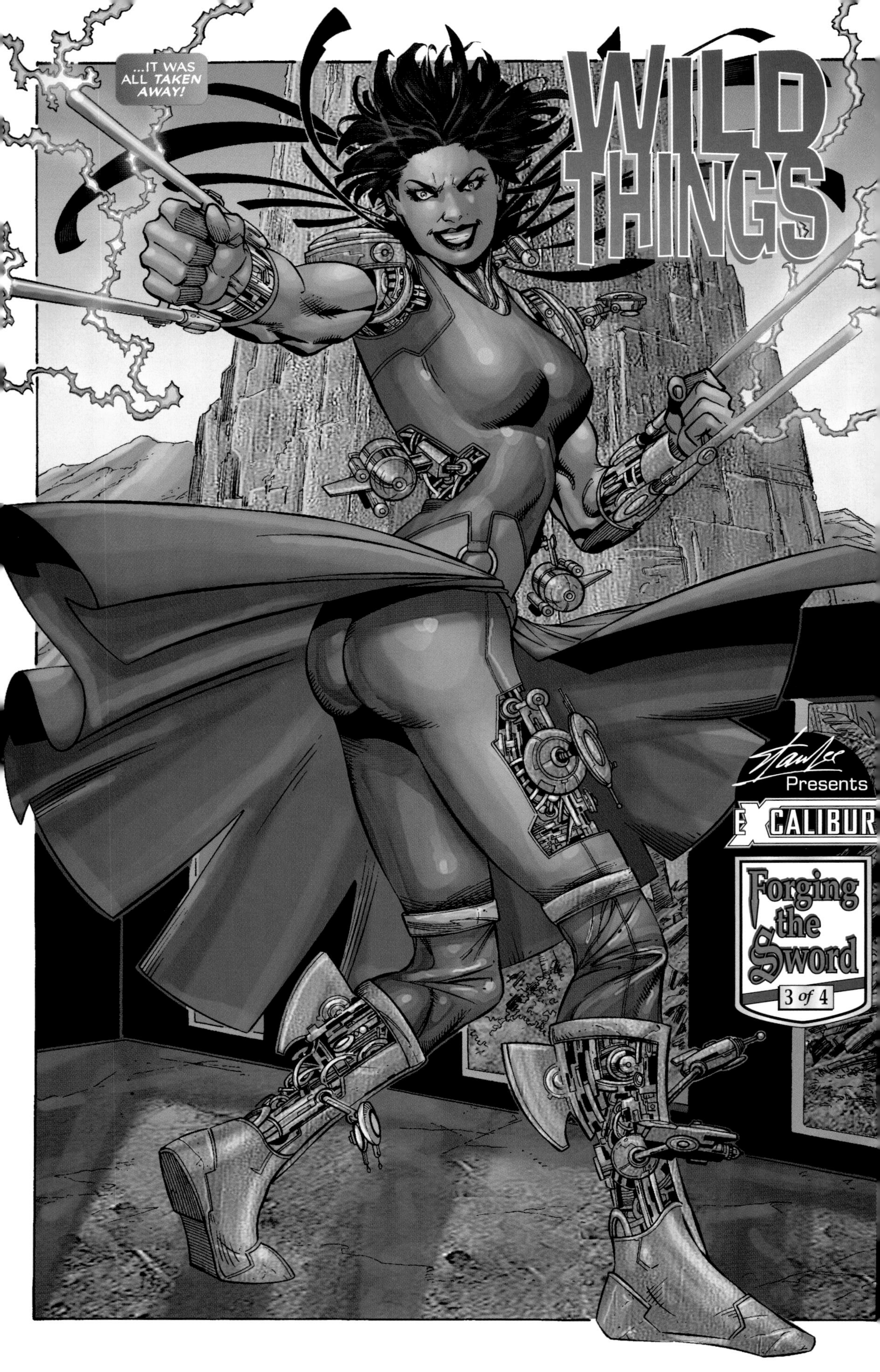

...IT WAS ALL TAKEN AWAY!
WILD THINGS
Stan Lee Presents
EXCALIBUR
Forging the Sword
3 of 4

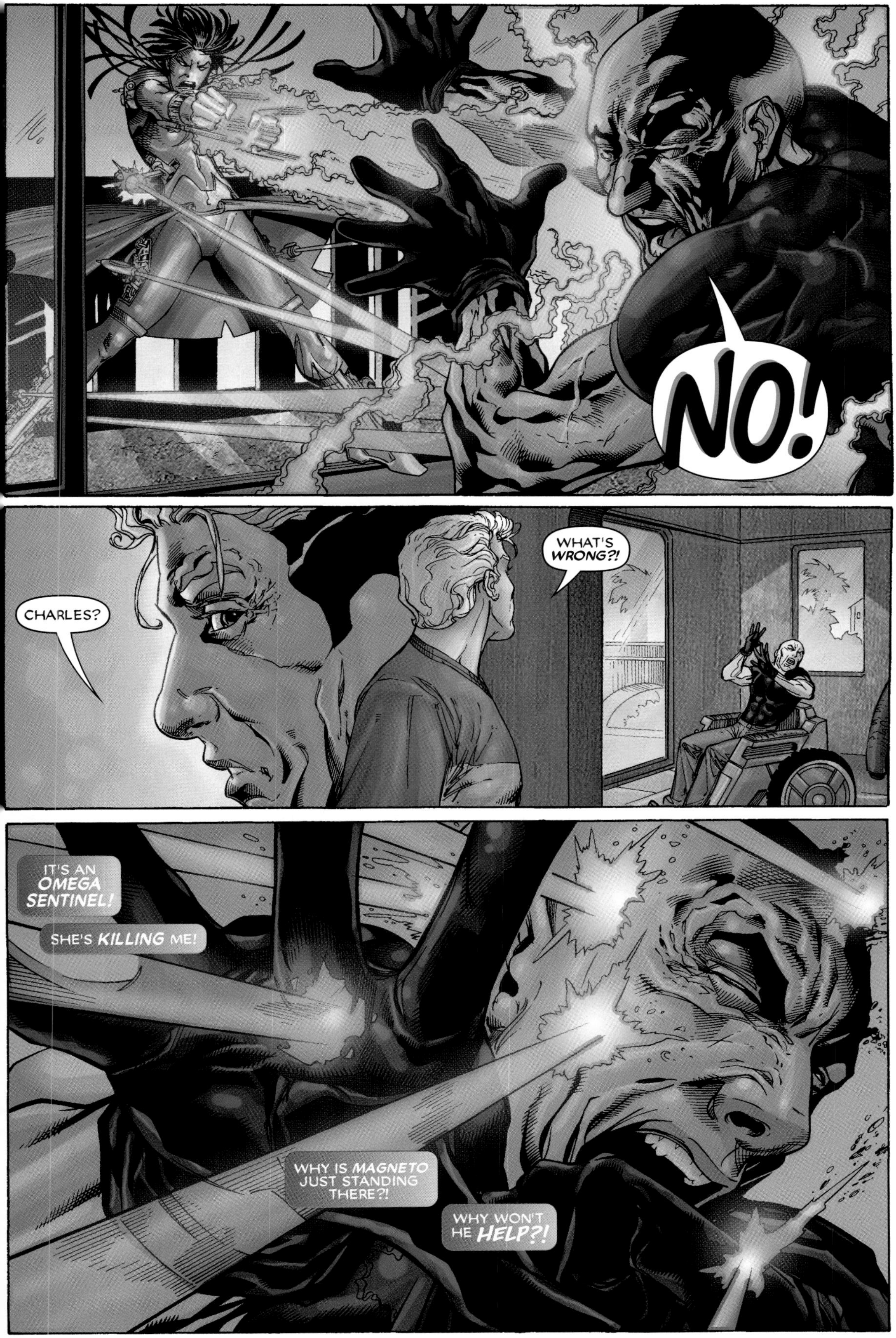
NO!
CHARLES?
WHAT'S WRONG?!
IT'S AN OMEGA SENTINEL!
SHE'S KILLING ME!
WHY IS MAGNETO JUST STANDING THERE?!
WHY WON'T HE HELP?!

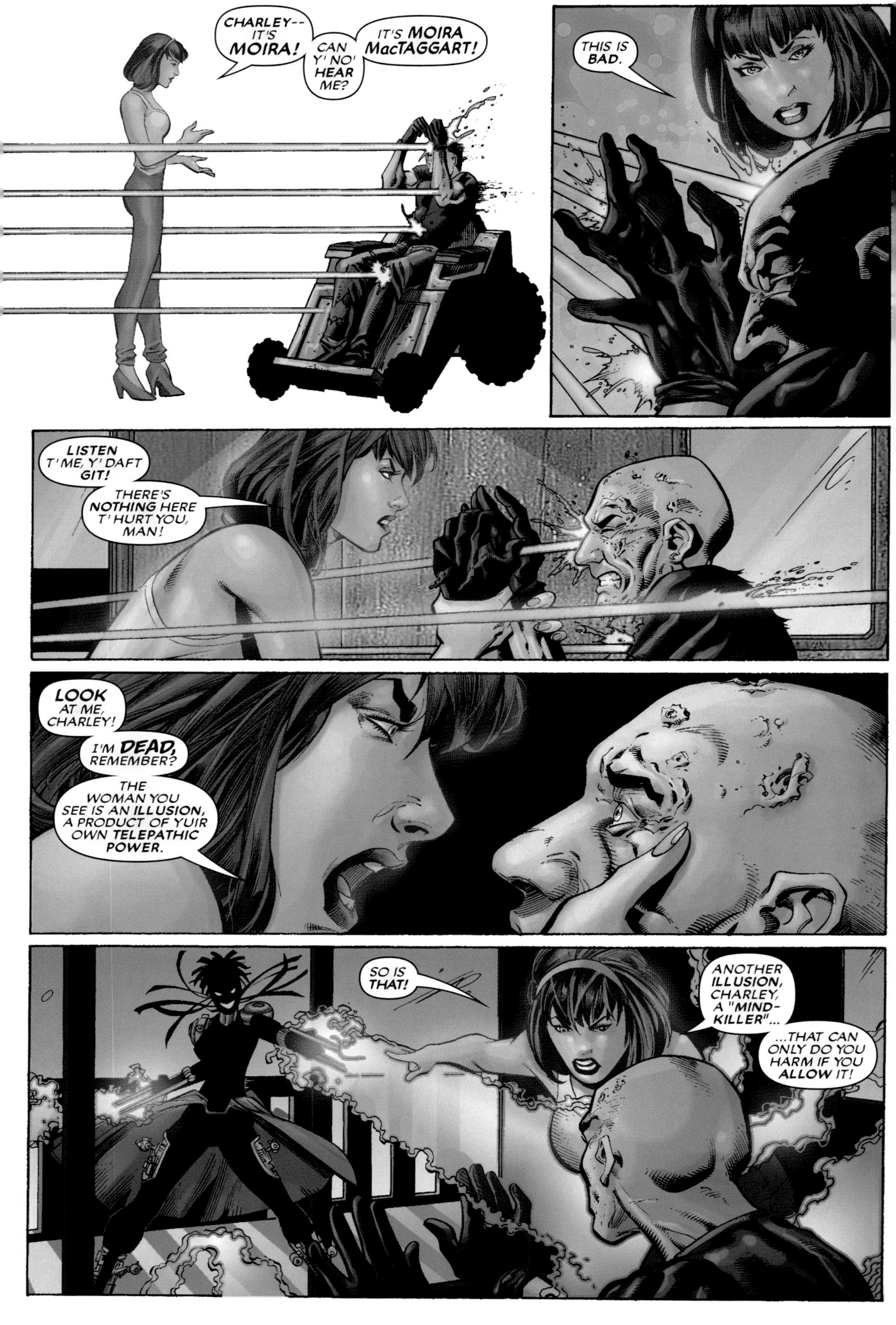
CHARLEY-- IT'S MOIRA!
CAN Y' NO' HEAR ME?
IT'S MOIRA MacTAGGART!
THIS IS BAD.
LISTEN T' ME, Y' DAFT GIT!
THERE'S NOTHING HERE T' HURT YOU, MAN!
LOOK AT ME, CHARLEY!
I'M DEAD, REMEMBER?
THE WOMAN YOU SEE IS AN ILLUSION, A PRODUCT OF YUIR OWN TELEPATHIC POWER.
SO IS THAT!
ANOTHER ILLUSION, CHARLEY, A "MIND-KILLER"...
...THAT CAN ONLY DO YOU HARM IF YOU ALLOW IT!

CHARLES-- OLD FRIEND-- ARE YOU *ALL RIGHT?*

USE YUIR *EYES,* CHARLEY, USE YUIR *INTELLECT.*

IF THIS IS *REAL,* WHY ISN'T *MAGNETO* AFFECTED?

ERIK?

YES, CHARLES?

YOU SUDDENLY SEEM VERY *UPSET.* CAN I *HELP?*

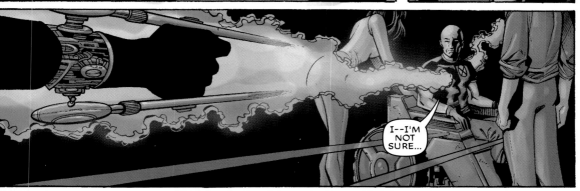

I--I'M NOT SURE...

THA'S *BETTER,* ME OL' DARLIN'.

...BUT I THINK YOU ALREADY *HAVE.*

WHAT ARE YOU *LOOKING* AT?

DO YOU *SEE* ANYTHING *THERE?*

ABSOLUTELY *NOTHING.*

AN *OMEGA SENTINEL* WAS STANDING ON THE DECK.

IT-- IT *KILLED* ME.

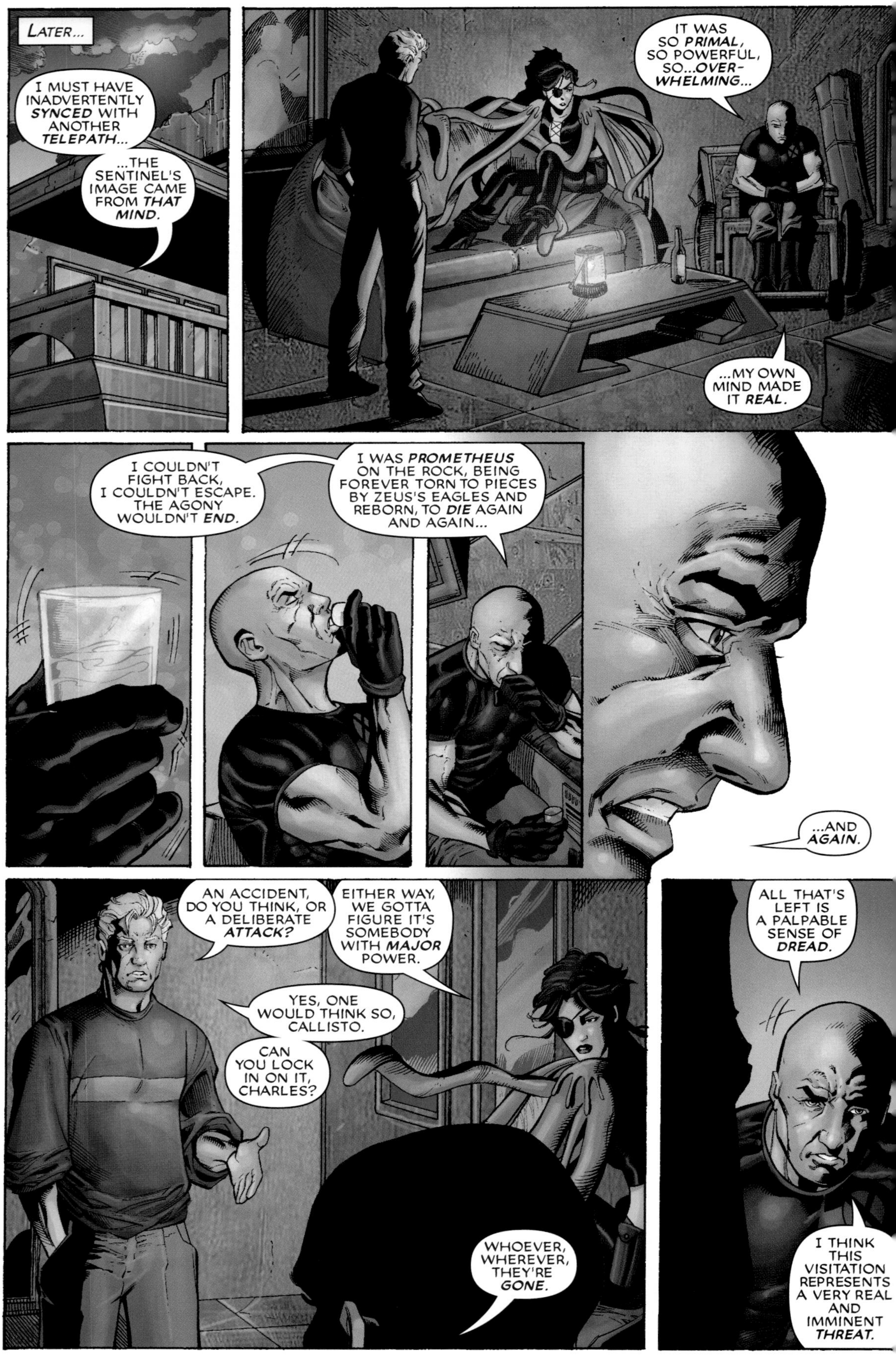
LATER...
I MUST HAVE INADVERTENTLY SYNCED WITH ANOTHER TELEPATH...
...THE SENTINEL'S IMAGE CAME FROM THAT MIND.
IT WAS SO PRIMAL, SO POWERFUL, SO...OVER-WHELMING...
...MY OWN MIND MADE IT REAL.
I COULDN'T FIGHT BACK, I COULDN'T ESCAPE. THE AGONY WOULDN'T END.
I WAS PROMETHEUS ON THE ROCK, BEING FOREVER TORN TO PIECES BY ZEUS'S EAGLES AND REBORN, TO DIE AGAIN AND AGAIN...
...AND AGAIN.
AN ACCIDENT, DO YOU THINK, OR A DELIBERATE ATTACK?
EITHER WAY, WE GOTTA FIGURE IT'S SOMEBODY WITH MAJOR POWER.
YES, ONE WOULD THINK SO, CALLISTO.
CAN YOU LOCK IN ON IT, CHARLES?
WHOEVER, WHEREVER, THEY'RE GONE.
ALL THAT'S LEFT IS A PALPABLE SENSE OF DREAD.
I THINK THIS VISITATION REPRESENTS A VERY REAL AND IMMINENT THREAT.

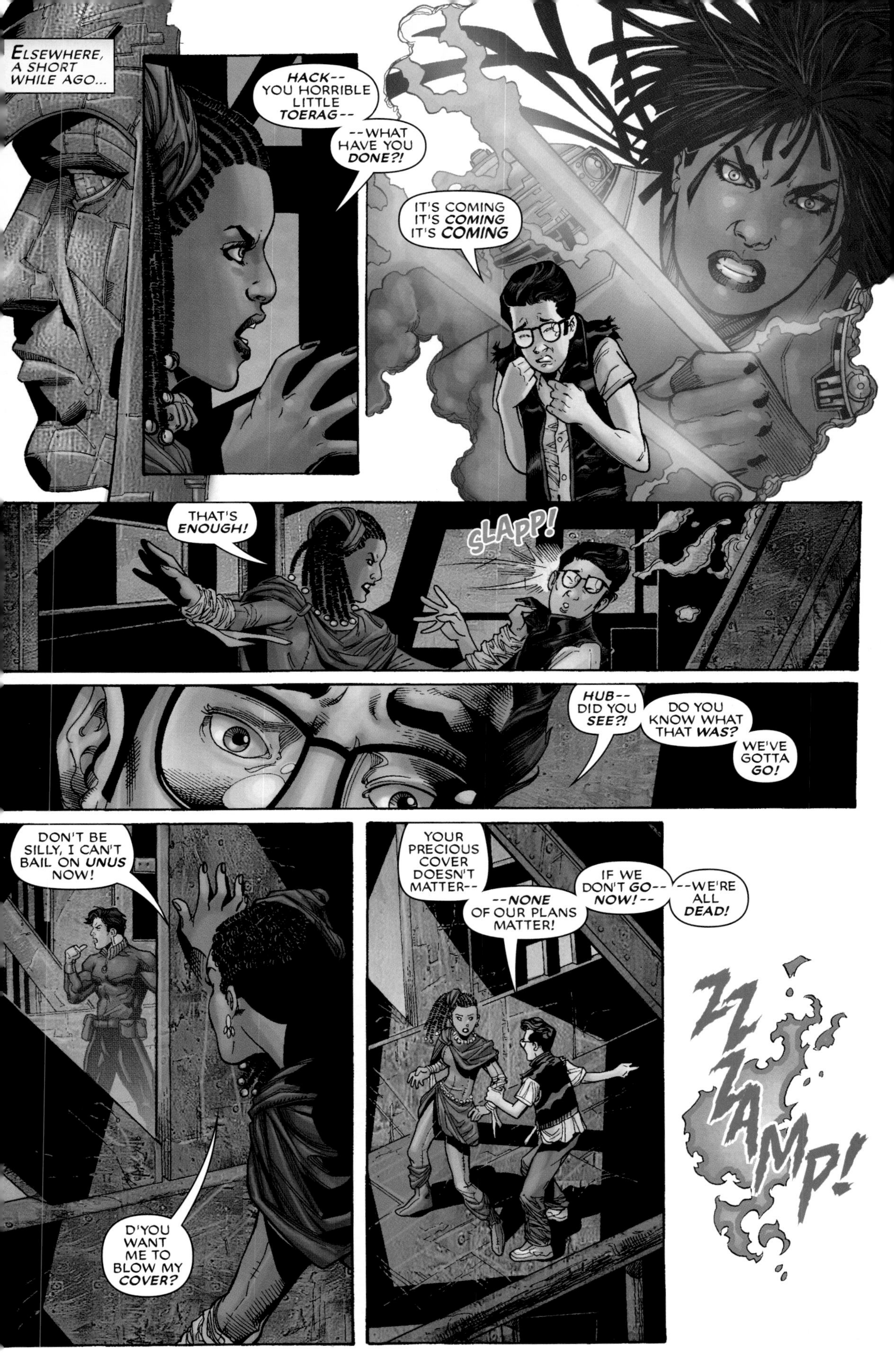
ELSEWHERE, A SHORT WHILE AGO...
HACK-- YOU HORRIBLE LITTLE TOERAG--
--WHAT HAVE YOU DONE?!
IT'S COMING IT'S COMING IT'S COMING
THAT'S ENOUGH!
SLAPP!
HUB-- DID YOU SEE?!
DO YOU KNOW WHAT THAT WAS?
WE'VE GOTTA GO!
DON'T BE SILLY, I CAN'T BAIL ON UNUS NOW!
D'YOU WANT ME TO BLOW MY COVER?
YOUR PRECIOUS COVER DOESN'T MATTER--
--NONE OF OUR PLANS MATTER!
IF WE DON'T GO-- NOW!--
--WE'RE ALL DEAD!
ZZZAMP!

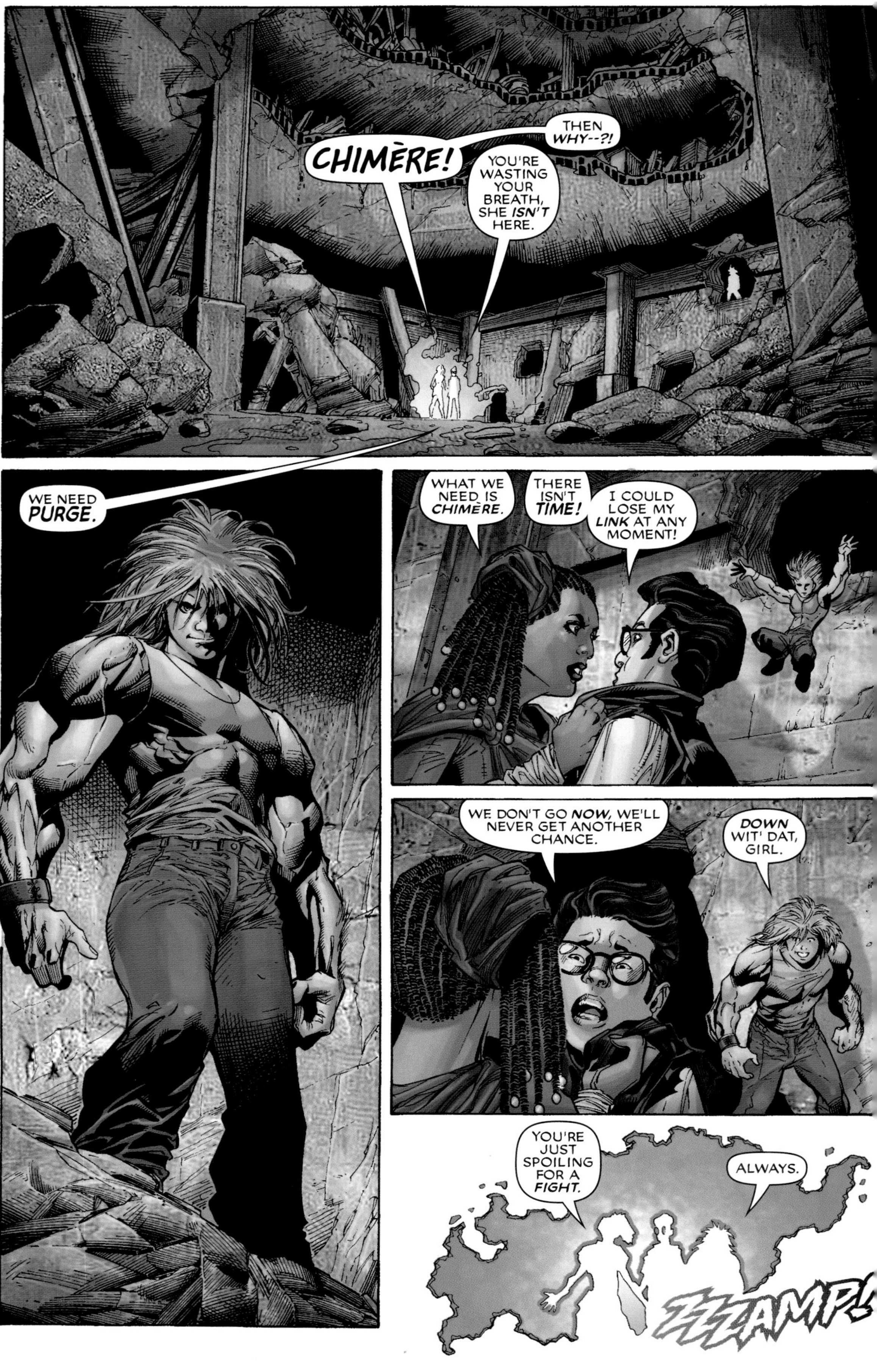
CHIMÈRE!
THEN WHY--?!
YOU'RE WASTING YOUR BREATH, SHE ISN'T HERE.
WE NEED PURGE.
WHAT WE NEED IS CHIMÈRE.
THERE ISN'T TIME!
I COULD LOSE MY LINK AT ANY MOMENT!
WE DON'T GO NOW, WE'LL NEVER GET ANOTHER CHANCE.
DOWN WIT' DAT, GIRL.
YOU'RE JUST SPOILING FOR A FIGHT.
ALWAYS.
ZZZAMP!

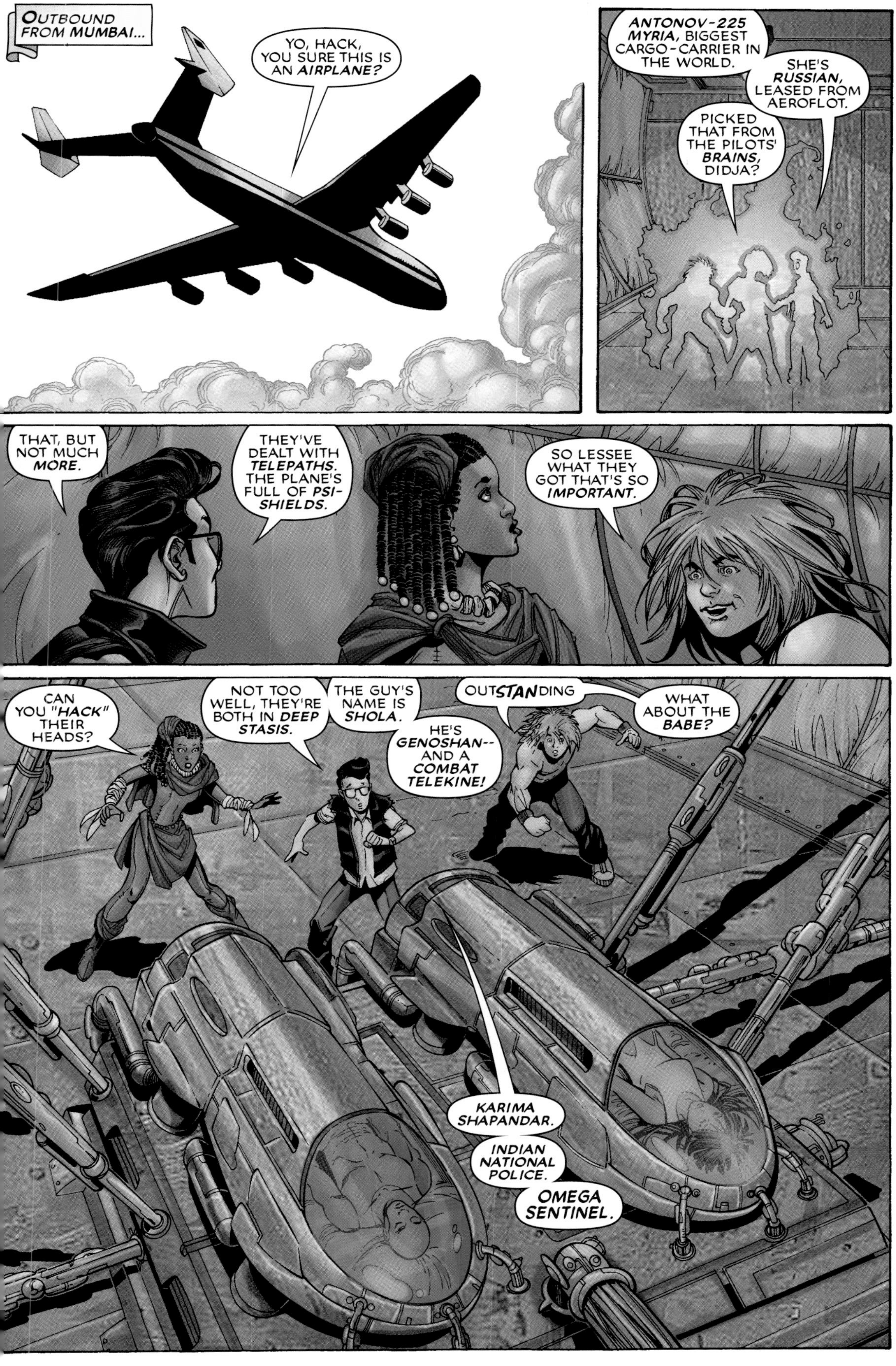
OUTBOUND FROM MUMBAI...
YO, HACK, YOU SURE THIS IS AN AIRPLANE?
ANTONOV-225 MYRIA, BIGGEST CARGO-CARRIER IN THE WORLD.
SHE'S RUSSIAN, LEASED FROM AEROFLOT.
PICKED THAT FROM THE PILOTS' BRAINS, DIDJA?
THAT, BUT NOT MUCH MORE.
THEY'VE DEALT WITH TELEPATHS. THE PLANE'S FULL OF PSI-SHIELDS.
SO LESSEE WHAT THEY GOT THAT'S SO IMPORTANT.
CAN YOU "HACK" THEIR HEADS?
NOT TOO WELL, THEY'RE BOTH IN DEEP STASIS.
THE GUY'S NAME IS SHOLA.
HE'S GENOSHAN-- AND A COMBAT TELEKINE!
OUTSTANDING
WHAT ABOUT THE BABE?
KARIMA SHAPANDAR.
INDIAN NATIONAL POLICE.
OMEGA SENTINEL.

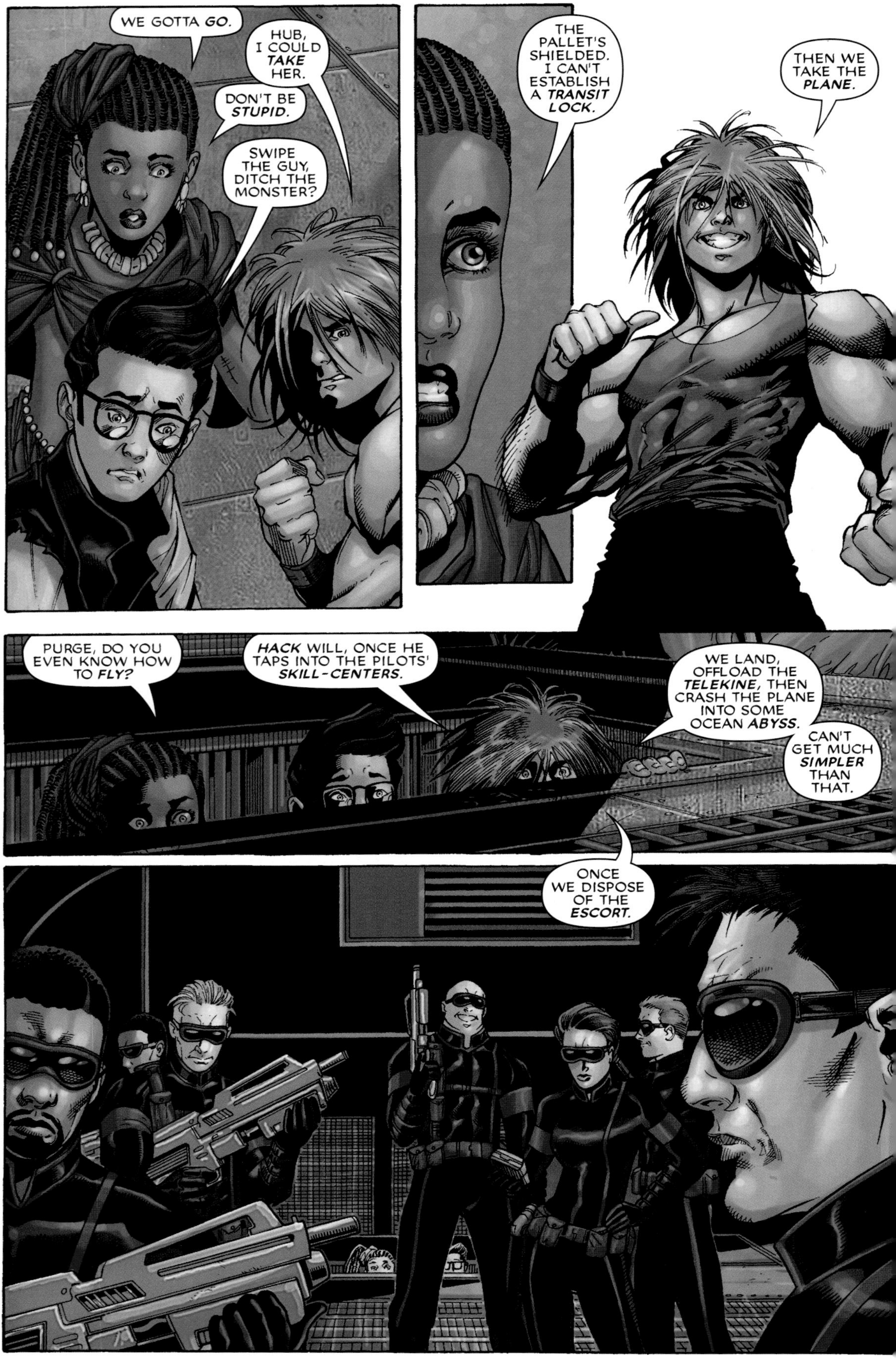
WE GOTTA *GO*.
HUB, I COULD *TAKE* HER.
DON'T BE *STUPID*.
SWIPE THE GUY, DITCH THE MONSTER?
THE PALLET'S SHIELDED. I CAN'T ESTABLISH A *TRANSIT LOCK*.
THEN WE TAKE THE *PLANE*.
PURGE, DO YOU EVEN KNOW HOW TO *FLY?*
HACK WILL, ONCE HE TAPS INTO THE PILOTS' *SKILL-CENTERS*.
WE LAND, OFFLOAD THE *TELEKINE*, THEN CRASH THE PLANE INTO SOME OCEAN *ABYSS*.
CAN'T GET MUCH *SIMPLER* THAN THAT.
ONCE WE DISPOSE OF THE *ESCORT*.

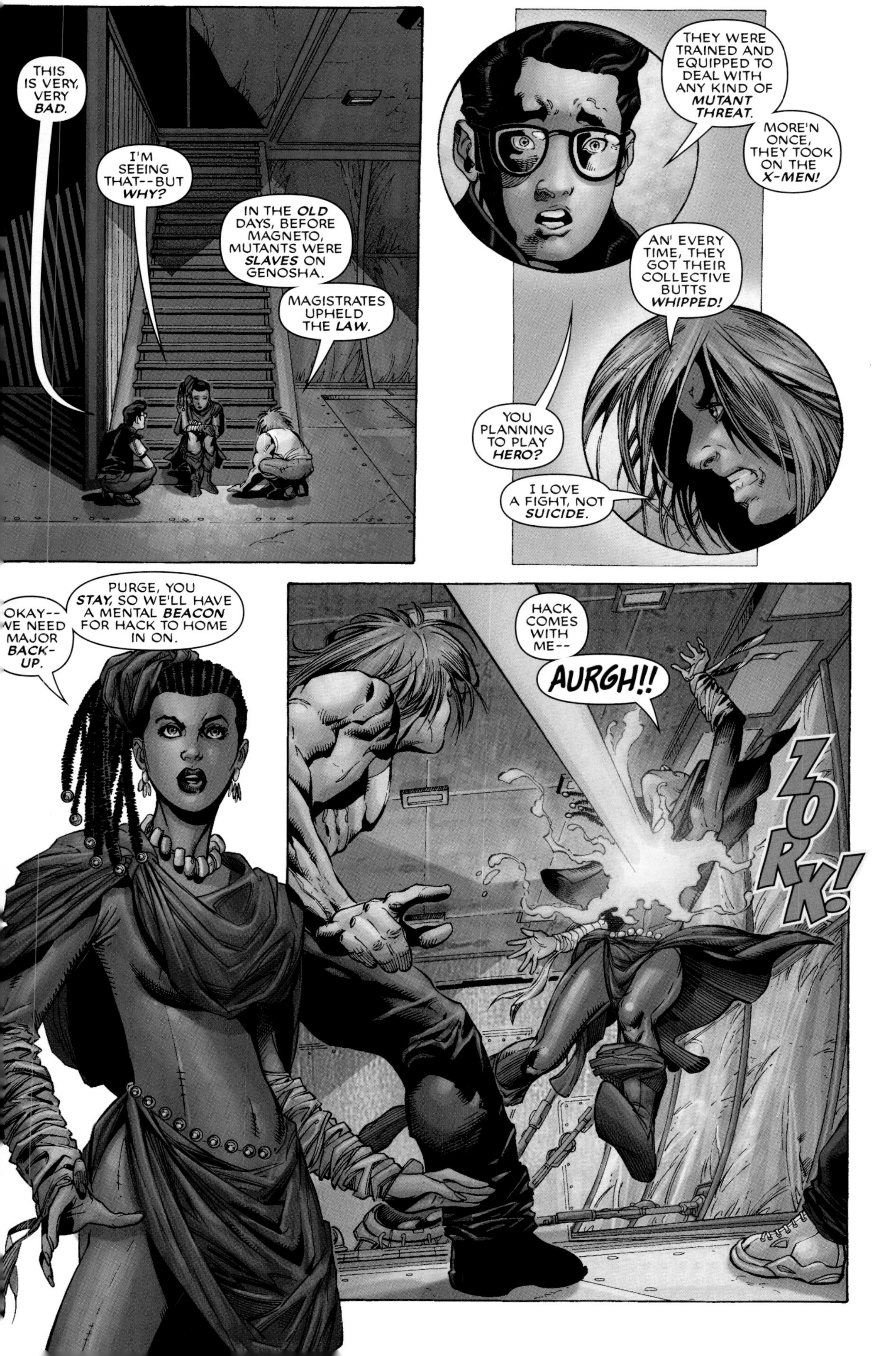

THIS IS VERY, VERY *BAD*.
I'M SEEING THAT--BUT *WHY?*
IN THE *OLD* DAYS, BEFORE MAGNETO, MUTANTS WERE *SLAVES* ON GENOSHA.
MAGISTRATES UPHELD THE *LAW*.
THEY WERE TRAINED AND EQUIPPED TO DEAL WITH ANY KIND OF *MUTANT THREAT*.
MORE'N ONCE, THEY TOOK ON THE *X-MEN!*
AN' EVERY TIME, THEY GOT THEIR COLLECTIVE BUTTS *WHIPPED!*
YOU PLANNING TO PLAY *HERO?*
I LOVE A FIGHT, NOT *SUICIDE*.
OKAY-- WE NEED MAJOR *BACK-UP*.
PURGE, YOU *STAY*, SO WE'LL HAVE A MENTAL *BEACON* FOR HACK TO HOME IN ON.
HACK COMES WITH ME--
AURGH!!
ZORK!

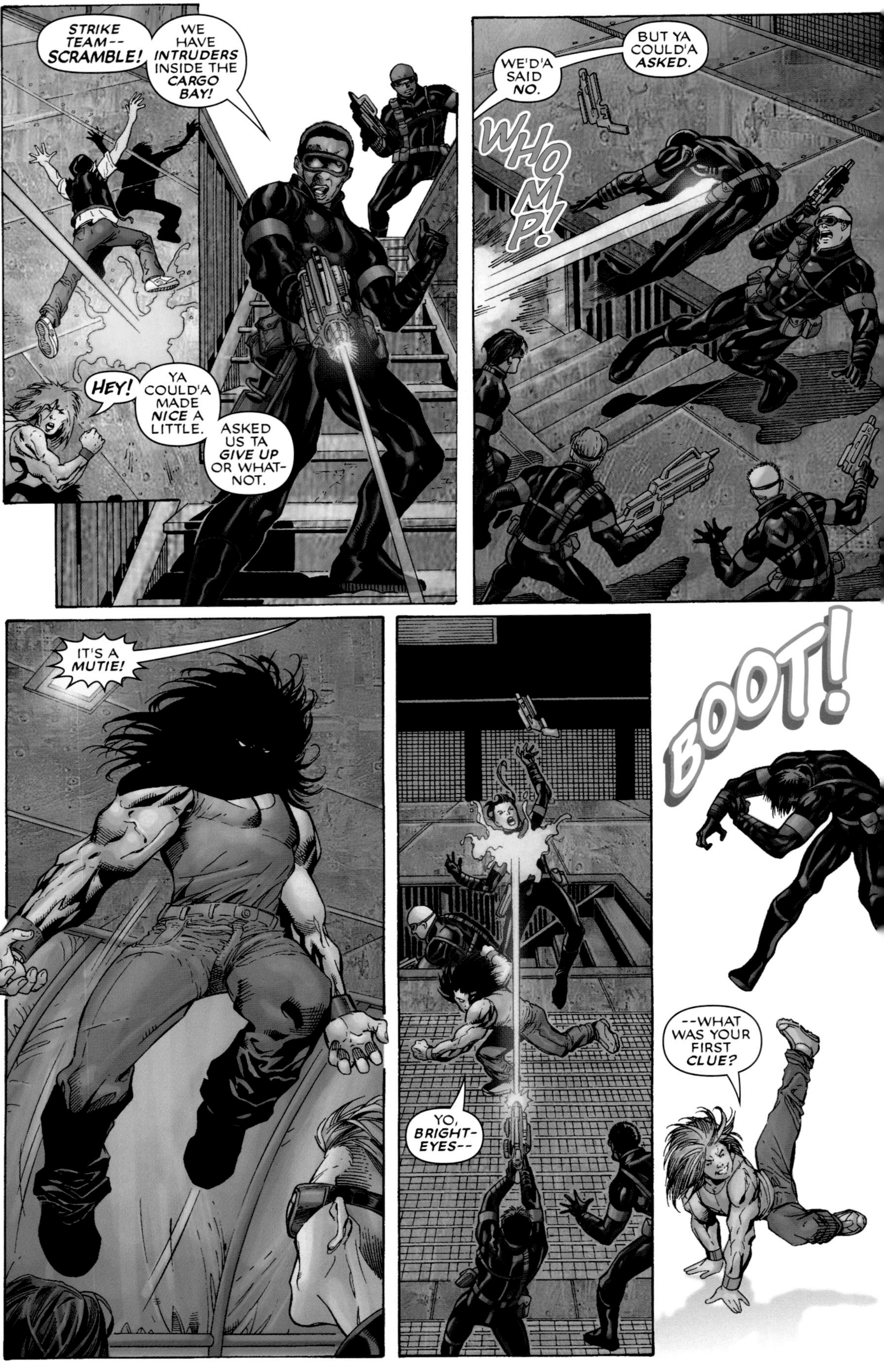
STRIKE TEAM--SCRAMBLE!
WE HAVE INTRUDERS INSIDE THE CARGO BAY!
HEY!
YA COULD'A MADE NICE A LITTLE.
ASKED US TA GIVE UP OR WHAT-NOT.
WE'D'A SAID NO.
BUT YA COULD'A ASKED.
WHOMP!
IT'S A MUTIE!
YO, BRIGHT-EYES--
BOOT!
--WHAT WAS YOUR FIRST CLUE?

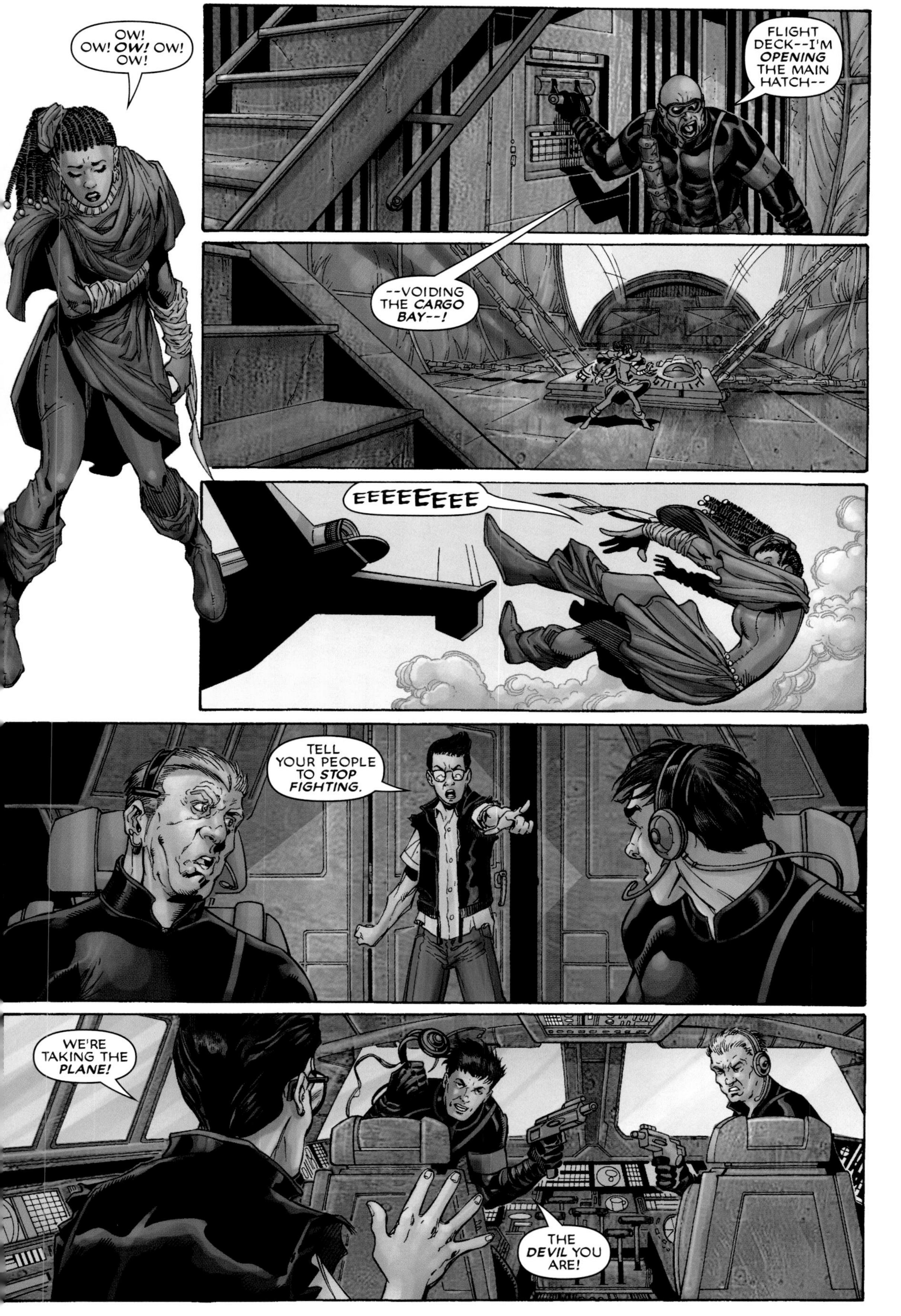
OW! OW! *OW!* OW! OW!
FLIGHT DECK--I'M *OPENING* THE MAIN HATCH--
--VOIDING THE *CARGO BAY*--!
EEEEEEEE
TELL YOUR PEOPLE TO *STOP FIGHTING*.
WE'RE TAKING THE *PLANE!*
THE *DEVIL* YOU ARE!

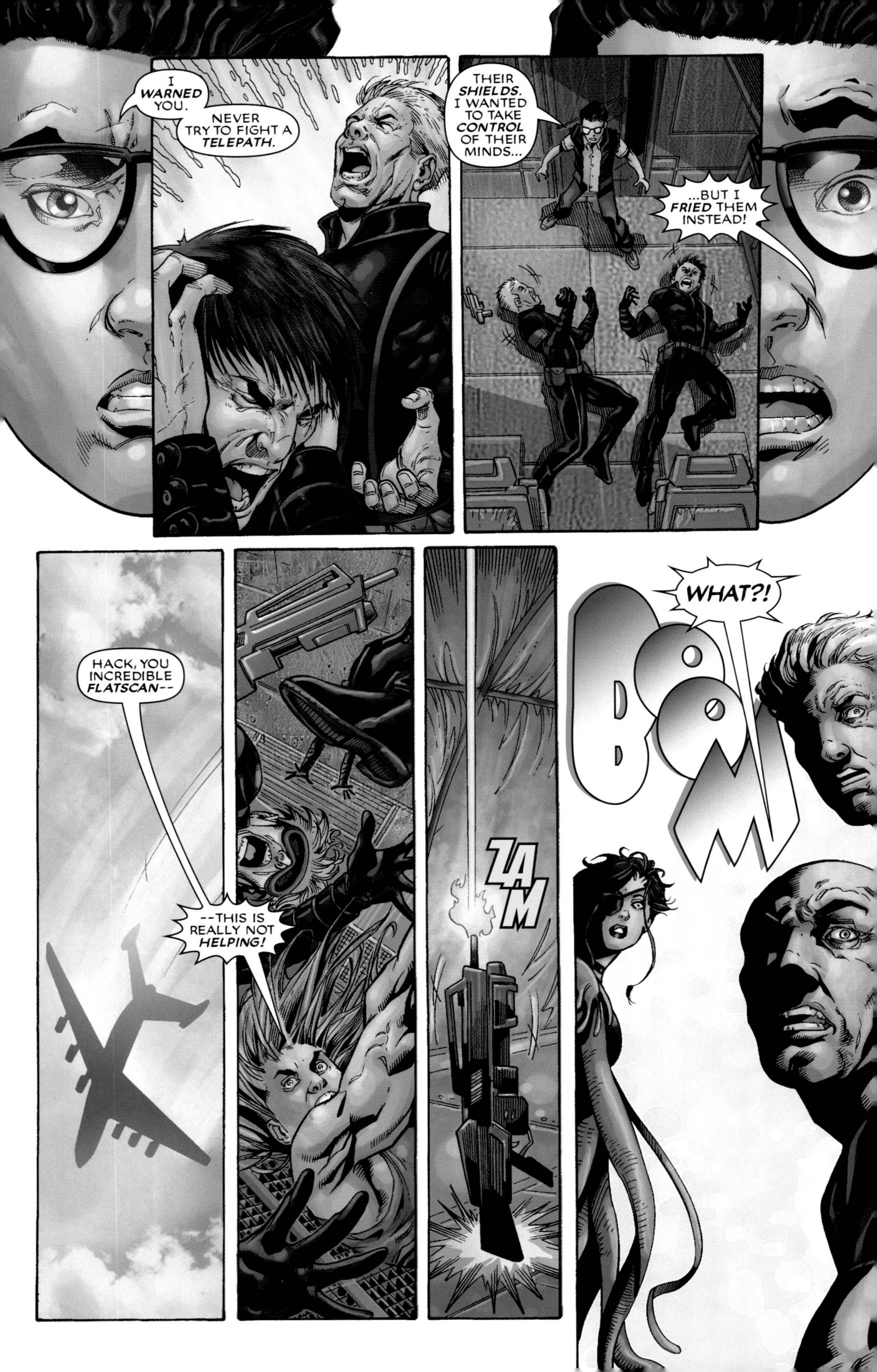
I WARNED YOU.
NEVER TRY TO FIGHT A TELEPATH.
THEIR SHIELDS. I WANTED TO TAKE CONTROL OF THEIR MINDS...
...BUT I FRIED THEM INSTEAD!
HACK, YOU INCREDIBLE FLATSCAN--
--THIS IS REALLY NOT HELPING!
ZAM
WHAT?!
BOOM

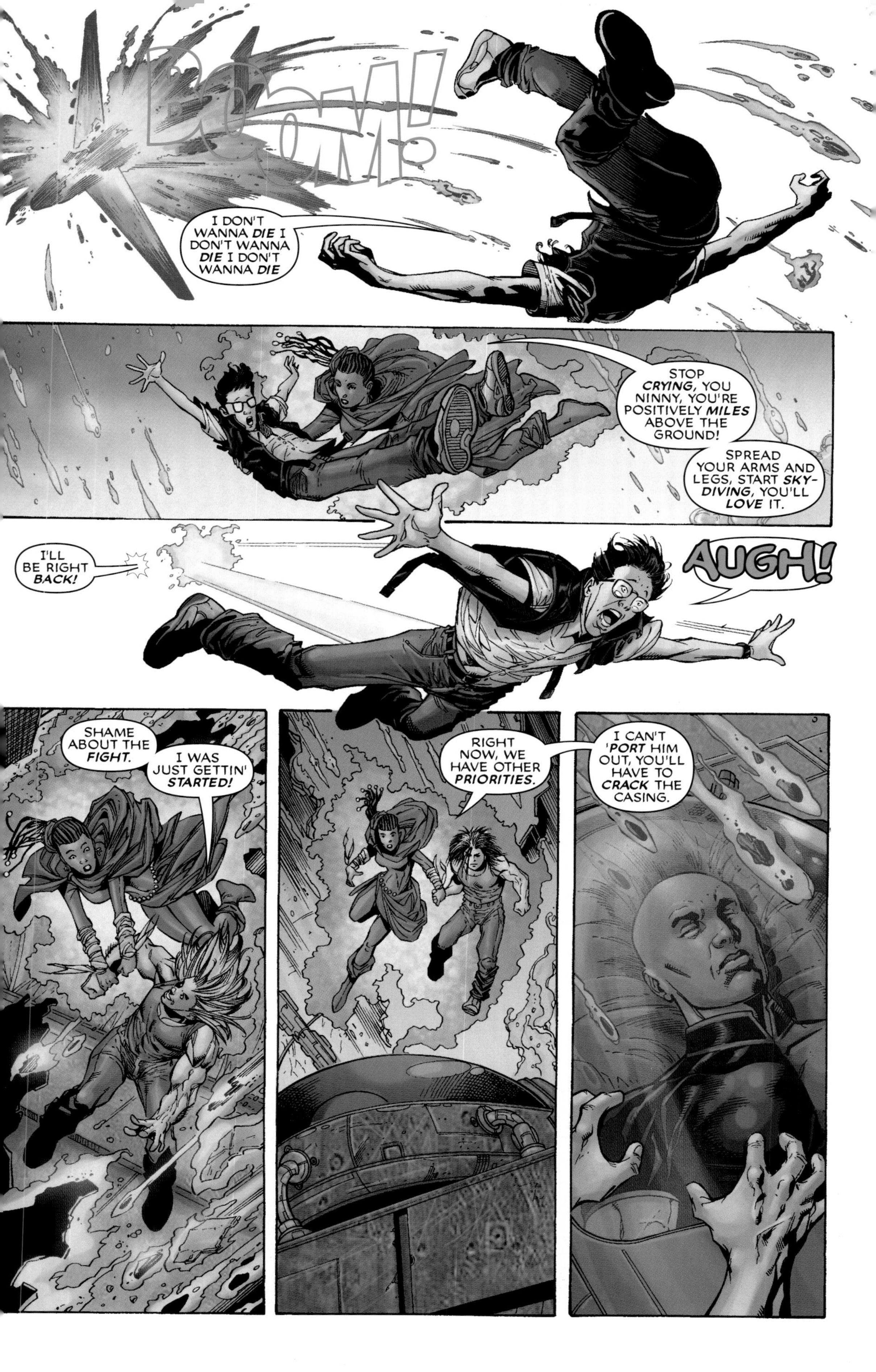
BOOM!
I DON'T WANNA DIE I DON'T WANNA DIE I DON'T WANNA DIE
STOP CRYING, YOU NINNY, YOU'RE POSITIVELY MILES ABOVE THE GROUND!
SPREAD YOUR ARMS AND LEGS, START SKY-DIVING, YOU'LL LOVE IT.
I'LL BE RIGHT BACK!
AUGH!
SHAME ABOUT THE FIGHT.
I WAS JUST GETTIN' STARTED!
RIGHT NOW, WE HAVE OTHER PRIORITIES.
I CAN'T 'PORT HIM OUT, YOU'LL HAVE TO CRACK THE CASING.

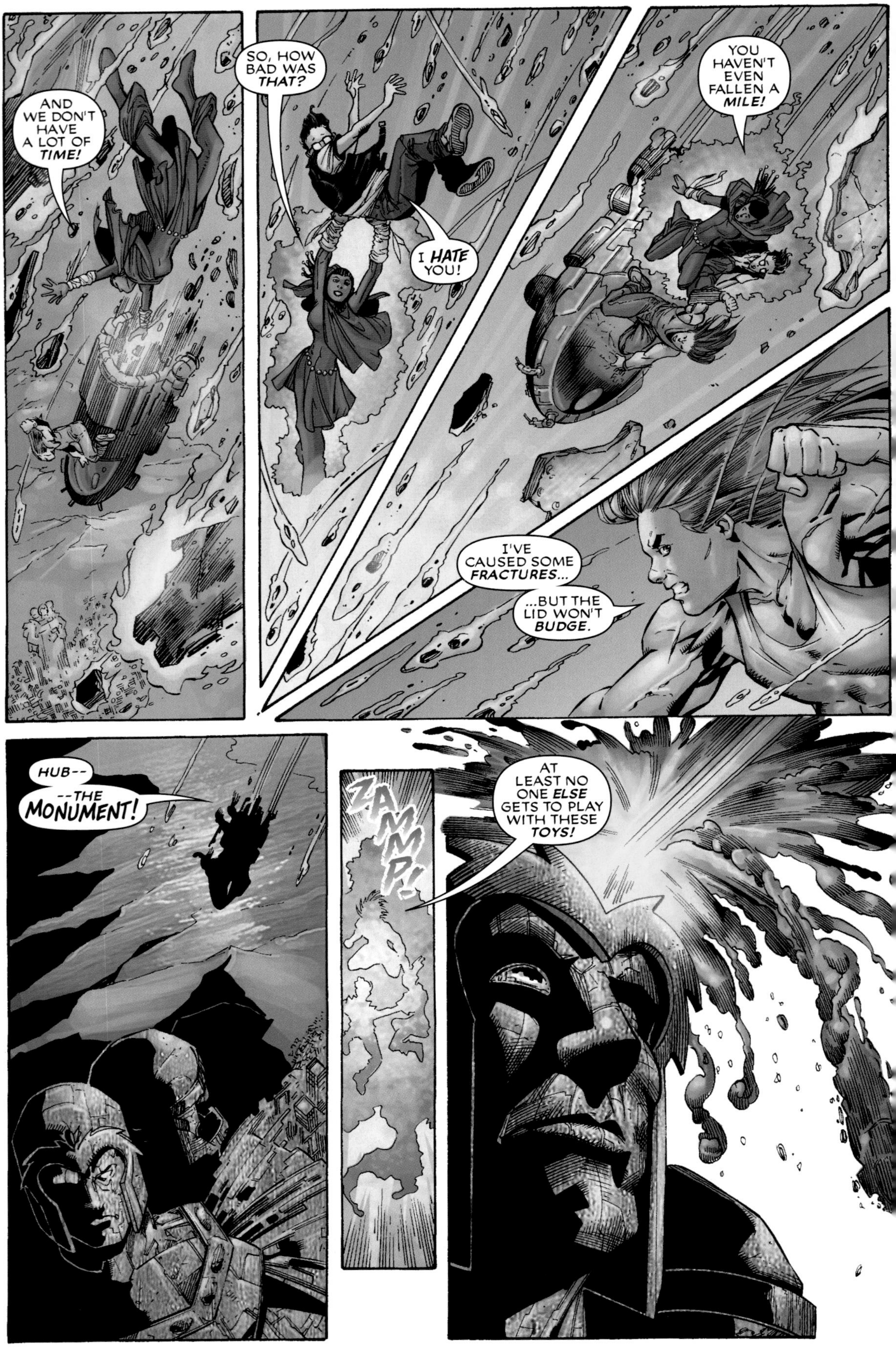
AND WE DON'T HAVE A LOT OF *TIME!*
SO, HOW BAD WAS *THAT?*
I ***HATE*** YOU!
YOU HAVEN'T EVEN FALLEN A ***MILE!***
I'VE CAUSED SOME *FRACTURES...*
...BUT THE LID WON'T *BUDGE.*
HUB--
--THE **MONUMENT!**
ZAMMP!
AT LEAST NO ONE *ELSE* GETS TO PLAY WITH THESE *TOYS!*

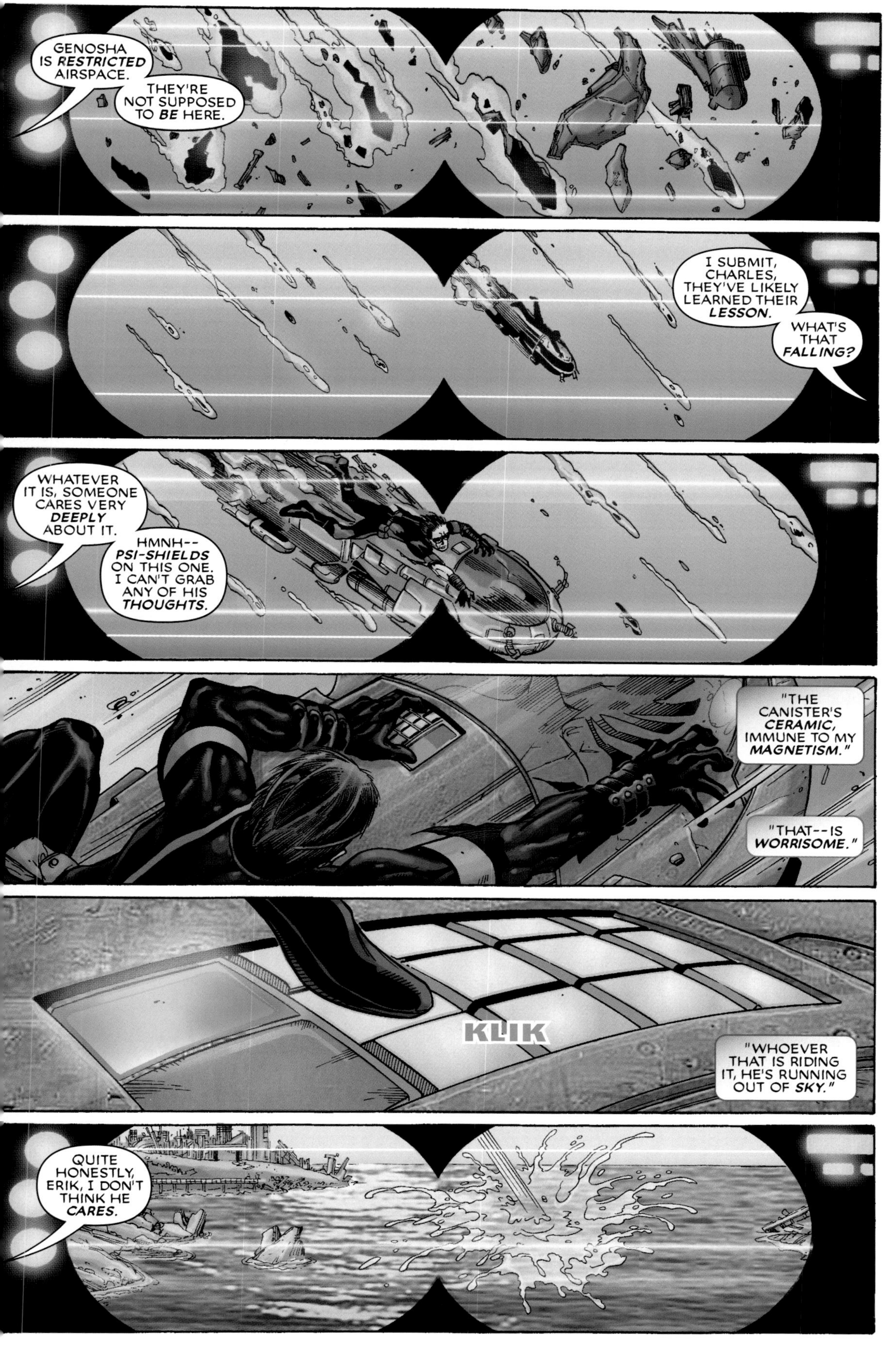
GENOSHA IS RESTRICTED AIRSPACE.
THEY'RE NOT SUPPOSED TO BE HERE.
I SUBMIT, CHARLES, THEY'VE LIKELY LEARNED THEIR LESSON.
WHAT'S THAT FALLING?
WHATEVER IT IS, SOMEONE CARES VERY DEEPLY ABOUT IT.
HMNH-- PSI-SHIELDS ON THIS ONE. I CAN'T GRAB ANY OF HIS THOUGHTS.
"THE CANISTER'S CERAMIC, IMMUNE TO MY MAGNETISM."
"THAT--IS WORRISOME."
KLIK
"WHOEVER THAT IS RIDING IT, HE'S RUNNING OUT OF SKY."
QUITE HONESTLY, ERIK, I DON'T THINK HE CARES.

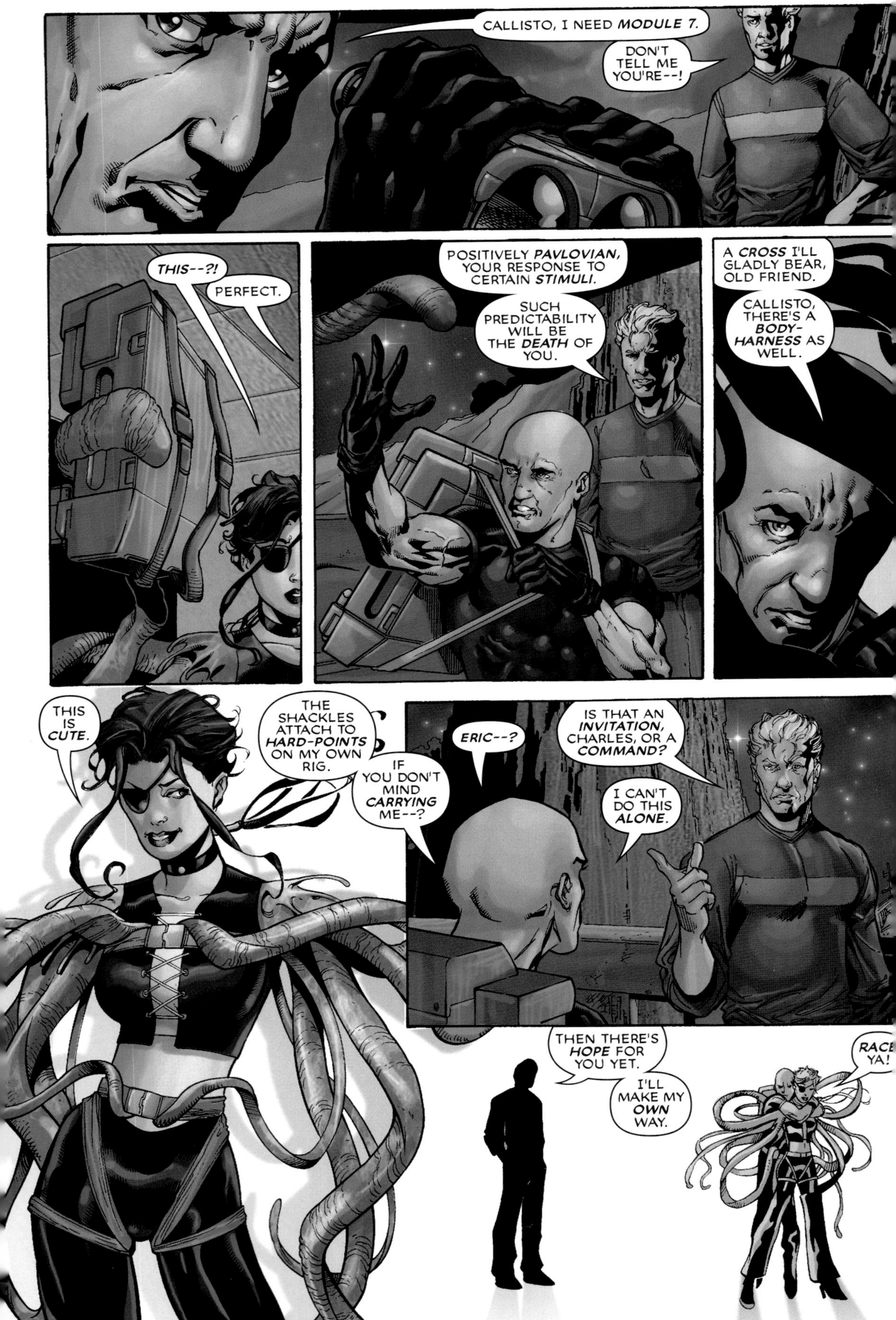
CALLISTO, I NEED *MODULE 7.*
DON'T TELL ME YOU'RE--!
THIS--?!
PERFECT.
POSITIVELY *PAVLOVIAN,* YOUR RESPONSE TO CERTAIN *STIMULI.*
SUCH PREDICTABILITY WILL BE THE *DEATH* OF YOU.
A *CROSS* I'LL GLADLY BEAR, OLD FRIEND.
CALLISTO, THERE'S A *BODY-HARNESS* AS WELL.
THIS IS *CUTE.*
THE SHACKLES ATTACH TO *HARD-POINTS* ON MY OWN RIG.
IF YOU DON'T MIND *CARRYING* ME--?
ERIC--?
IS THAT AN *INVITATION,* CHARLES, OR A *COMMAND?*
I CAN'T DO THIS *ALONE.*
THEN THERE'S *HOPE* FOR YOU YET.
I'LL MAKE MY *OWN* WAY.
RACE YA!

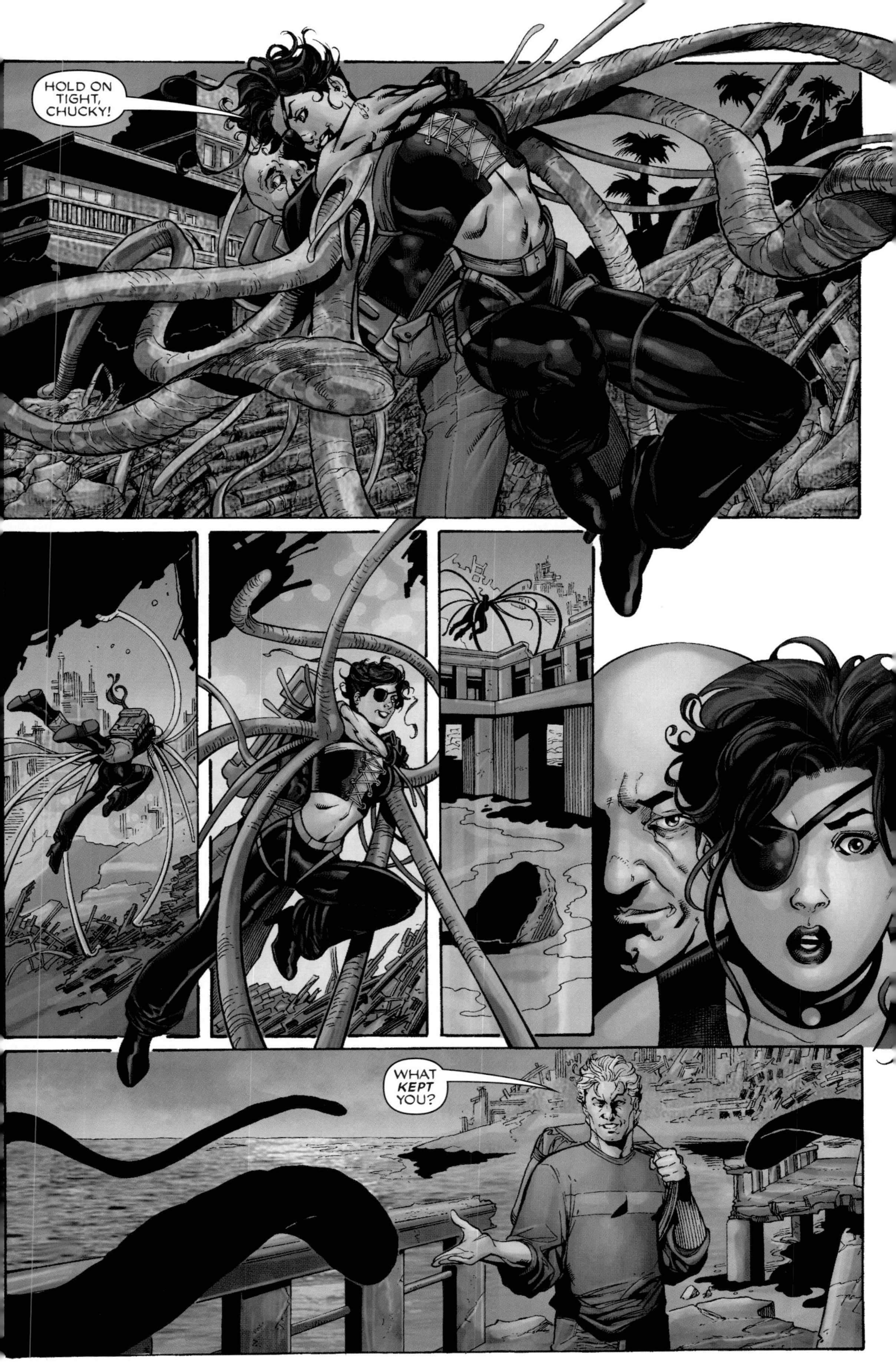
HOLD ON TIGHT, CHUCKY!
WHAT KEPT YOU?

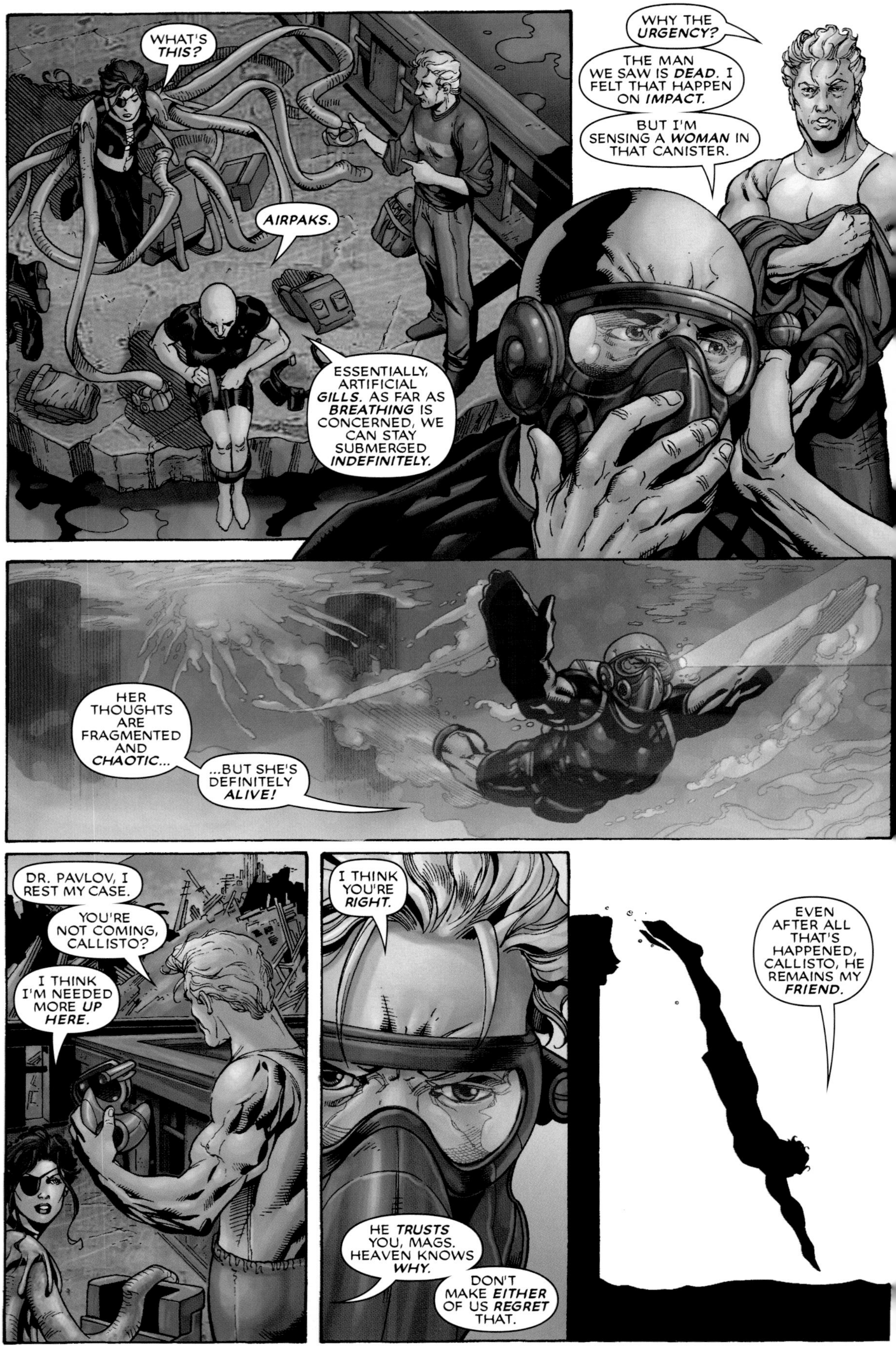
WHAT'S THIS?
AIRPAKS.
ESSENTIALLY, ARTIFICIAL GILLS. AS FAR AS BREATHING IS CONCERNED, WE CAN STAY SUBMERGED INDEFINITELY.
WHY THE URGENCY?
THE MAN WE SAW IS DEAD. I FELT THAT HAPPEN ON IMPACT.
BUT I'M SENSING A WOMAN IN THAT CANISTER.
HER THOUGHTS ARE FRAGMENTED AND CHAOTIC...
...BUT SHE'S DEFINITELY ALIVE!
DR. PAVLOV, I REST MY CASE.
YOU'RE NOT COMING, CALLISTO?
I THINK I'M NEEDED MORE UP HERE.
I THINK YOU'RE RIGHT.
HE TRUSTS YOU, MAGS. HEAVEN KNOWS WHY.
DON'T MAKE EITHER OF US REGRET THAT.
EVEN AFTER ALL THAT'S HAPPENED, CALLISTO, HE REMAINS MY FRIEND.

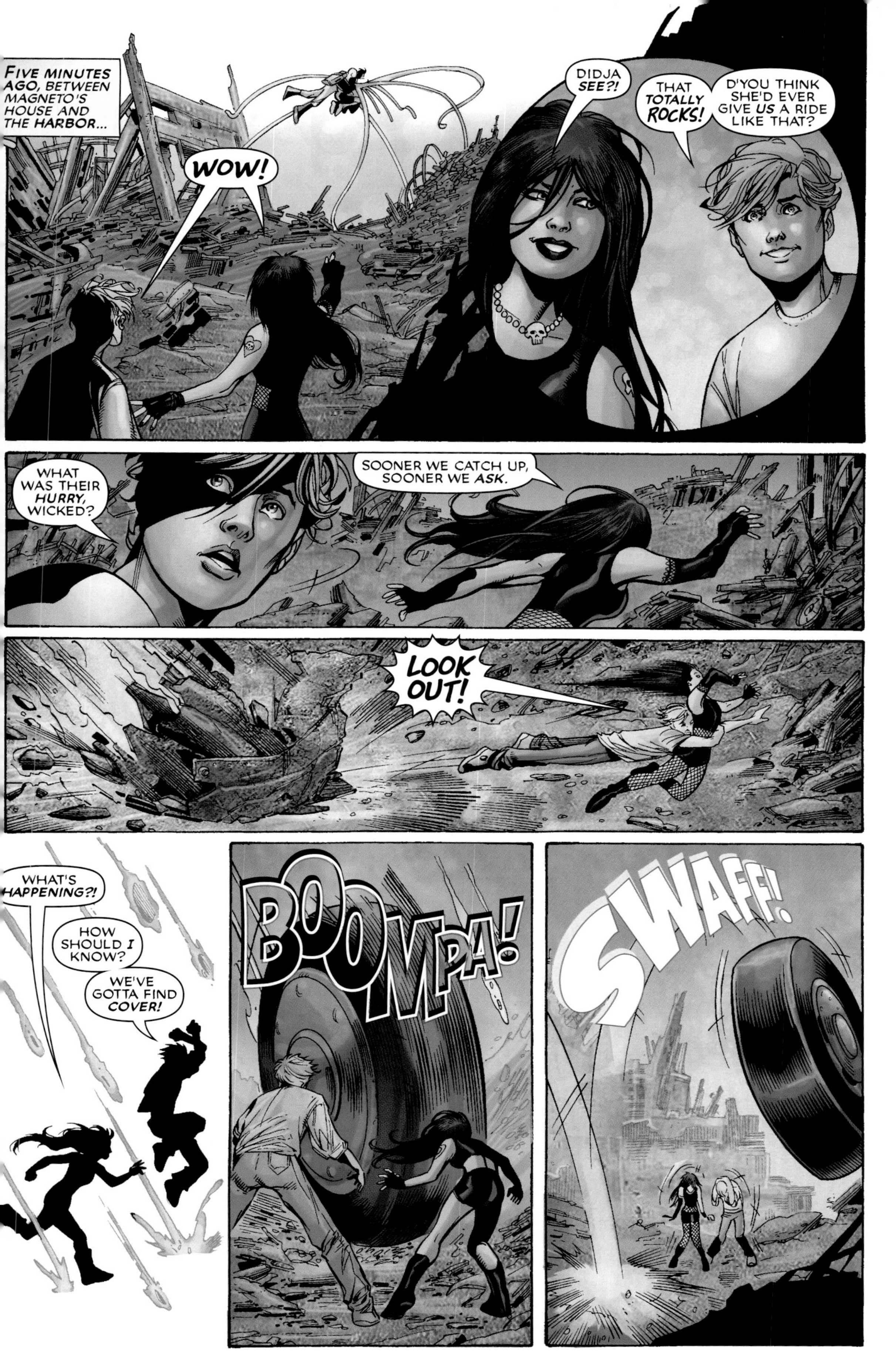
FIVE MINUTES AGO, BETWEEN MAGNETO'S HOUSE AND THE HARBOR...
WOW!
DIDJA SEE?!
THAT TOTALLY ROCKS!
D'YOU THINK SHE'D EVER GIVE US A RIDE LIKE THAT?
WHAT WAS THEIR HURRY, WICKED?
SOONER WE CATCH UP, SOONER WE ASK.
LOOK OUT!
WHAT'S HAPPENING?!
HOW SHOULD I KNOW?
WE'VE GOTTA FIND COVER!
BOOMPA!
SWAFF!

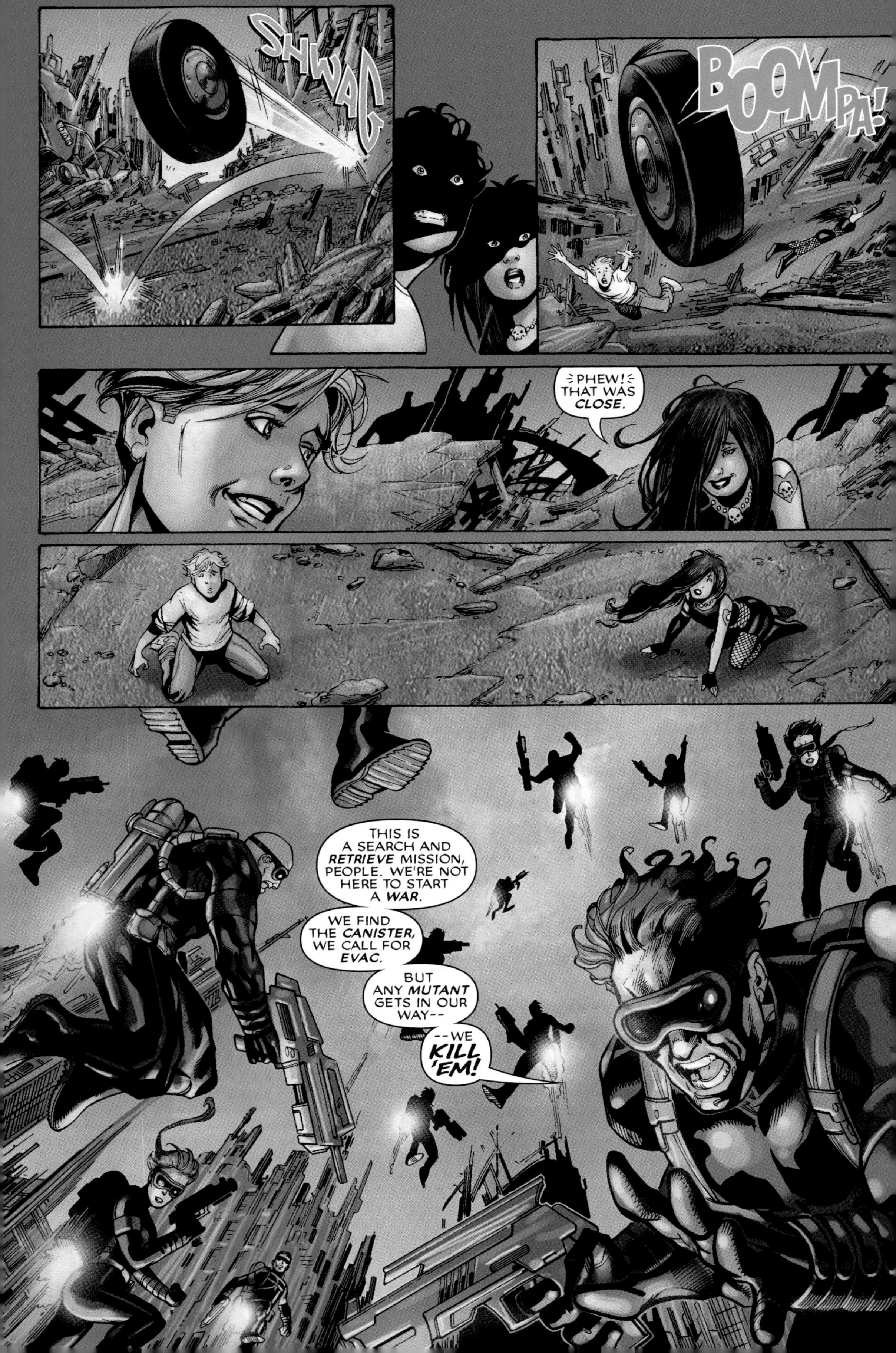
SHWAG
BOOMPA!
PHEW! THAT WAS CLOSE.
THIS IS A SEARCH AND RETRIEVE MISSION, PEOPLE. WE'RE NOT HERE TO START A WAR.
WE FIND THE CANISTER, WE CALL FOR EVAC.
BUT ANY MUTANT GETS IN OUR WAY--
--WE KILL 'EM!

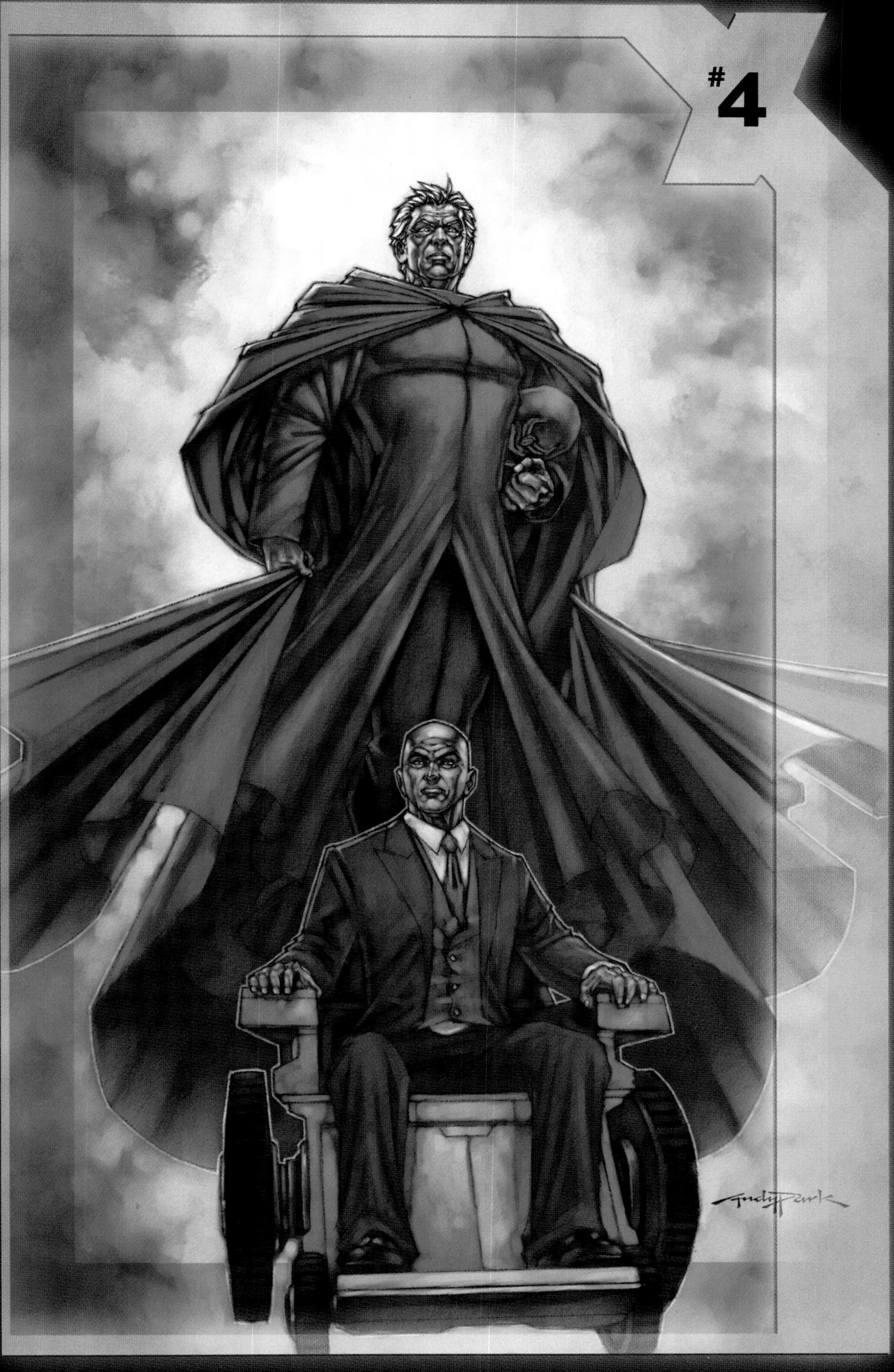
#4

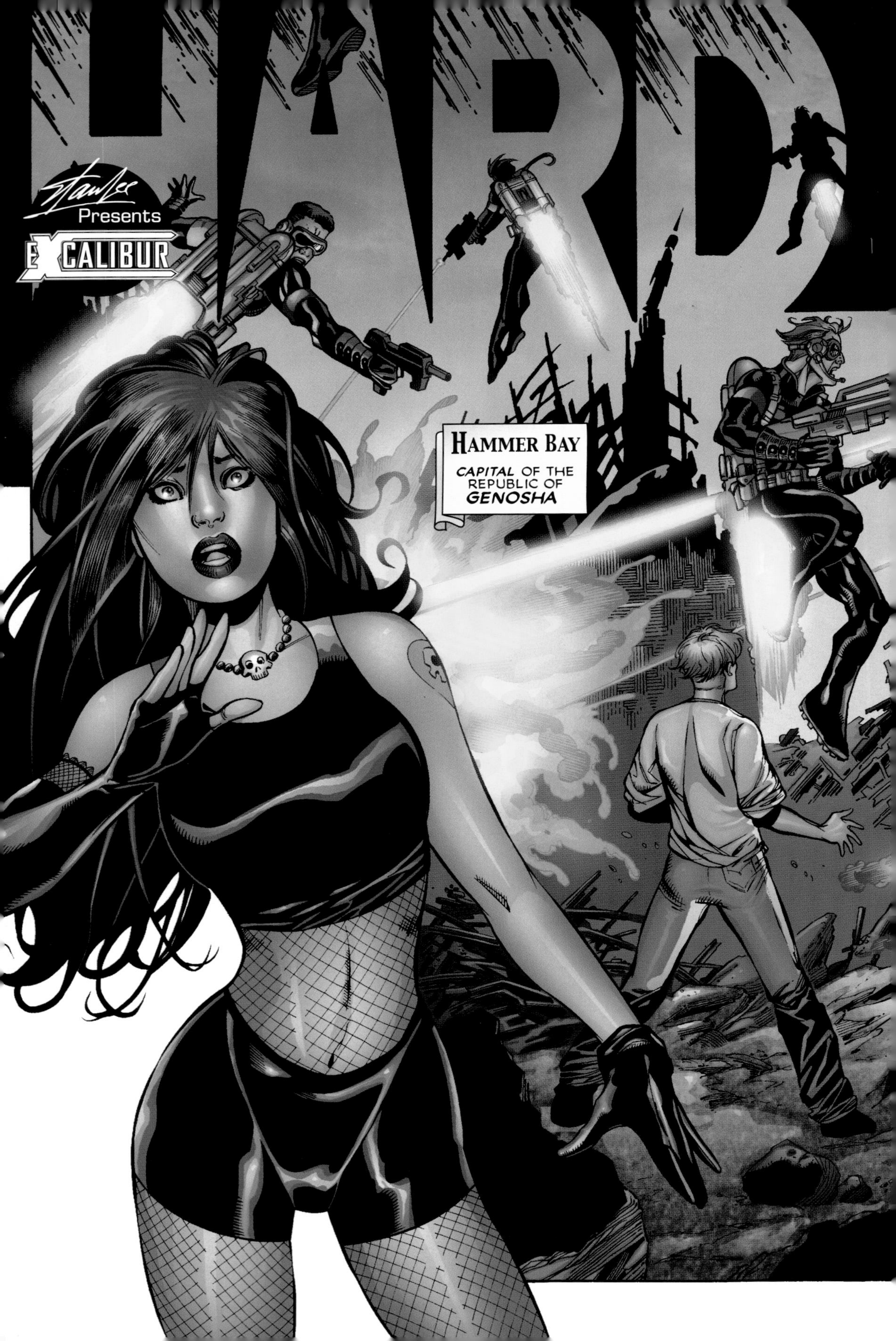
Presents
EXCALIBUR
HAMMER BAY
CAPITAL OF THE REPUBLIC OF GENOSHA

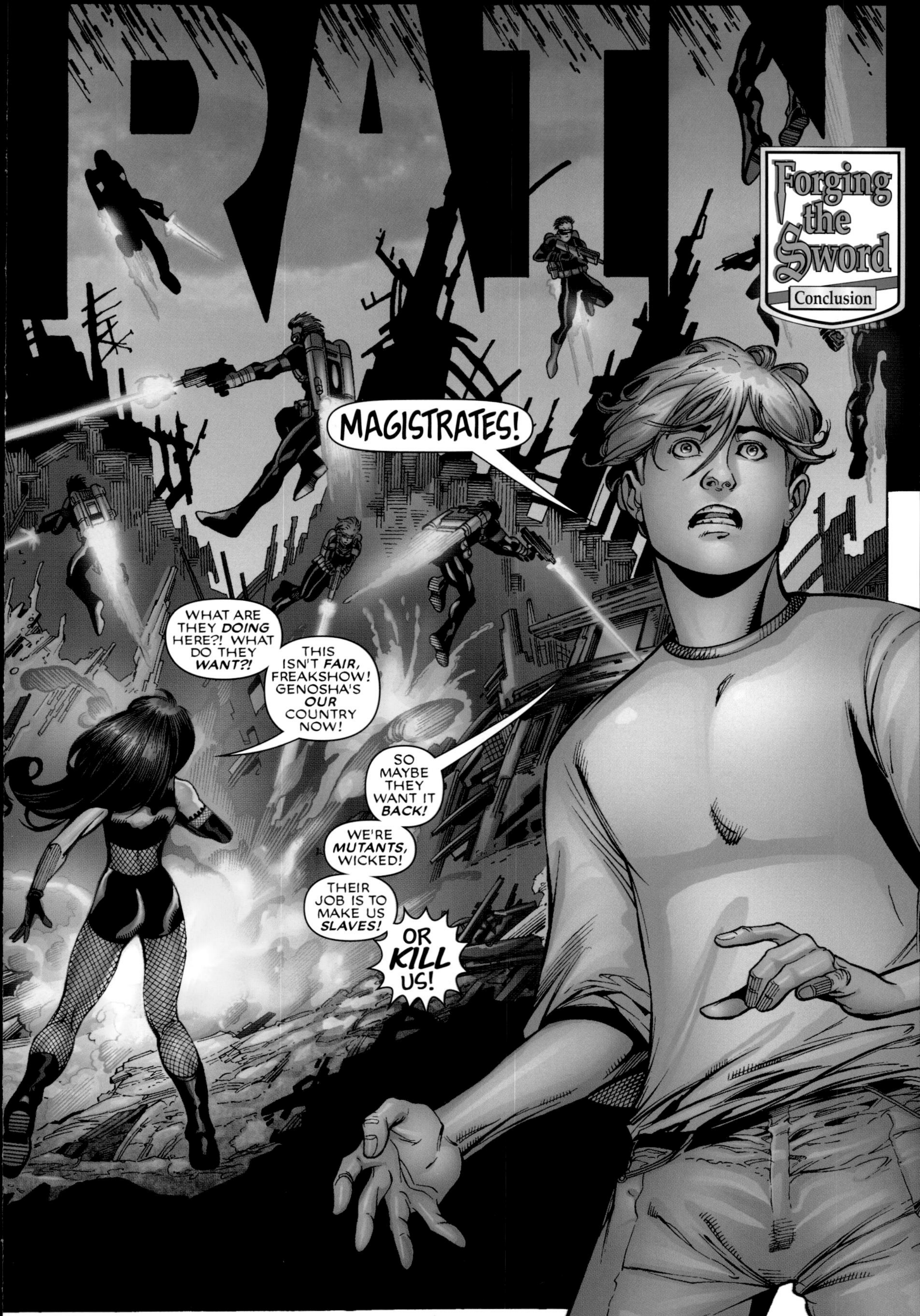
Forging the Sword
Conclusion
MAGISTRATES!
WHAT ARE THEY DOING HERE?! WHAT DO THEY WANT?!
THIS ISN'T FAIR, FREAKSHOW! GENOSHA'S OUR COUNTRY NOW!
SO MAYBE THEY WANT IT BACK!
WE'RE MUTANTS, WICKED!
THEIR JOB IS TO MAKE US SLAVES!
OR KILL US!

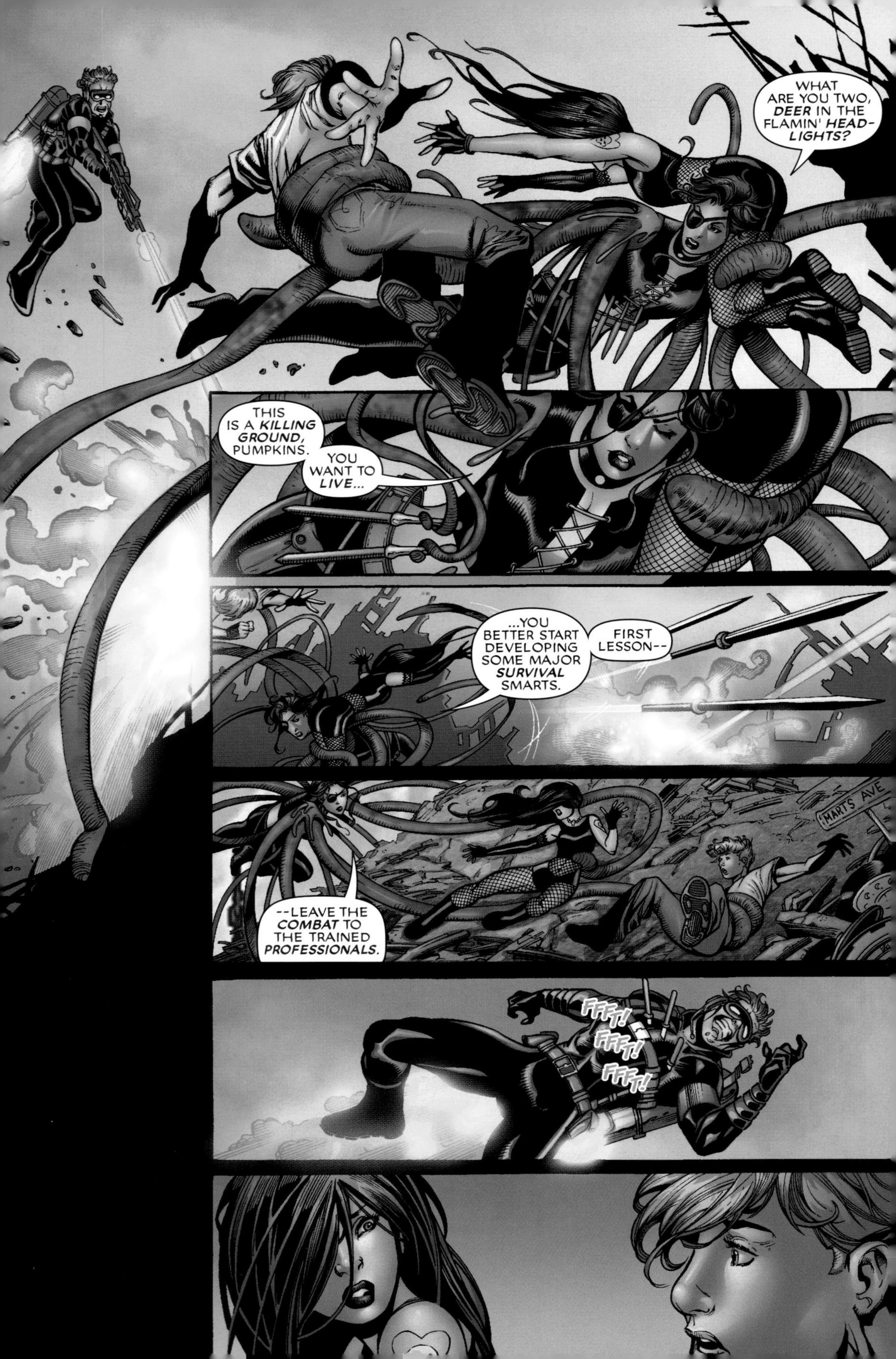
WHAT ARE YOU TWO, *DEER* IN THE FLAMIN' *HEAD-LIGHTS?*
THIS IS A *KILLING GROUND,* PUMPKINS.
YOU WANT TO *LIVE...*
...YOU BETTER START DEVELOPING SOME MAJOR *SURVIVAL* SMARTS.
FIRST LESSON--
MARTS AVE
--LEAVE THE *COMBAT* TO THE TRAINED *PROFESSIONALS.*
FFFT!
FFFT!
FFFT!

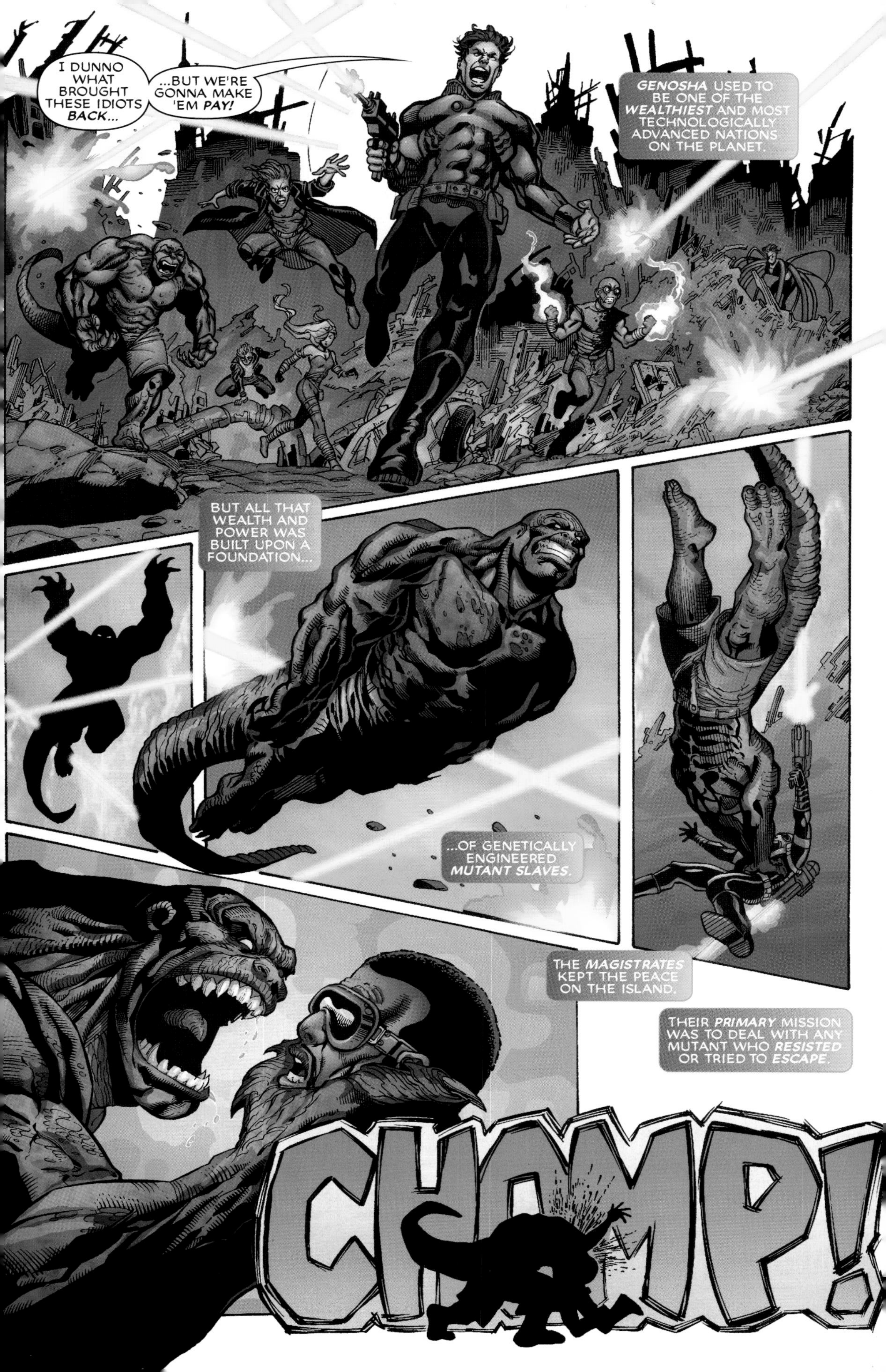
I DUNNO WHAT BROUGHT THESE IDIOTS *BACK*...
...BUT WE'RE GONNA MAKE 'EM *PAY!*
GENOSHA USED TO BE ONE OF THE *WEALTHIEST* AND MOST TECHNOLOGICALLY ADVANCED NATIONS ON THE PLANET.
BUT ALL THAT WEALTH AND POWER WAS BUILT UPON A FOUNDATION...
...OF GENETICALLY ENGINEERED *MUTANT SLAVES.*
THE *MAGISTRATES* KEPT THE PEACE ON THE ISLAND.
THEIR *PRIMARY* MISSION WAS TO DEAL WITH ANY MUTANT WHO *RESISTED* OR TRIED TO *ESCAPE.*
CHOMP!

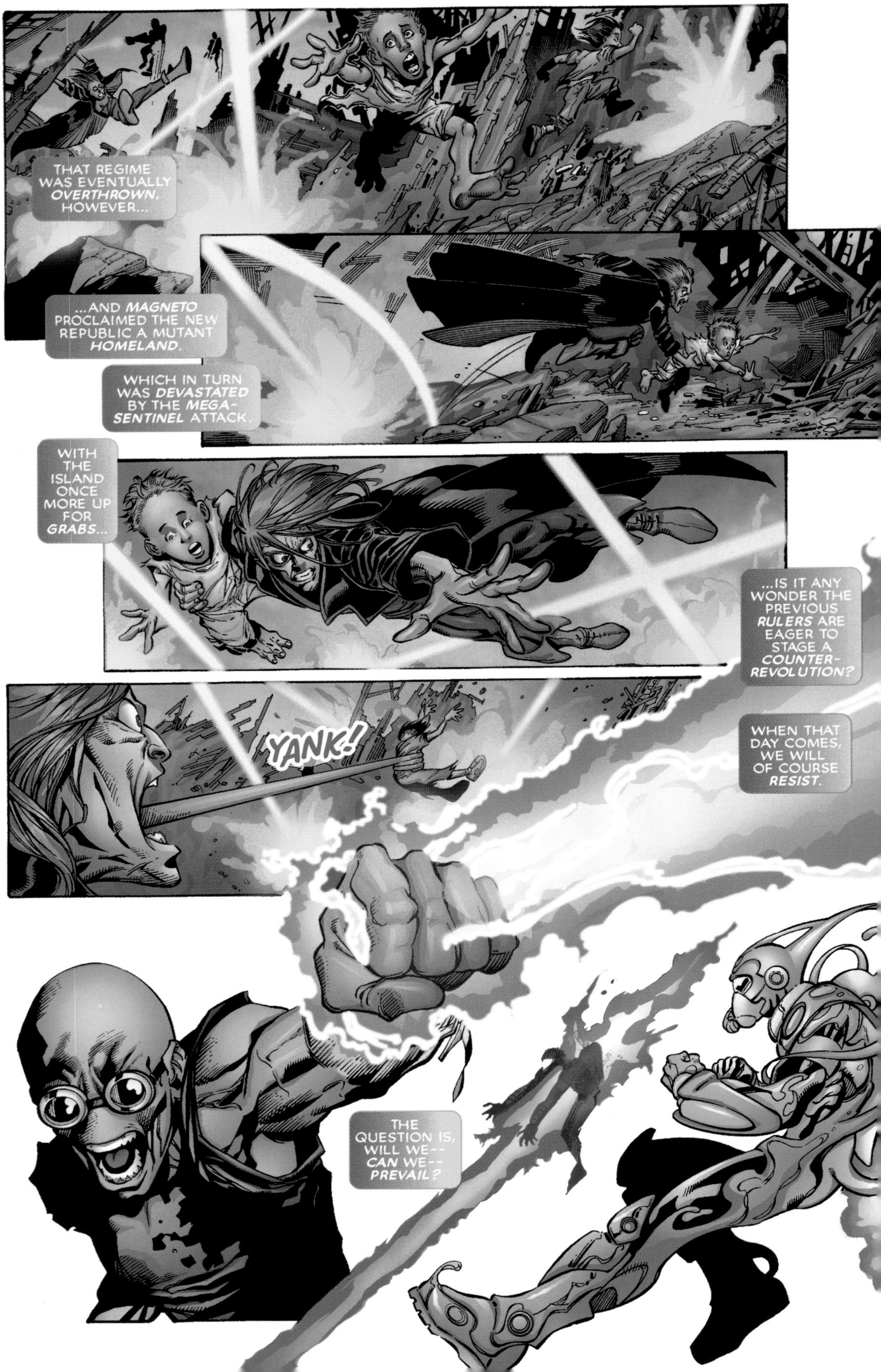
THAT REGIME WAS EVENTUALLY OVERTHROWN, HOWEVER...
...AND MAGNETO PROCLAIMED THE NEW REPUBLIC A MUTANT HOMELAND.
WHICH IN TURN WAS DEVASTATED BY THE MEGA-SENTINEL ATTACK.
WITH THE ISLAND ONCE MORE UP FOR GRABS...
...IS IT ANY WONDER THE PREVIOUS RULERS ARE EAGER TO STAGE A COUNTER-REVOLUTION?
YANK!
WHEN THAT DAY COMES, WE WILL OF COURSE RESIST.
THE QUESTION IS, WILL WE-- CAN WE-- PREVAIL?

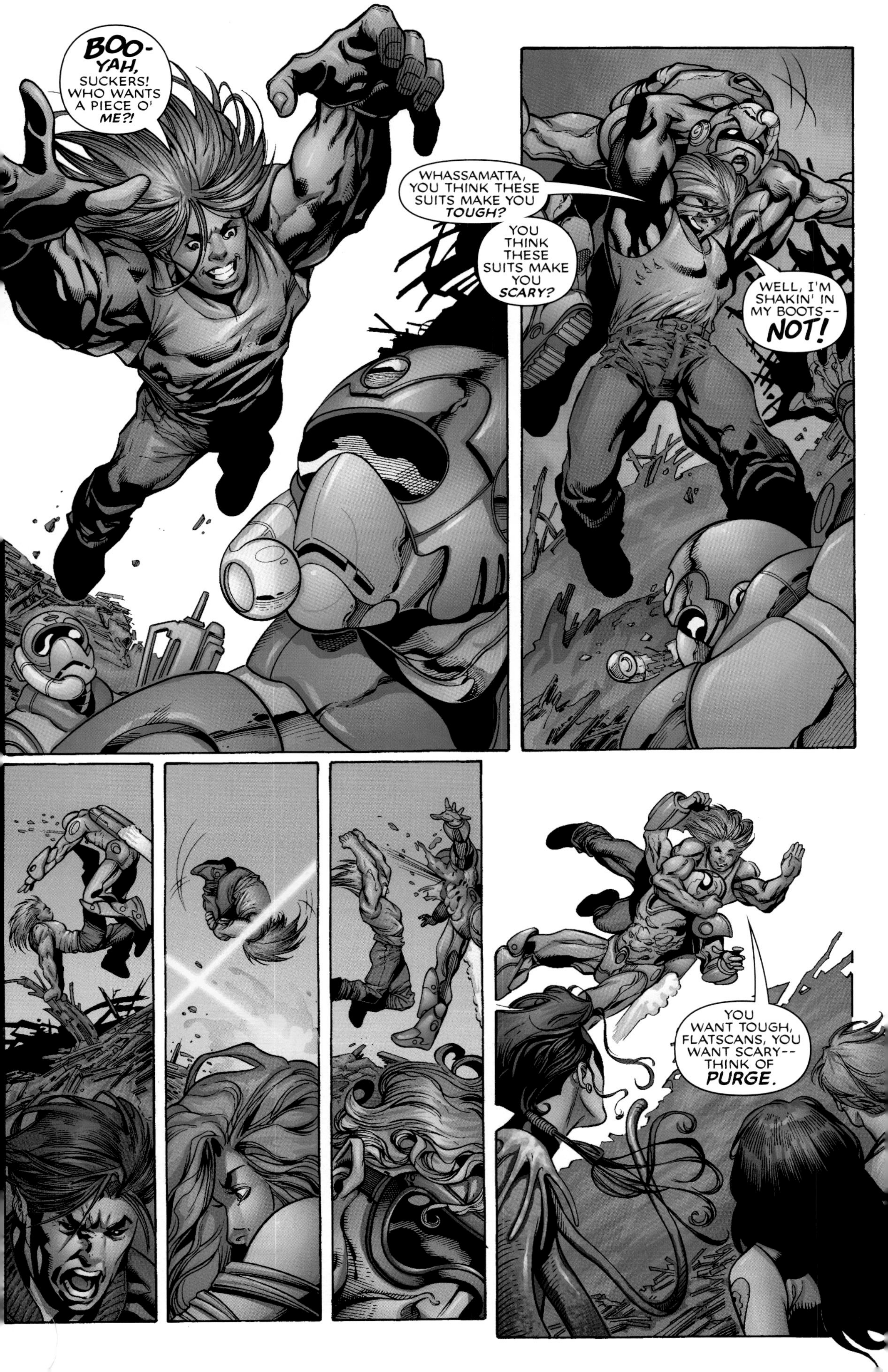

BOO-YAH, SUCKERS! WHO WANTS A PIECE O' ME?!
WHASSAMATTA, YOU THINK THESE SUITS MAKE YOU TOUGH?
YOU THINK THESE SUITS MAKE YOU SCARY?
WELL, I'M SHAKIN' IN MY BOOTS-- NOT!
YOU WANT TOUGH, FLATSCANS, YOU WANT SCARY-- THINK OF PURGE.

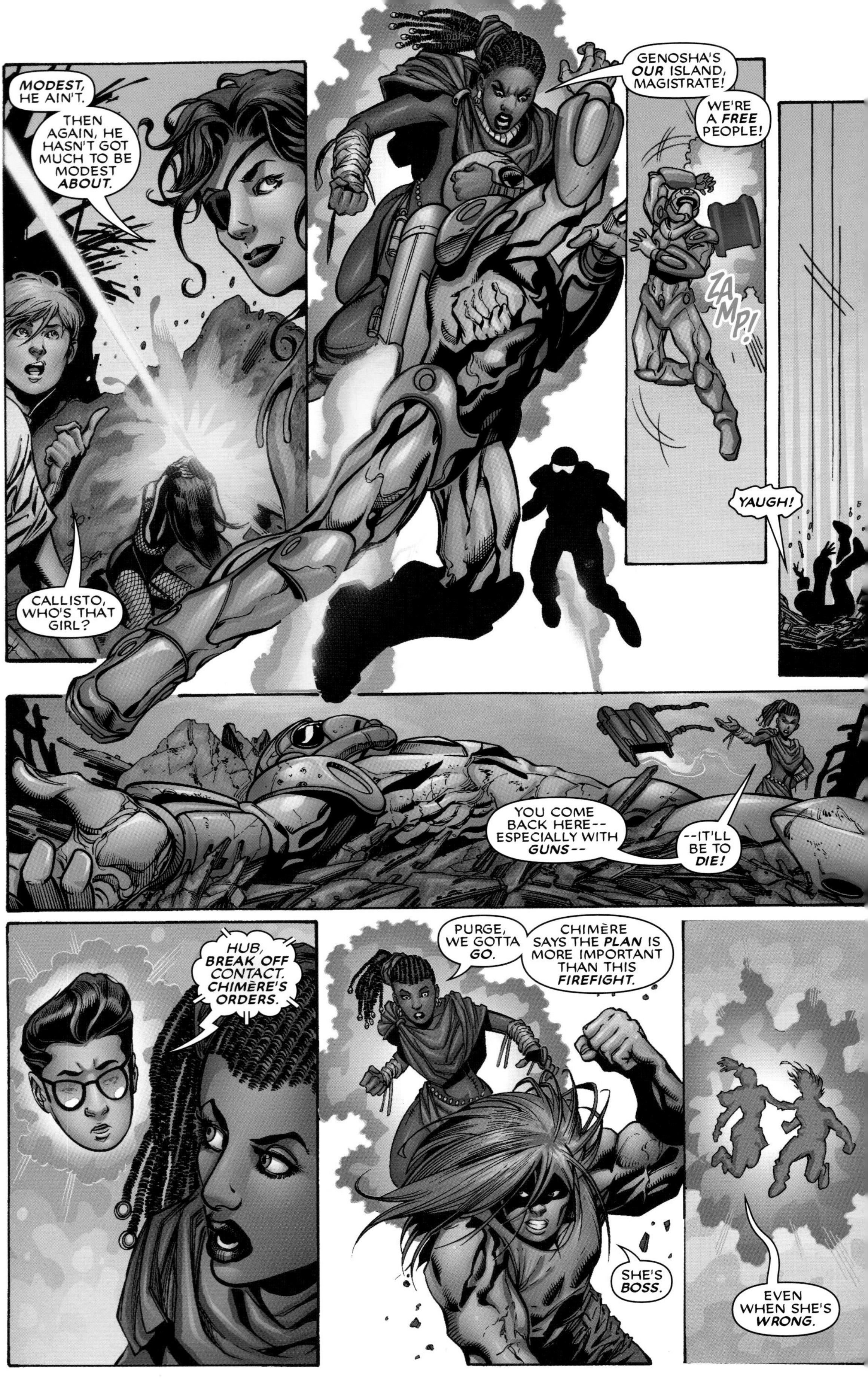
MODEST, HE AIN'T.
THEN AGAIN, HE HASN'T GOT MUCH TO BE MODEST ABOUT.
CALLISTO, WHO'S THAT GIRL?
GENOSHA'S OUR ISLAND, MAGISTRATE!
WE'RE A FREE PEOPLE!
ZAMP!
YAUGH!
YOU COME BACK HERE-- ESPECIALLY WITH GUNS--
--IT'LL BE TO DIE!
HUB, BREAK OFF CONTACT. CHIMÈRE'S ORDERS.
PURGE, WE GOTTA GO.
CHIMÈRE SAYS THE PLAN IS MORE IMPORTANT THAN THIS FIREFIGHT.
SHE'S BOSS.
EVEN WHEN SHE'S WRONG.

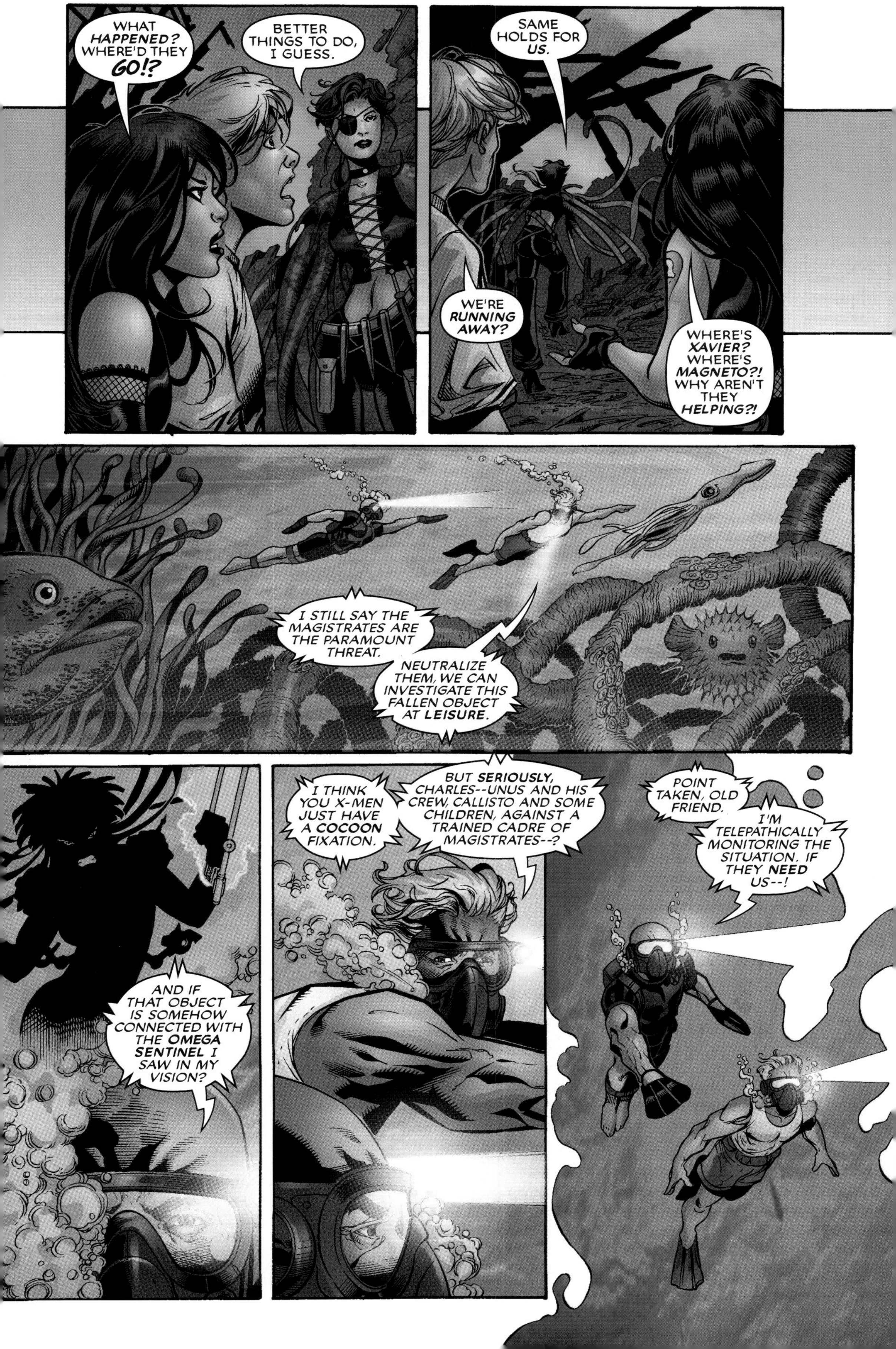
WHAT HAPPENED? WHERE'D THEY GO!?
BETTER THINGS TO DO, I GUESS.
SAME HOLDS FOR US.
WE'RE RUNNING AWAY?
WHERE'S XAVIER? WHERE'S MAGNETO?! WHY AREN'T THEY HELPING?!
I STILL SAY THE MAGISTRATES ARE THE PARAMOUNT THREAT.
NEUTRALIZE THEM, WE CAN INVESTIGATE THIS FALLEN OBJECT AT LEISURE.
AND IF THAT OBJECT IS SOMEHOW CONNECTED WITH THE OMEGA SENTINEL I SAW IN MY VISION?
I THINK YOU X-MEN JUST HAVE A COCOON FIXATION.
BUT SERIOUSLY, CHARLES--UNUS AND HIS CREW, CALLISTO AND SOME CHILDREN, AGAINST A TRAINED CADRE OF MAGISTRATES--?
POINT TAKEN, OLD FRIEND.
I'M TELEPATHICALLY MONITORING THE SITUATION. IF THEY NEED US--!

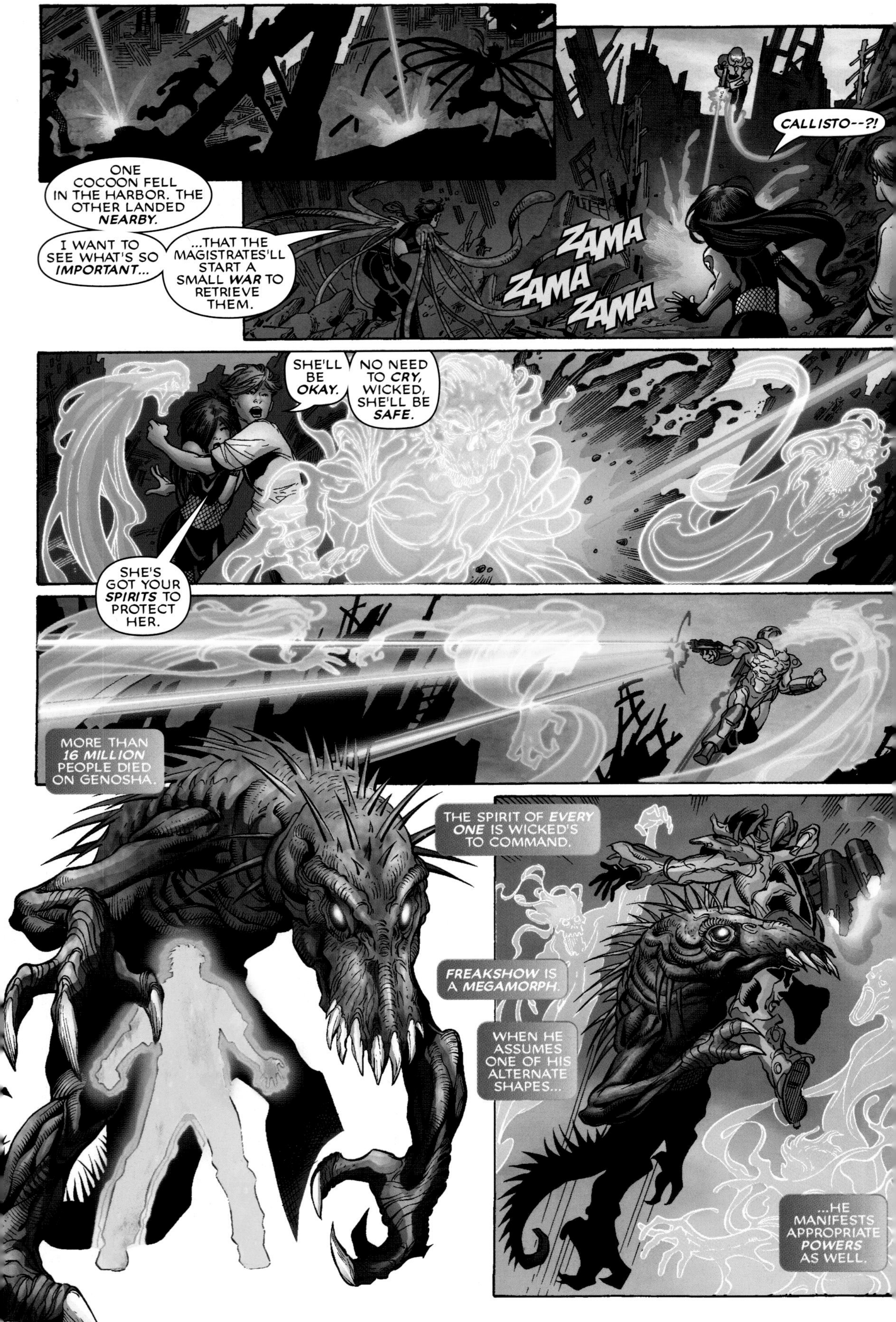

ONE COCOON FELL IN THE HARBOR. THE OTHER LANDED NEARBY.
I WANT TO SEE WHAT'S SO IMPORTANT...
...THAT THE MAGISTRATES'LL START A SMALL WAR TO RETRIEVE THEM.
ZAMA ZAMA ZAMA ZAMA
CALLISTO--?!
SHE'LL BE OKAY.
NO NEED TO CRY, WICKED, SHE'LL BE SAFE.
SHE'S GOT YOUR SPIRITS TO PROTECT HER.
MORE THAN 16 MILLION PEOPLE DIED ON GENOSHA.
THE SPIRIT OF EVERY ONE IS WICKED'S TO COMMAND.
FREAKSHOW IS A MEGAMORPH.
WHEN HE ASSUMES ONE OF HIS ALTERNATE SHAPES...
...HE MANIFESTS APPROPRIATE POWERS AS WELL.

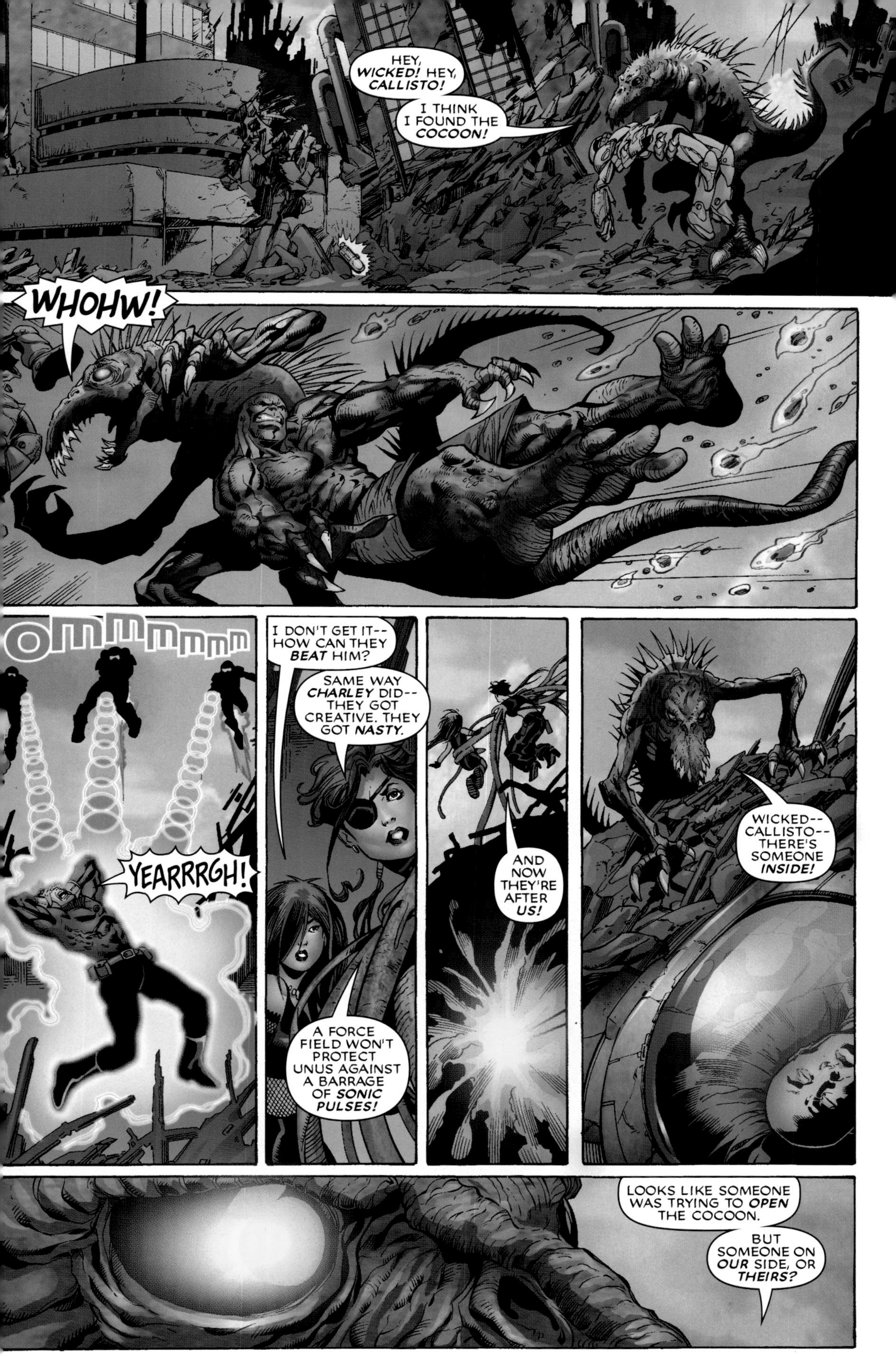

HEY, *WICKED!* HEY, *CALLISTO!*
I THINK I FOUND THE *COCOON!*
WHOHW!
OMMMMMM
I DON'T GET IT-- HOW CAN THEY *BEAT* HIM?
SAME WAY *CHARLEY* DID-- THEY GOT CREATIVE. THEY GOT *NASTY.*
YEARRRGH!
A FORCE FIELD WON'T PROTECT UNUS AGAINST A BARRAGE OF *SONIC PULSES!*
AND NOW THEY'RE AFTER *US!*
WICKED-- CALLISTO-- THERE'S SOMEONE *INSIDE!*
LOOKS LIKE SOMEONE WAS TRYING TO *OPEN* THE COCOON.
BUT SOMEONE ON *OUR* SIDE, OR *THEIRS?*

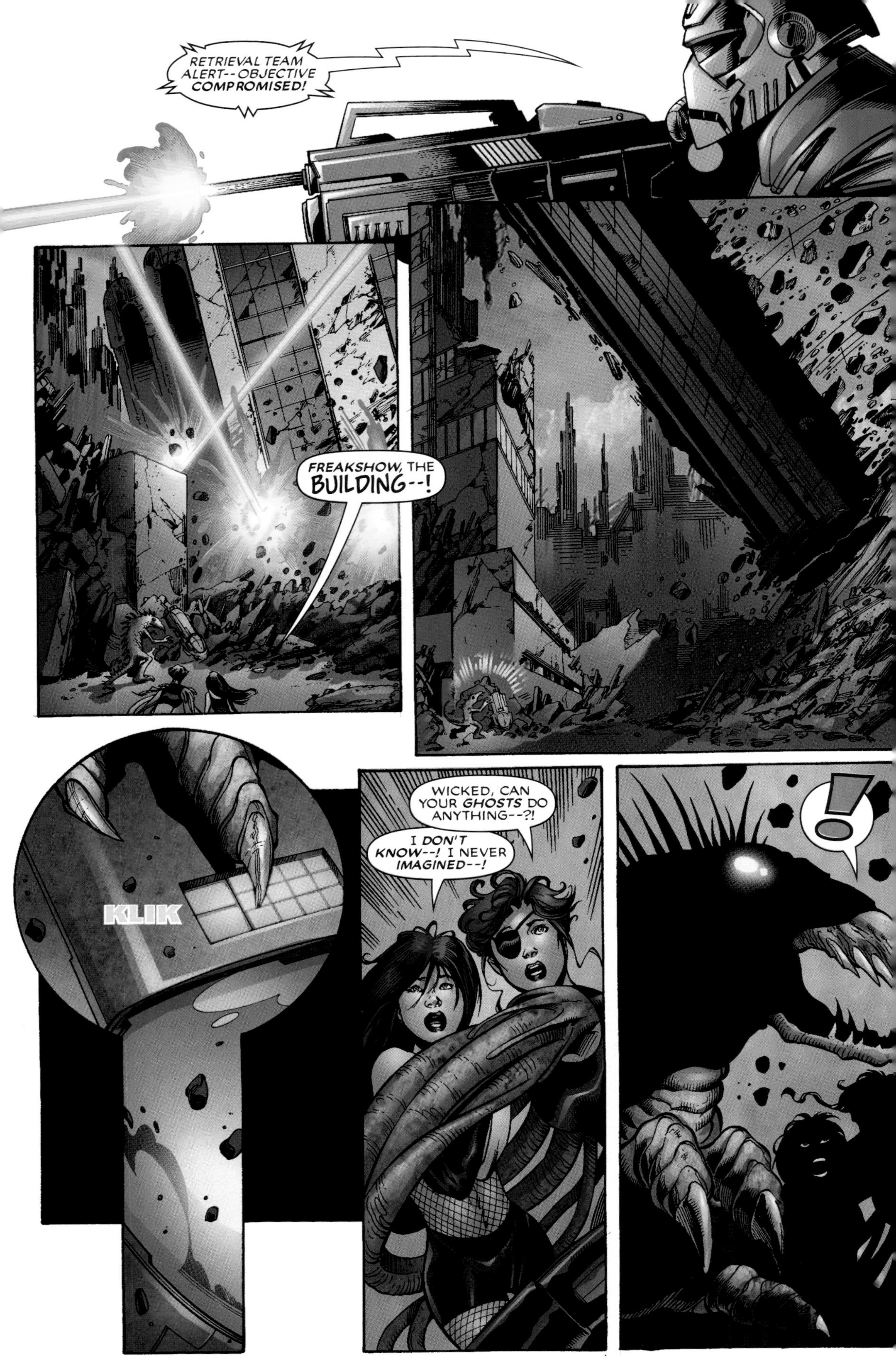
RETRIEVAL TEAM ALERT--OBJECTIVE COMPROMISED!
FREAKSHOW, THE BUILDING--!
KLIK
WICKED, CAN YOUR GHOSTS DO ANYTHING--?!
I DON'T KNOW--! I NEVER IMAGINED--!
!

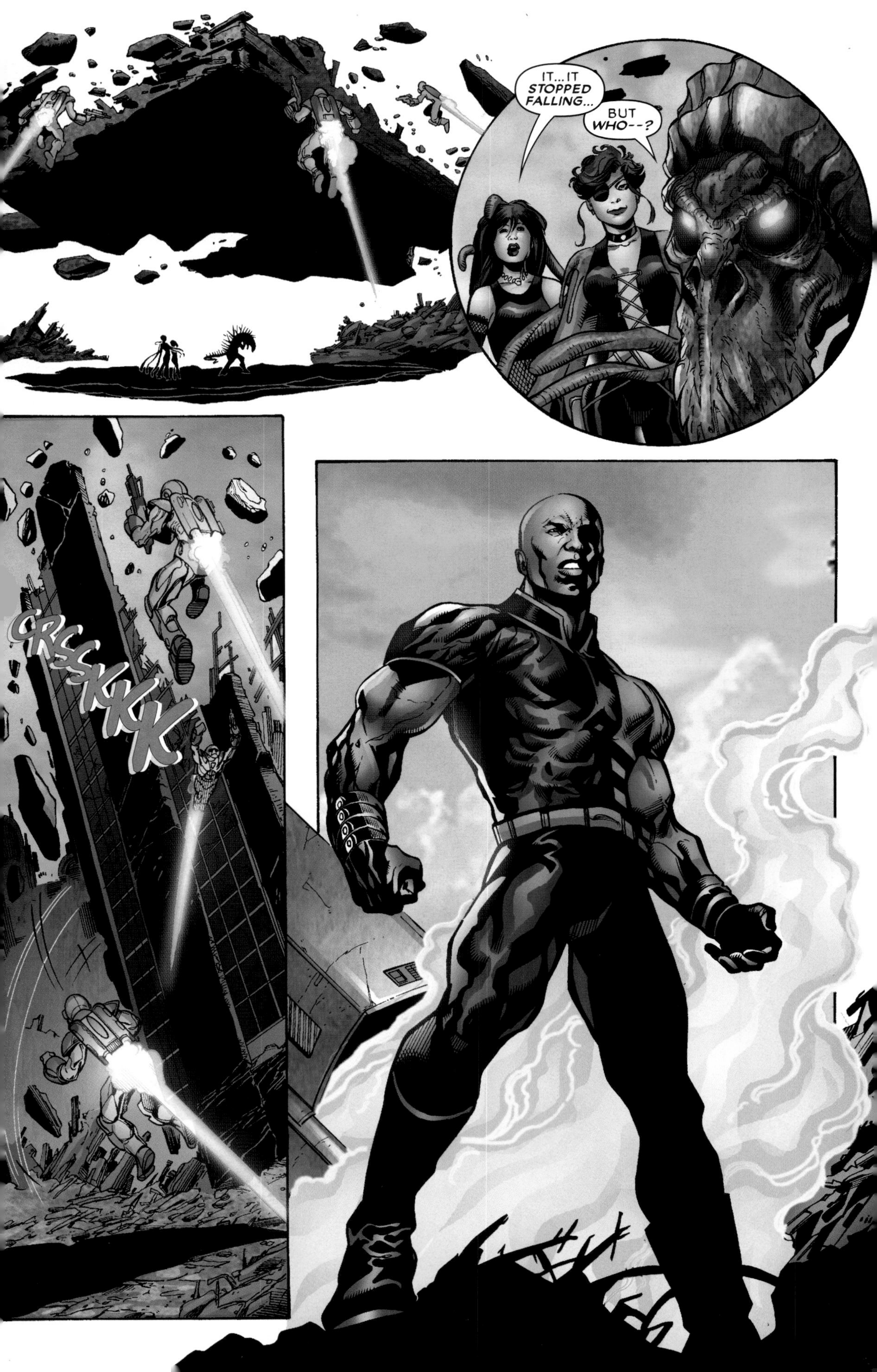
IT...IT STOPPED FALLING...
BUT WHO--?
CRSSKKK

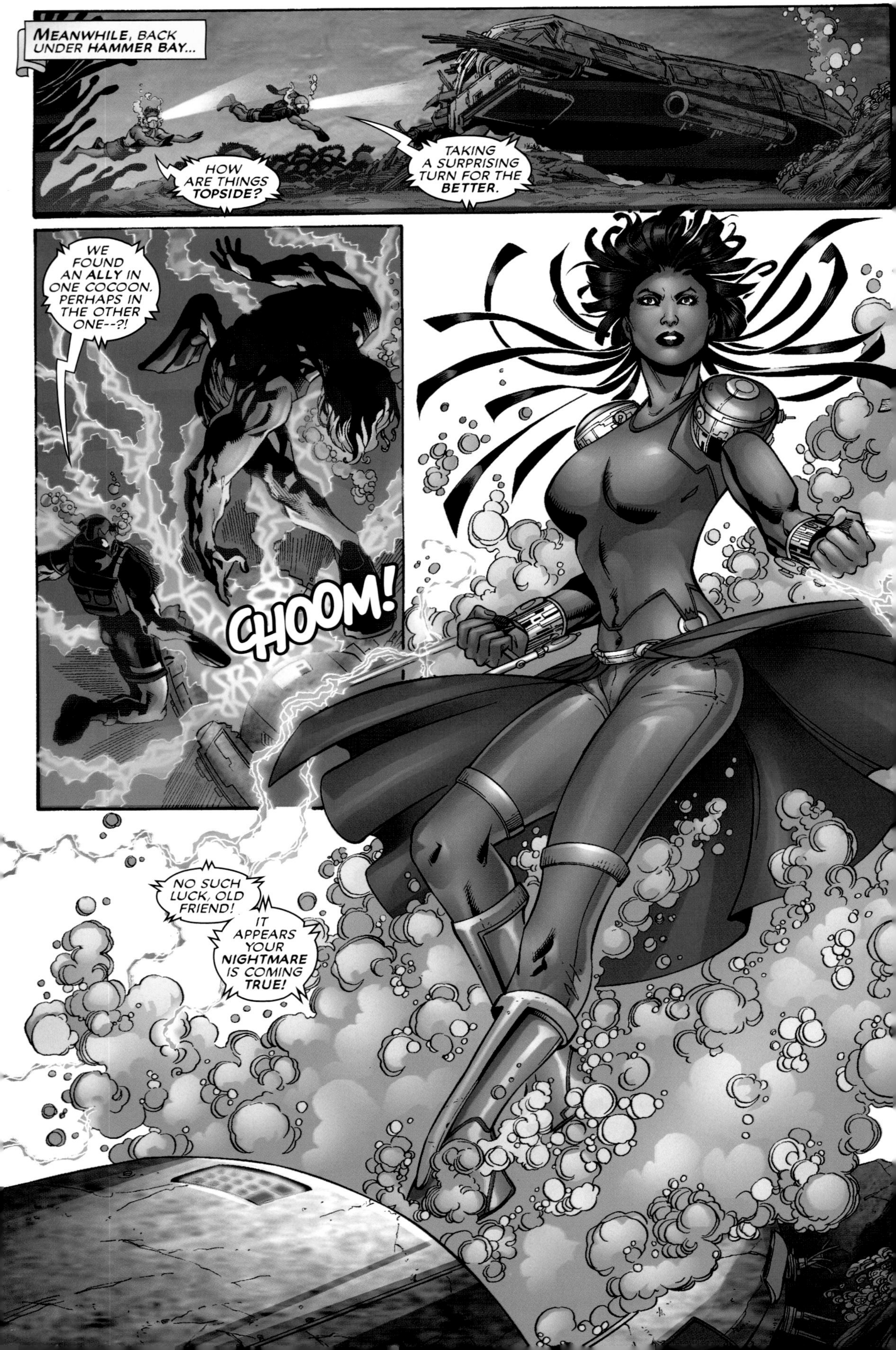
MEANWHILE, BACK UNDER HAMMER BAY...
HOW ARE THINGS TOPSIDE?
TAKING A SURPRISING TURN FOR THE BETTER.
WE FOUND AN ALLY IN ONE COCOON. PERHAPS IN THE OTHER ONE--?!
CHOOM!
NO SUCH LUCK, OLD FRIEND!
IT APPEARS YOUR NIGHTMARE IS COMING TRUE!

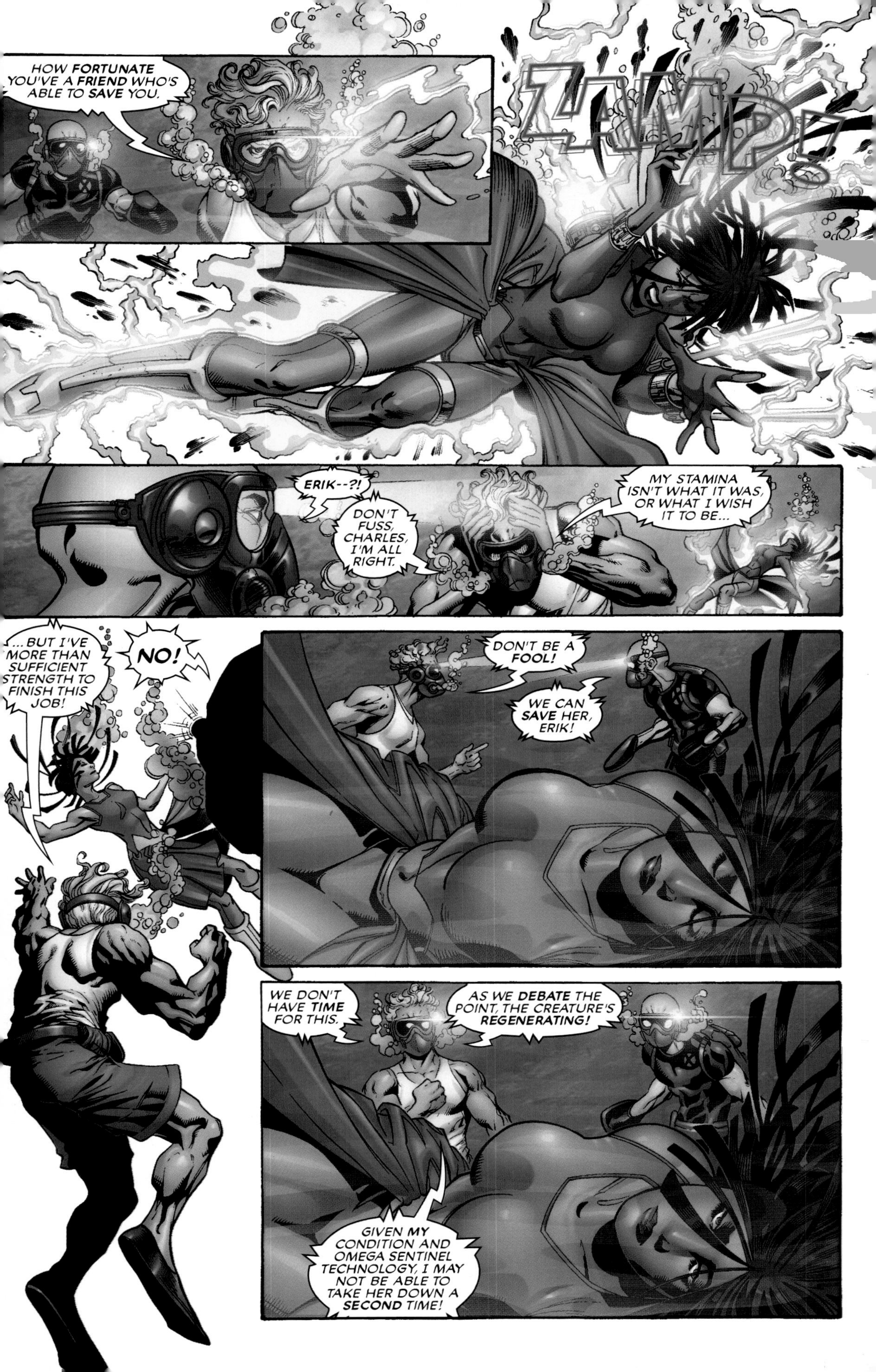
HOW FORTUNATE YOU'VE A FRIEND WHO'S ABLE TO SAVE YOU.
ZAMP!
ERIK--?!
DON'T FUSS, CHARLES, I'M ALL RIGHT.
MY STAMINA ISN'T WHAT IT WAS, OR WHAT I WISH IT TO BE...
...BUT I'VE MORE THAN SUFFICIENT STRENGTH TO FINISH THIS JOB!
NO!
DON'T BE A FOOL!
WE CAN SAVE HER, ERIK!
WE DON'T HAVE TIME FOR THIS.
AS WE DEBATE THE POINT, THE CREATURE'S REGENERATING!
GIVEN MY CONDITION AND OMEGA SENTINEL TECHNOLOGY, I MAY NOT BE ABLE TO TAKE HER DOWN A SECOND TIME!

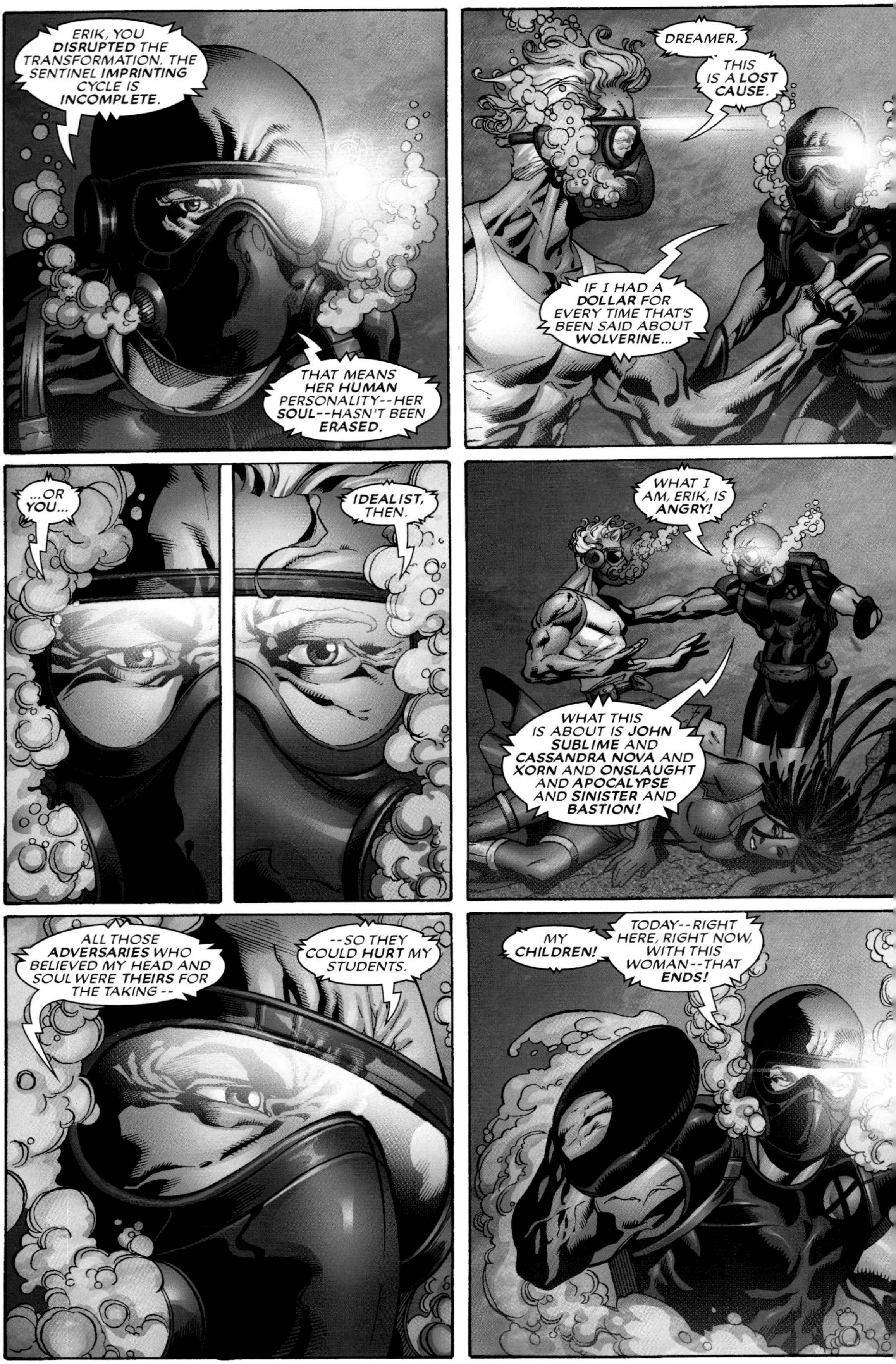
ERIK, YOU DISRUPTED THE TRANSFORMATION. THE SENTINEL IMPRINTING CYCLE IS INCOMPLETE.
THAT MEANS HER HUMAN PERSONALITY--HER SOUL--HASN'T BEEN ERASED.
DREAMER.
THIS IS A LOST CAUSE.
IF I HAD A DOLLAR FOR EVERY TIME THAT'S BEEN SAID ABOUT WOLVERINE...
...OR YOU...
IDEALIST, THEN.
WHAT I AM, ERIK, IS ANGRY!
WHAT THIS IS ABOUT IS JOHN SUBLIME AND CASSANDRA NOVA AND XORN AND ONSLAUGHT AND APOCALYPSE AND SINISTER AND BASTION!
ALL THOSE ADVERSARIES WHO BELIEVED MY HEAD AND SOUL WERE THEIRS FOR THE TAKING--
--SO THEY COULD HURT MY STUDENTS.
MY CHILDREN!
TODAY--RIGHT HERE, RIGHT NOW, WITH THIS WOMAN--THAT ENDS!

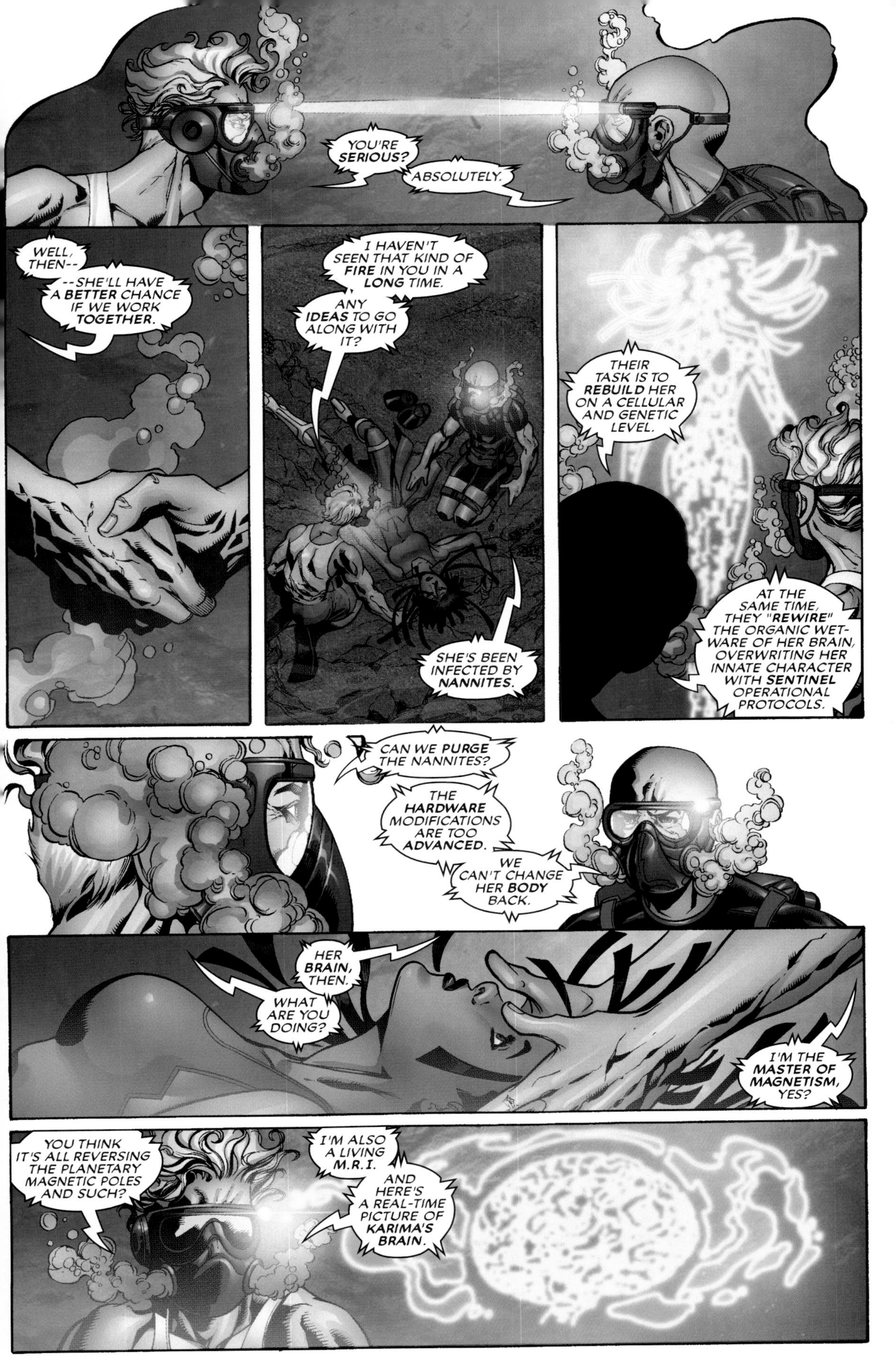
YOU'RE SERIOUS?
ABSOLUTELY.
WELL, THEN--
--SHE'LL HAVE A BETTER CHANCE IF WE WORK TOGETHER.
I HAVEN'T SEEN THAT KIND OF FIRE IN YOU IN A LONG TIME.
ANY IDEAS TO GO ALONG WITH IT?
SHE'S BEEN INFECTED BY NANNITES.
THEIR TASK IS TO REBUILD HER ON A CELLULAR AND GENETIC LEVEL.
AT THE SAME TIME, THEY "REWIRE" THE ORGANIC WET-WARE OF HER BRAIN, OVERWRITING HER INNATE CHARACTER WITH SENTINEL OPERATIONAL PROTOCOLS.
CAN WE PURGE THE NANNITES?
THE HARDWARE MODIFICATIONS ARE TOO ADVANCED.
WE CAN'T CHANGE HER BODY BACK.
HER BRAIN, THEN.
WHAT ARE YOU DOING?
I'M THE MASTER OF MAGNETISM, YES?
YOU THINK IT'S ALL REVERSING THE PLANETARY MAGNETIC POLES AND SUCH?
I'M ALSO A LIVING M.R.I.
AND HERE'S A REAL-TIME PICTURE OF KARIMA'S BRAIN.

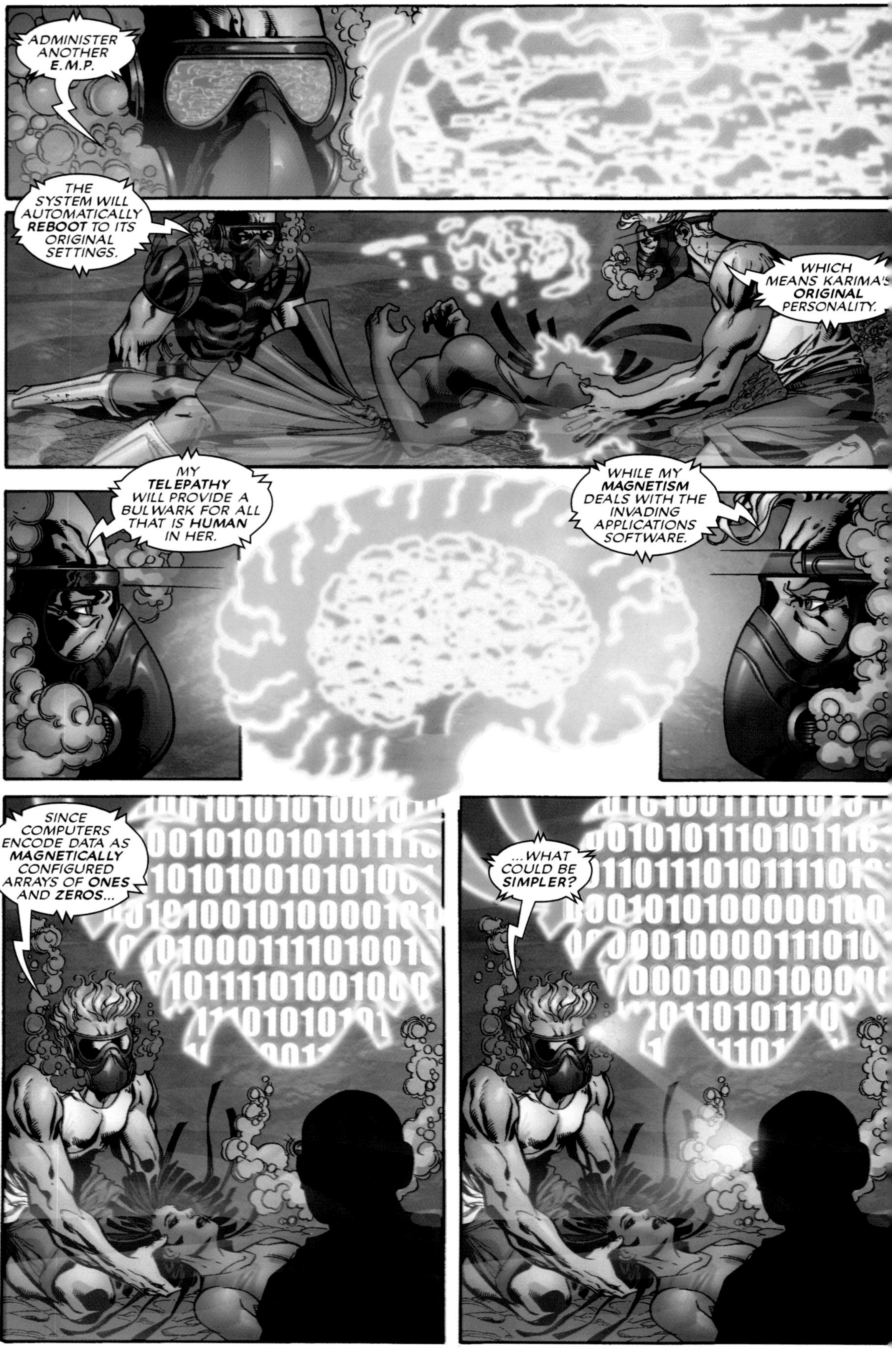
ADMINISTER ANOTHER E.M.P.
THE SYSTEM WILL AUTOMATICALLY REBOOT TO ITS ORIGINAL SETTINGS.
WHICH MEANS KARIMA'S ORIGINAL PERSONALITY.
MY TELEPATHY WILL PROVIDE A BULWARK FOR ALL THAT IS HUMAN IN HER.
WHILE MY MAGNETISM DEALS WITH THE INVADING APPLICATIONS SOFTWARE.
SINCE COMPUTERS ENCODE DATA AS MAGNETICALLY CONFIGURED ARRAYS OF ONES AND ZEROS...
...WHAT COULD BE SIMPLER?

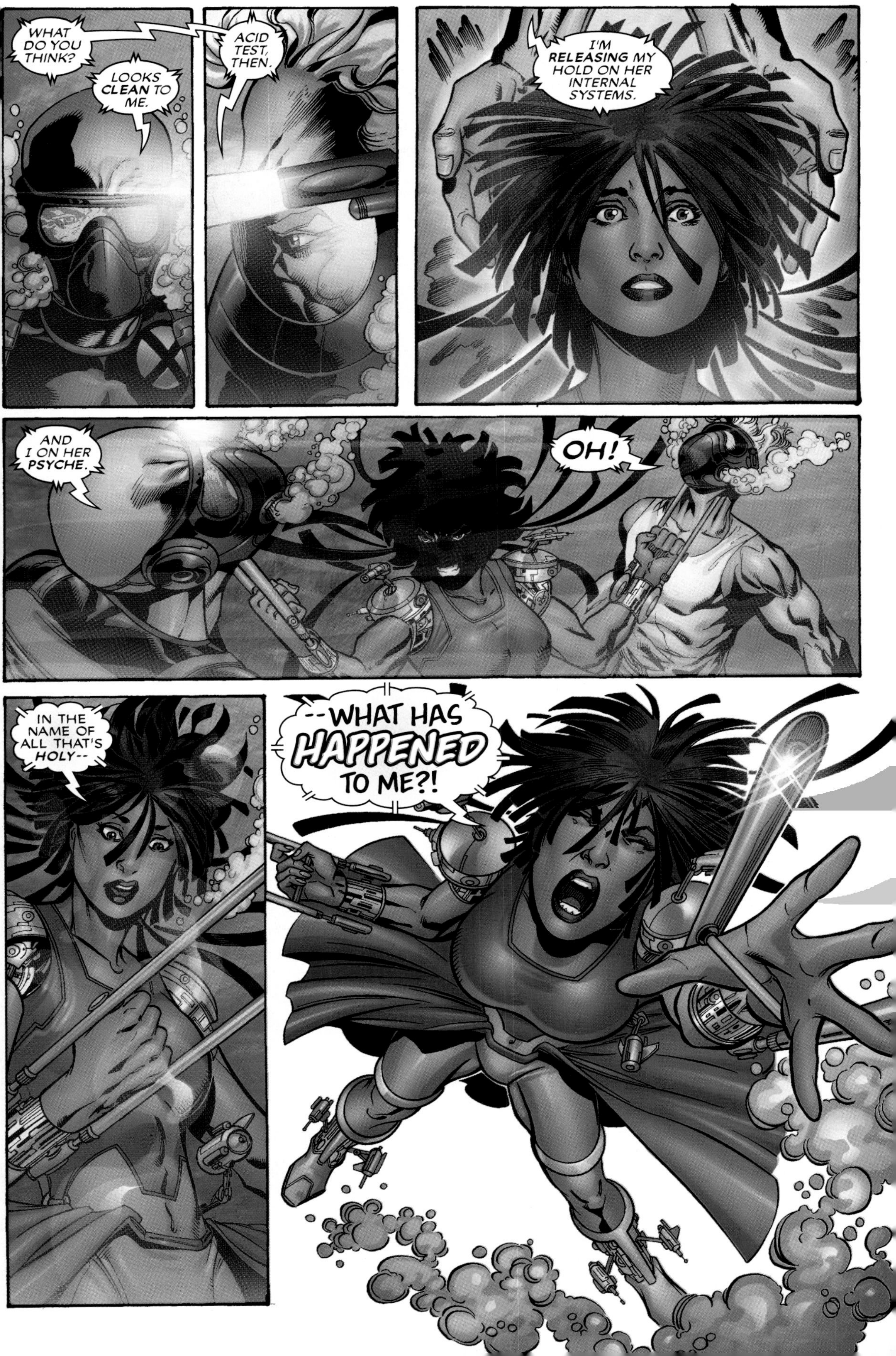
WHAT DO YOU THINK?
LOOKS CLEAN TO ME.
ACID TEST, THEN.
I'M RELEASING MY HOLD ON HER INTERNAL SYSTEMS.
AND I ON HER PSYCHE.
OH!
IN THE NAME OF ALL THAT'S HOLY--
--WHAT HAS HAPPENED TO ME?!

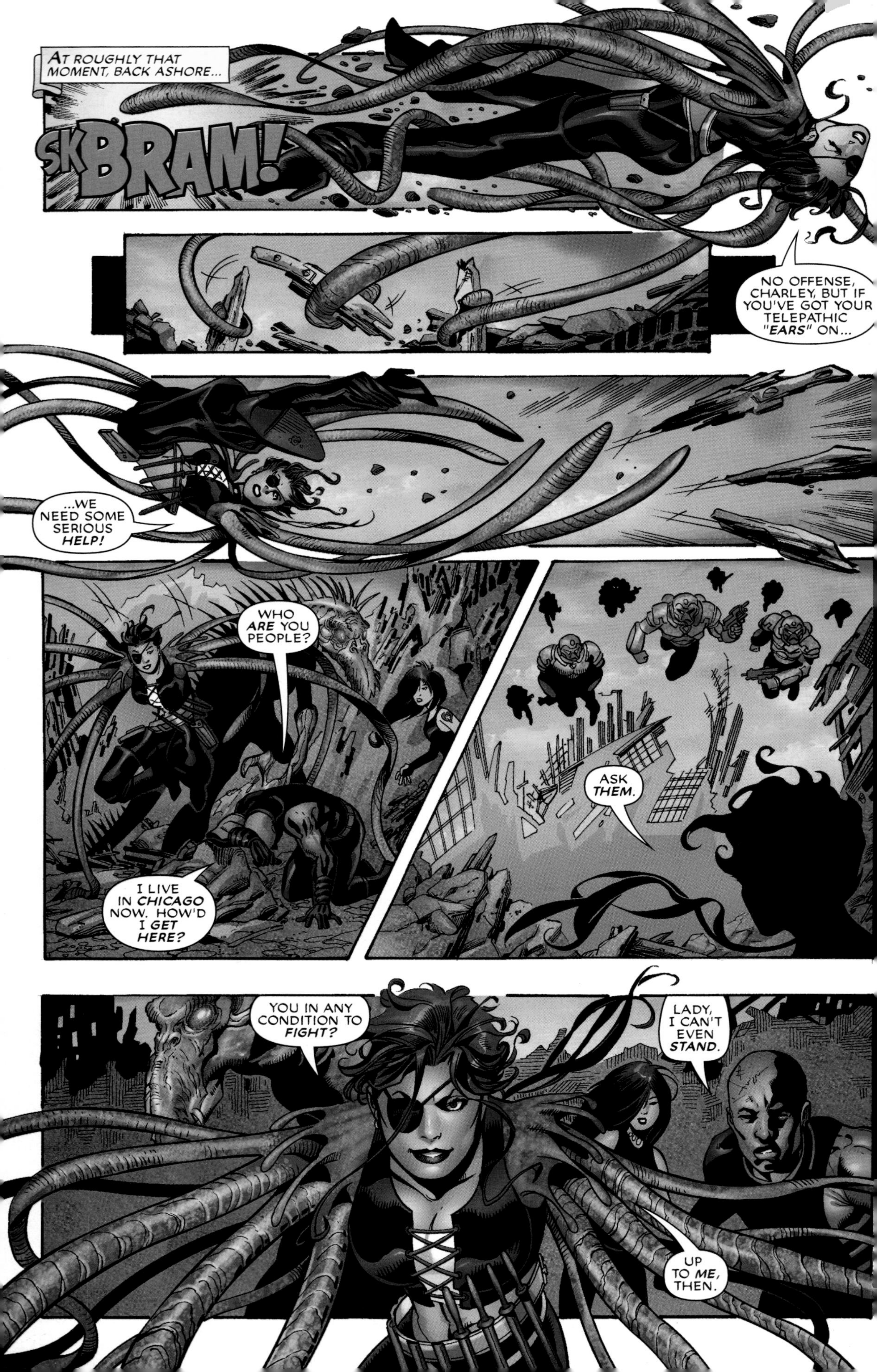

AT ROUGHLY THAT MOMENT, BACK ASHORE...
SKBRAM!
NO OFFENSE, CHARLEY, BUT IF YOU'VE GOT YOUR TELEPATHIC "EARS" ON...
...WE NEED SOME SERIOUS HELP!
WHO ARE YOU PEOPLE?
I LIVE IN CHICAGO NOW. HOW'D I GET HERE?
ASK THEM.
YOU IN ANY CONDITION TO FIGHT?
LADY, I CAN'T EVEN STAND.
UP TO ME, THEN.

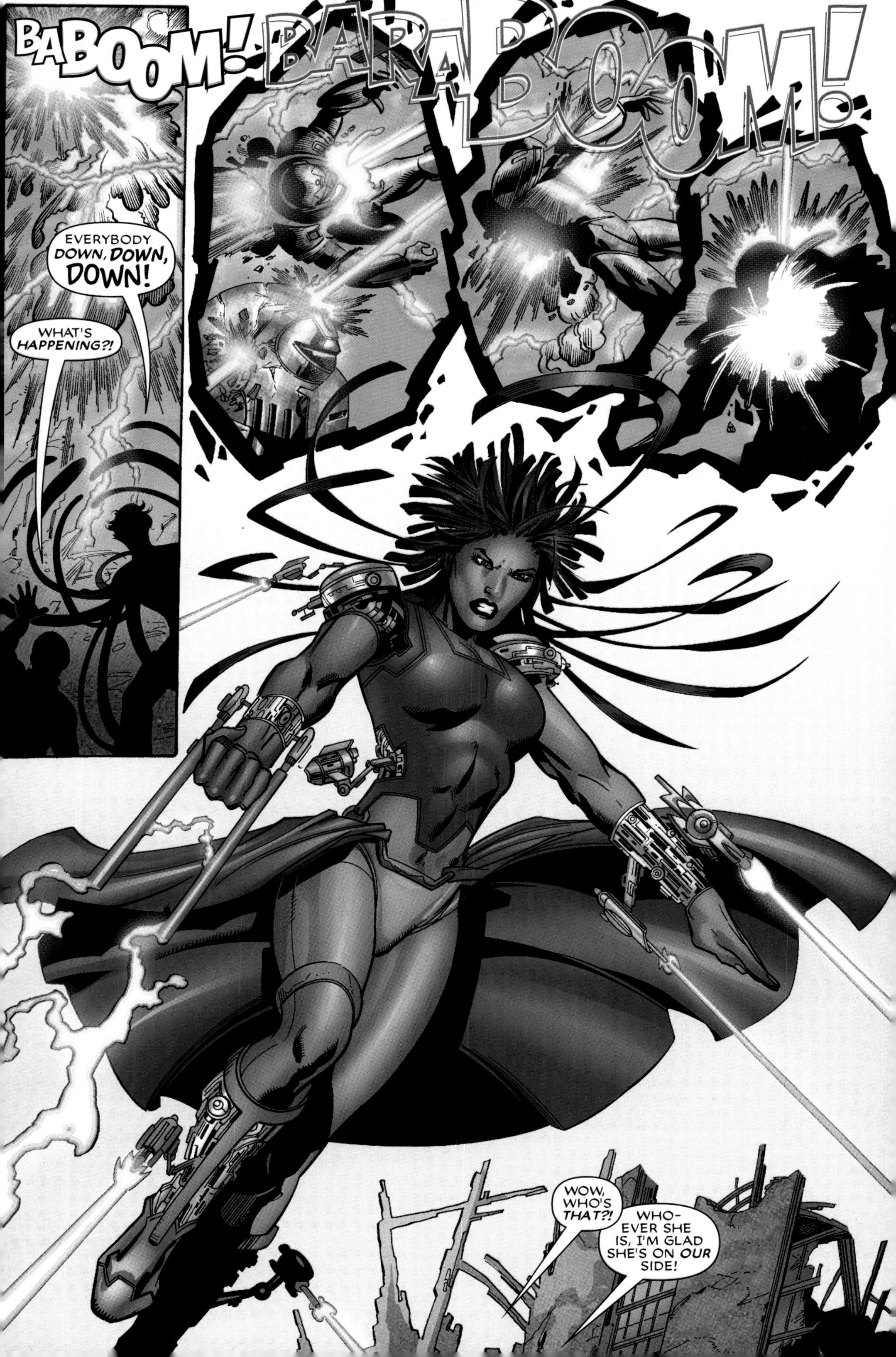

BABOOM!
BARADBOOM!
EVERYBODY DOWN, DOWN, DOWN!
WHAT'S HAPPENING?!
WOW, WHO'S THAT?!
WHO-EVER SHE IS, I'M GLAD SHE'S ON OUR SIDE!

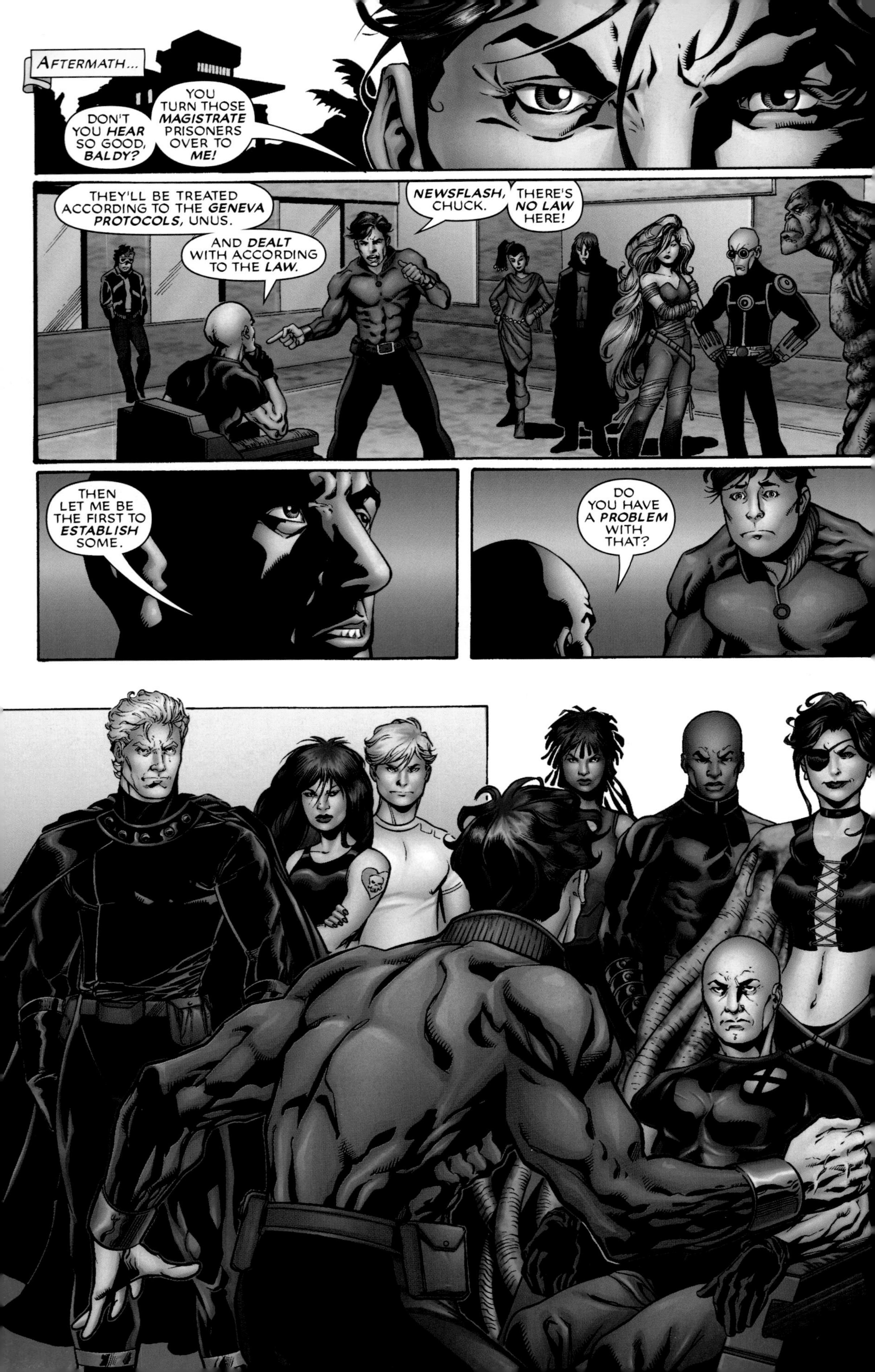
AFTERMATH...
YOU TURN THOSE MAGISTRATE PRISONERS OVER TO ME!
DON'T YOU HEAR SO GOOD, BALDY?
THEY'LL BE TREATED ACCORDING TO THE GENEVA PROTOCOLS, UNUS.
AND DEALT WITH ACCORDING TO THE LAW.
NEWSFLASH, CHUCK.
THERE'S NO LAW HERE!
THEN LET ME BE THE FIRST TO ESTABLISH SOME.
DO YOU HAVE A PROBLEM WITH THAT?

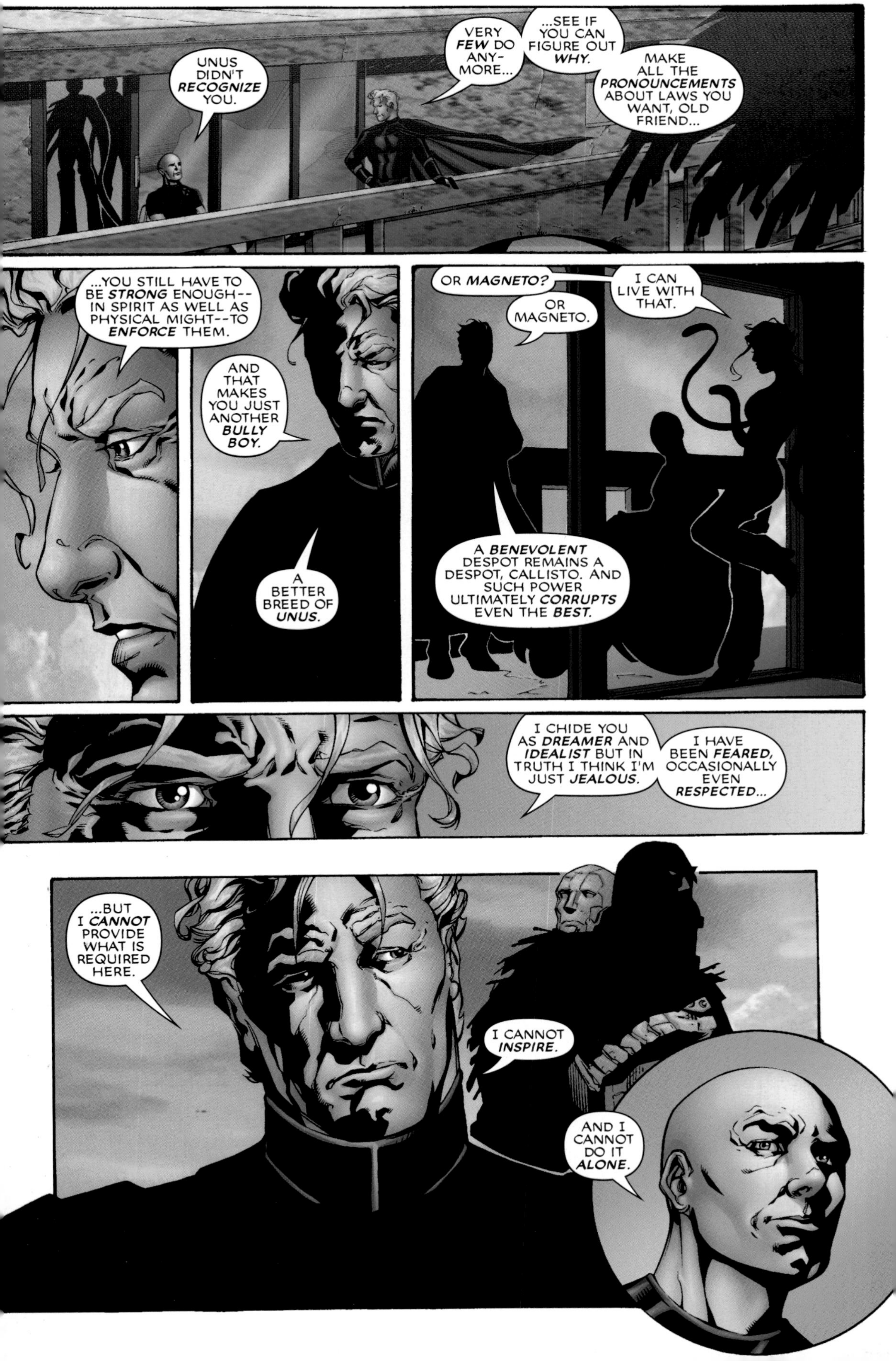
UNUS DIDN'T RECOGNIZE YOU.
VERY FEW DO ANY-MORE...
...SEE IF YOU CAN FIGURE OUT WHY.
MAKE ALL THE PRONOUNCEMENTS ABOUT LAWS YOU WANT, OLD FRIEND...
...YOU STILL HAVE TO BE STRONG ENOUGH--IN SPIRIT AS WELL AS PHYSICAL MIGHT--TO ENFORCE THEM.
AND THAT MAKES YOU JUST ANOTHER BULLY BOY.
A BETTER BREED OF UNUS.
OR MAGNETO?
OR MAGNETO.
I CAN LIVE WITH THAT.
A BENEVOLENT DESPOT REMAINS A DESPOT, CALLISTO. AND SUCH POWER ULTIMATELY CORRUPTS EVEN THE BEST.
I CHIDE YOU AS DREAMER AND IDEALIST BUT IN TRUTH I THINK I'M JUST JEALOUS.
I HAVE BEEN FEARED, OCCASIONALLY EVEN RESPECTED...
...BUT I CANNOT PROVIDE WHAT IS REQUIRED HERE.
I CANNOT INSPIRE.
AND I CANNOT DO IT ALONE.

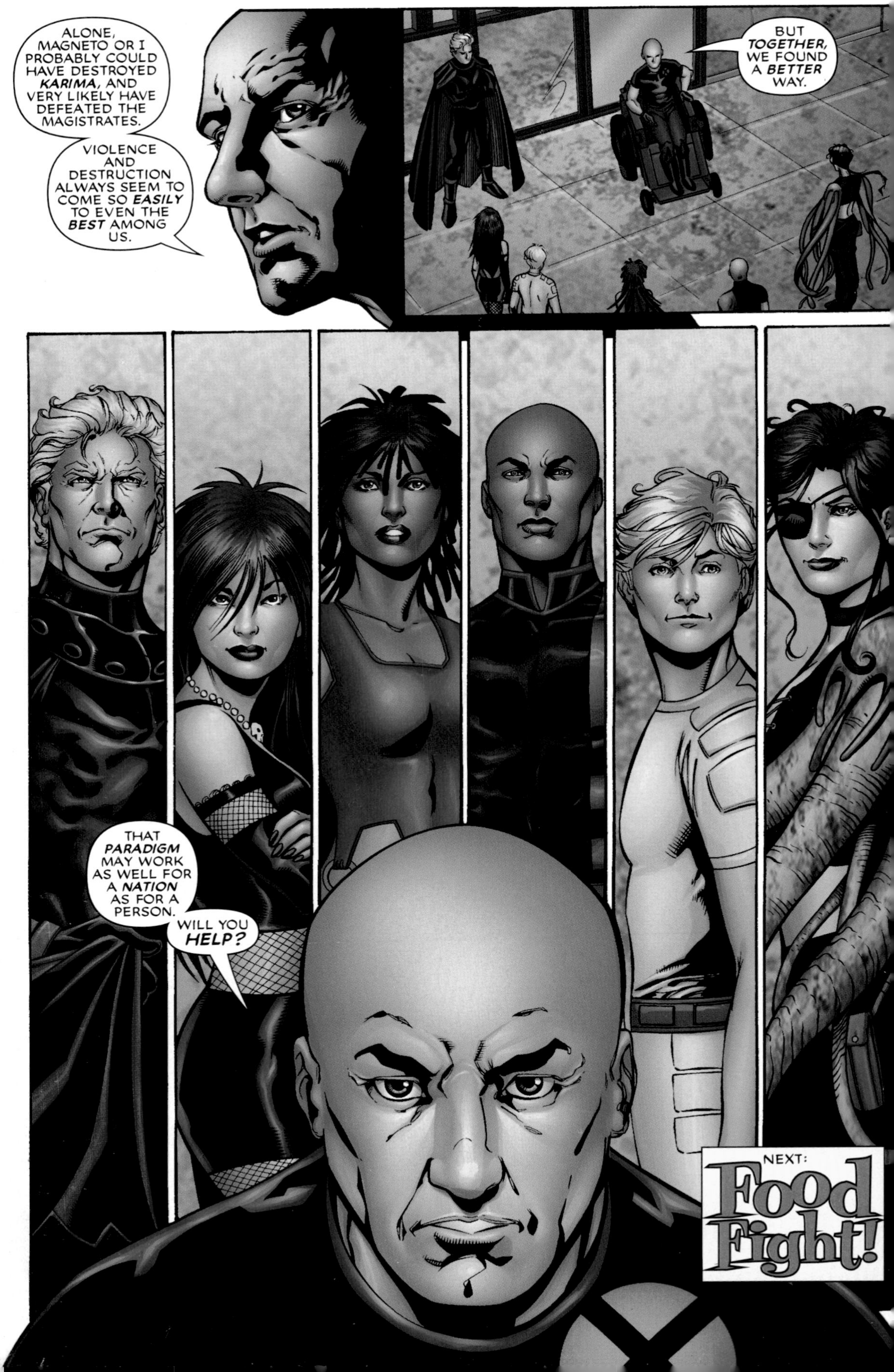
ALONE, MAGNETO OR I PROBABLY COULD HAVE DESTROYED KARIMA, AND VERY LIKELY HAVE DEFEATED THE MAGISTRATES.
VIOLENCE AND DESTRUCTION ALWAYS SEEM TO COME SO EASILY TO EVEN THE BEST AMONG US.
BUT TOGETHER, WE FOUND A BETTER WAY.
THAT PARADIGM MAY WORK AS WELL FOR A NATION AS FOR A PERSON.
WILL YOU HELP?
NEXT:
Food Fight!